HAVERFORD ESSAYS

HAVERFORD ESSAYS

Studies in Modern Literature

Prepared by Some Former Pupils of

PROFESSOR FRANCIS B. GUMMERE

In Honor of the Completion of the Twentieth
Year of his Teaching in Haverford College

62572

Essay Index Reprint Series

BOOKS FOR LIBRARIES PRESS
FREEPORT, NEW YORK

First Published 1909
First Reprinting in this Series 1967
Second Reprinting 1969

STANDARD BOOK NUMBER:
8369-0519-9

LIBRARY OF CONGRESS CATALOG CARD NUMBER:
67-23227

PRINTED IN THE UNITED STATES OF AMERICA

INDEX

THE LOGIC OF ARGUMENT.

By Clarence Gilbert Hoag, A.M.

THE LOGIC OF ARGUMENT.

Argument or, as it is called in the text-books, argumentation is now made the subject of regular courses of study in American colleges. A correct view of its logical structure is therefore much to be desired.

The views presented in most of the current special text-books[1] and in the chapters on argument in the current books on general rhetoric are evidently based largely on the pioneer text-book in this field, Professor G. P. Baker's *Principles of Argumentation,*[2] revised by Baker and Huntington in 1905. And in that book the logic of argument is not explained, it seems to me, either correctly or adequately.

Works on logic furnished to the authors of this book theories enough of the isolated syllogism and the isolated induction, but no adequate account of the logic of extended discourse. Works on legal evidence furnished them with principles normally applicable to a legal case but usually inapplicable to what the book was especially intended to give instruction on, namely arguments on questions of public discussion or academic debate: in a legal case the conclusion in question usually covers a concrete fact, for example, *Smith is guilty of murder in the first degree* or *Jones owes Brown fifty dollars,* and the evidence is usually some kind of testimony, whereas in arguments

---

[1] *The Art of Debate,* by R. M. Alden, Henry Holt, 1900.
The Essentials of Argumentation, by E. J. MacEwen, Heath, 1900.
Argumentation and Debate, by C. Laycock and R. L. Scales, Macmillan, 1904.
[2] Ginn and Company, 1895.

on questions of public discussion or academic debate the
conclusion usually covers a proposal as to what should be
done, for example, *Chicago should buy and operate her
street railways* or *United States Senators should be elected
by direct vote of the people,* and the evidence is usually
not testimony of any kind. And these writers made the
mistake, it seems to me, of taking over into their own
book part of what the logics taught on the isolated single
step in reasoning and of what the legal works taught
on the principles of legal evidence without sufficiently
working over the two bodies of material and correlating
them to each other and to the third body of material
which they developed more independently, that is, the
principles of brief-drawing. The result is that their book
is far astray in respect even to so fundamental a matter
as the application to argument of the distinction between
induction and deduction and that its teachings in respect
to the principles of logic, the principles of legal evidence,
and the principles of brief-drawing or structure, are almost altogether uncorrelated with each other.

I make these criticisms not in a carping spirit but only
to justify my present attempt to analyze the logic of
argument anew.

To substantiate my criticisms briefly, I will simply cite
and comment on some passages from Baker and Huntington's influential book.

The following passage is from page 109:

"SUMMARY OF THE KINDS OF EVIDENCE. Evidence, as
we have seen, consisting of facts, the opinions of authorities, and reasoning (inferences from the facts or opinions) can be classified as testimonial and circumstantial,
facts and opinions being testimonial and inferences being
circumstantial. Testimonial evidence needs no sub-

division beyond the natural division into facts and the opinions of authorities, since the same tests are applicable to all witnesses and to all authorities. Circumstantial evidence, however, can be more surely tested if we subdivide it into deductive and inductive reasoning. Deductive reasoning, moreover, for our purposes may be tested without considering the subdivisions which formal logic applies to it. Inductive reasoning, on the other hand, it is helpful to separate somewhat arbitrarily into generalizations, arguments based on a causal relationship, and arguments based on resemblance. In the section that follows it will be well to bear these classifications in mind, for they are helpful as guides to the tests to be applied."

This makes "reasoning" a "kind of evidence," co-ordinate with "facts" and "opinions" grouped together. But surely reasoning is not a kind of evidence at all but the process of reaching a conclusion from evidence. Moreover, the passage makes induction and deduction subdivisions of circumstantial evidence and consequently exclusive of testimonial evidence. But induction and deduction play, of course, exactly the same part with testimonial evidence that they do with circumstantial. When I reason "from authority," for example, to the conclusion, *Such and such an act is treason,* I am reasoning deductively from the two premises, say, *Whatever Blackstone says is treason is treason* and *Blackstone says that such and such an act is treason.* And the deductive syllogism is involved in the same way in the case of reasoning from ordinary testimonial evidence not classed as evidence "from authority:" when I reason to the conclusion, *Jones was the murderer,* from the testimony of Smith and Brown, I am reasoning deductively from two such premises as these, first, *Whatever Smith and Brown agree on without collusion, in a case in which they have no motive to lie, in which they had good opportunity to observe the facts, etc., etc., is true,* and second, *Smith and Brown agree that Jones was the murderer, without collusion, having no motive to lie, etc., etc.*

The passage makes "generalizations" a subdivision of inductive argument. Now, of course, the conclusions reached by inductive reasoning, in other words those based on inductive argument or evidence, are generalizations, but inductive arguments themselves are not generalizations necessarily, or even usually. Consider, too, what it means to make "arguments based on a causal relationship" a *subdivision* of inductive arguments. I have not the space here to go into a full discussion of the point—and as it is fully covered by treatises on logic it would be superfluous to do so—but it may be said sweepingly that inductive reasoning is absolutely meaningless except as based on supposed causal relationships.

The failure of the book to correlate the principles of logic with those of brief-drawing means nothing less than that the scheme of brief-drawing taught is given no sound logical basis. That failure is illustrated by the comparison of a passage from pages 91 and 92 about "deductive argument" with one of the "good briefs" presented as models in the later chapter on brief-drawing. The teaching of the passage and the practice of the briefs are inconsistent. In this case it is the teaching that is wrong, the practice being right though its logical nature is altogether unexplained.

Here is the passage from pages 91 and 92. Its teaching is that deduction is used but little in most arguments such as the book is concerned with.

"THE USE OF DEDUCTIVE ARGUMENT. Deductive argument, depending as it does for its effectiveness largely upon the assumption that its fundamental generalizations will be accepted without argument, is especially serviceable where there is close agreement between the writer and his readers in regard to the principles underlying the argument; a philosopher or a scientist arguing with those of the same school of thought, a lawyer arguing before a bench of judges, a clergyman trying to convince others who accept his fundamental creed,—all these can make free use of deductive reasoning based on broad principles accepted by their audience. But in cases where there is wide divergence in views the safer method is to establish the basal generalizations by rapid and well-selected inductive reasoning from significant special instances and to use the deductive process, if at all, chiefly to summarize results."

"Good Brief," pp. 257-275, omitting the introduction, the conclusion, and the arguments supporting those numbered with arabic numerals:

"*Resolved*: *That the Annexation of Canada by Treaty with Great Britain would be Economically Advantageous to the United States.*

Brief Proper.

"I. From an economic standpoint Annexation would be advantageous, for

"A. Our present tariff makes our commercial relations with Canada precarious, for

1. The tariff in itself is unfair.
2. Trade figures show it to be unfair.
3. The Canadians evidently realize this unfairness.

4. It is in Canada's power to equalize these tariff and trade conditions.

"B. Our tariff is harmful in many cases.

1. It is almost prohibitive on many articles which are really needed in the United States.

"C. These tariff evils would be removed by annexation.

1. The tariff would be removed altogether.

"D. Thus, with tariff removed, our home trade would increase naturally.

1. Our markets would have the preference on all Canadian products.

2. We should get all of Canada's trade now coming under the head of imports into Canada.

"E. The wealth of the United States would be very materially increased by annexation.

1. Developed Canada has a very considerable wealth.

2. The vast undeveloped natural wealth of Canada, in lumber, minerals, fertile soil, and in natural waterways for transportation, is beyond even the possibility of doubt.

3. This natural wealth would be developed by our capital and enterprise.

"F. As far as the export trade of a country shows the economic wealth we should not lose by annexation.

1. Our export trade would be increased.

"G. The argument that annexation, by opening our markets to Canadian competition, would hurt our manufacturers and producers, is worthless.

THE LOGIC OF ARGUMENT.

1. Iron, coal, lumber, fish and farm products are the principal products of Canada.
2. Canadian iron could not hurt our producers or our manufacturers.
3. Canadian coal could not injure our producers.
4. Canadian lumber cannot hurt our producers.
5. The argument that our producers would be unable to compete against Canadian farm products and Canadian fish does not hold in case of annexation.

"H. We can strengthen our argument for annexation by comparing annexation with Reciprocity and Free Trade.

1. Such a comparison will show that all of these methods improve trade conditions through the tariff.
2. It will show that in some cases any one of these methods would prove equally effective.
3. It will show that our export trade would be increased by any one of these methods.
4. It will prove that only annexation would make all tariff conditions fair to both countries.
5. It will prove that only by annexation could the vast wealth of Canada benefit the United States.
6. It will prove that all the advantages of either Reciprocity or Free Trade would be realized by annexation."

Now, as will be clearer later when we have analyzed the relation of deductive arguments to the conclusions they support, every one of these arguments is deductive. And the same is true of the "good briefs" printed as models on pages 272-285, 483-493 and 493-502. In short, the briefs generally throughout the book are inconsistent with the passage about deductive argument on pages 91 and 92.

I will now present my own view of the logic of argument. In doing so I must repeat some of the most elementary principles of logic, and for this I ask the reader's indulgence.

We shall discover the nature of argument best, perhaps, by first asking how it is that we come to hold any proposition to be true or to be untrue. If we find out by what road we ourselves arrive at a conclusion, we shall be in the way of learning how to guide the minds of others to a conclusion, that is, how to argue.

How do we come to believe that putting frost-bitten fingers into warm water makes them ache worse? By trying it a few times: what we find to be true a few times we infer to be true always. How do we come to believe that heating water over a hot fire will cause it to go off into the air as water vapor? By trying it a few times: in this case also what we find to be true a few times we infer to be true always. How do we come to believe that the time of vibration of a pendulum varies as the square root of the length? If we come to this belief through experiments merely, the answer is the same, by trying it a few times. These examples illustrate one of the ways by which we reach conclusions: what in actual experience we find to be true in some cases we infer to be true in all cases of the kind; our conclusion is simply an assertion so phrased as to cover not only the observed cases but all cases whatever of the kind. The act of jumping to such a general conclusion from some of the facts it covers is called inductive reasoning or induction.

But how, supposing we have never tried putting frost-bitten fingers into warm water, can we come to the conclusion that putting into warm water certain fingers, say those of a boy who comes into the house with fingers apparently frost-bitten, will make them ache worse? Evidently not by the process of reasoning just explained, for whereas by that we inferred a generalization from some of the observed facts it covers, in this case our conclusion is not a generalization at all, and the one fact it covers we have not observed. Yet it may be that we can come to the conclusion by good reasoning. What is the nature of the process? One of the grounds of our inference is the fact—for convenience I will call it a "fact" at this point, though in reality it is itself only a conclusion reached by such reasoning as I am now explaining—one of the grounds of our inference, I say, is the fact that *the particular fingers in question are frost-bitten fingers.* The other ground of inference is a generalization already stored up in our mind and now suggested or brought to our attention by the frost-bitten fingers. It is the generalization, *Putting frost-bitten fingers into warm water makes them ache worse*—the same generalization, it happens, that was the conclusion of the induction we considered first, though in the present case, as we have explicitly supposed no previous experience of the fact it covers, not the result of previous induction. Our process of reasoning here, you see, is distinctly different from that explained above as induction: it consists in the application of a generalization to a case or another generalization which it covers. This process of reasoning, the application of a generalization to a case or another generalization which it covers, is called deductive reasoning or deduction.

The grounds of induction are the facts showing that the conclusion, the generalization covering them, *is* true. The grounds of deduction are reasons why the conclusion *should be expected to be* true. The generalization applied may be itself the conclusion of an induction, as we have seen the very generalization in this case might have been, or it may not, as we have supposed in this case.

Induction and deduction are the only kinds of reasoning we use in coming to any conclusion. Let us proceed, then, with our examination of deduction, and then inquire into the bearing of both kinds of reasoning on argument.

In regard to deduction, it must be noted that to express in language the grounds of inference for such reasoning two assertions are required. We cannot reasonably conclude that *putting these fingers into warm water will make them ache worse* unless we believe not only the generalization already stored away in our mind that we call forth to apply to the case, namely, *Putting frost-bitten fingers into warm water makes them ache worse,* but also the fact, *These fingers are frost-bitten fingers.* Now the assertion which covers the generalization we apply in deduction is called the major premise, and the assertion which covers the fact coming under it is called the minor premise.

The major premise may take any one of several forms in language, but it must always be a generalization of some sort. The minor premise must, of course, conform to the major so as to make unmistakably clear the fact that it is covered by it. For the deductions we have been considering here are several forms of the major, together with forms of the minor and the conclusion to correspond.

1.

Major: Putting frost-bitten fingers into warm water makes them ache worse.

Minor: These fingers are frost-bitten fingers.

Conclusion: Putting these fingers into warm water will make them ache worse.

2.

Major: Frost-bitten fingers always ache worse when put into warm water.
Minor: These fingers are frost-bitten fingers.
Conclusion: These fingers will ache worse when put into warm water.

3.

Major: Frost-bitten fingers ache worse if put into warm water.
Minor: These fingers are frost-bitten.
Conclusion: These fingers will ache worse if put into warm water.

Of these groups of forms some are more simple and natural, others more labored. Perhaps the most simple and natural group is the third, that with the if-clause. This is worth noting, for this if-form is just as sound logically as any of the others, and on account of its naturalness it is in many cases the most desirable form rhetorically.

Such a group of assertions, the two premises and the conclusion of a deduction, is called by logicians, of course, a syllogism.

Thus far we have been considering reasoning. Let us now ask, What is argument? Argument is language expressing the grounds from which another can reason to the conclusion upheld by the person arguing. Now we have just seen what are the only grounds from which anybody can reason to any conclusion. They are either the facts from which it can be inferred, that is, reasoned to, inductively or the two premises from which it can be inferred deductively. No language is argument therefore, speaking very strictly, that does not express either such facts or such premises.

Consider some concrete examples. If you wanted to persuade me that in general putting frost-bitten fingers into warm water makes them ache worse, you would perhaps say: "It did so when I tried it; it did so when A tried it; it did so when B tried it." That, of course, is argument; and what does it consist in? Simply in the expression in language, in the form of assertions, of the facts of which the conclusion you want me to accept is the generalization. It is called, therefore, of course, inductive argument.

Perhaps, however, you might say: "The doctor knows all about such matters, and he says so." That is argument too; and if you consider it, you will see that it is the two premises from which you expect me to reason deductively to the same conclusion. This becomes clear if we change the wording to either of these forms:

If the doctor says that putting frost-bitten fingers into warm water makes them ache worse, it does make them ache worse (major).

The doctor says that putting frost-bitten fingers into warm water makes them ache worse (minor).

What the doctor says about such matters is true (major).

The doctor says that putting frost-bitten fingers into warm water makes them ache worse (minor).

If one tries to think of some other argument for this conclusion, one may think of several others readily, but they will all prove to be one of these two kinds, that is, the facts of which the assertion argued for is the generalization (inductive argument) or the premises from which it is the conclusion (deductive argument). As there are only two kinds of reasoning, there can be only two kinds of argument.

We have seen that every argument bears one of three possible relations to the assertion it argues for, the relation of facts covered by a generalization to the generalization itself (in inductive argument), the relation of major premise to conclusion (in deductive argument), and the relation of minor premise to conclusion (in deductive argument). Of these relations the first is so clear as to require no further treatment. The second and third, however, may not be; and a thorough grasp of these last two relations is the secret of a mastery of the logic of argument.

What, then, is the relation between a major and a minor premise? And what is the relation between each and the conclusion?

Suppose the conclusion, the assertion to be argued for, is this: *Mr. Roosevelt should not be nominated for the Presidency in 1908*. The two premises chosen as arguments, let us say, are these: *Mr. Roosevelt has served two terms already* and *Any man who has served two terms already should not be nominated for the Presidency*. The relations between these three assertions, from the point of view not of reasoning but of arguing, can be represented, I think, by a graphic method similar to that by which the mathematician Euler, in the instruction of a German princess in the eighteenth century, represented the relations between the three terms of a syllogism. The three circles of

Euler, each representing one of the three terms, will be remembered by everyone who has studied the old fashioned elementary logic.   The graphic representation of the relations to each other of the entire propositions is equally simple.   Let the assertion to be supported be represented by the ring called *Conclusion* in the figure below.   Let the mind of the person to be convinced of the truth of the assertion, whom for convenience I shall hereafter call simply the reader, be represented by the circle *M*.   The function of argument, then, the work it is to do, the supporting of the assertion in the mind of the reader, is the linking of *Conclusion* to *M*.   Note that well, for it is the heart of the whole matter: to argue is to link *Conclusion* to *M*.

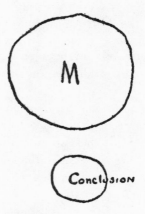

Now, if you will look back to the two premises, you will see that the second one is simply language expressing that part of the contents of the reader's mind which the conclusion can be linked to, and that the first one is simply the link.   Moreover, the second, you will note, is the major premise; the first, the minor. The complete figure, therefore, is this:

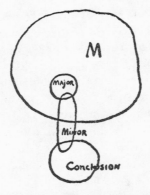

This figure represents all possible cases of single processes of deductive argument. To represent a chain of arguments it has only to be modified as I shall explain below. The process in all deductive arguments, that is, in all arguments whatever that are not inductive, is essentially that of linking the conclusion or assertion supported to what is already held as truth in the mind of the reader. Of what is held as truth in that mind, the part that is used to link the supported assertion to, when expressed in language, is called the major premise. The link is called the minor premise.

This graphic mode of representing deductive argument reveals some interesting points concerning it.

Evidently the adaptation of a deductive argument to the reader's mind is not important merely, but essential: if the link fails to connect the conclusion with something in his mind, it does no supporting whatever. This principle is fundamental for all arguing. Whether the major premise you are using is or is not really held as true in your own mind may be important, but only in respect to sincerity: what is important in respect to the performance of its work by the argument is whether the major you are using is or is not really held as true in the mind of the reader. With an audience of Christians, to use the good example of Professor G. P. Baker, it is useless to support an assertion by arguing that it is in the Koran, whereas with an audience of Mohammedans it is not. What is the difference from the point of view of my graphic representation of argument? It is this: the Christian does not have in his mind the ring, so to speak, namely, *What is in the Koran is true,* to which you are trying to link the conclusion; the Mohammedan does have it. So far as the mere effectiveness of the argument with the audience is concerned, it makes no difference whatever whether this ring is in the arguer's mind or not.

Deductive argument, to express the same point in different words, is argument based on the consistency which must rule the thinking of the reader. You want him to believe, for example, that he should not vote for B——— for Governor. "What," you ask yourself, "can I say that he will believe which will make it clear to him that what he believes already requires the truth of my proposition? He believes that he should not vote for anyone for Governor who has accepted a bribe. If, then, I can say that B——— accepted a bribe while in the Legislature, that is, if I can say it and make the reader believe it, consistency will require him to believe the original proposition, namely, that he should not vote for B——— for Governor." If, to take another example, the proposition is, *Chicago should buy and operate its street railways,* it is consistency, if anything, that will require my reader to accept it if I can say and make him believe that *Municipal ownership and operation of the street railways of Chicago will result in economic benefit to the people.*

This graphic mode of representing deductive argument makes it clear, too, that the minor premise, the link, is argument in a sense in which the major premise, the generalization linked to, the ring, is not. It shows that the minor premise may be altogether new to the reader, whereas the major, so far as we have yet seen, serves no purpose if it be not already part—whether or not it has ever been formulated in words—of the reader's store of accepted generalizations. And in this the graphic representation accords with the truth. Thus far, for the sake of explaining only one thing at a time, I have assumed that major as well as minor is actually expressed in arguing deductively. Three times out of four, however, the major is not expressed. The reason will now be clear. In supporting the proposition, *The city should own its street railways,* you would probably not say at all, *The city should own its street railways if owning them will result in economic benefit to the people.* Your economic argument you would cover by the minor only, *Municipal ownership will result in economic benefit to the people*: you would trust that the major above would do its work (of serving as the ring for the conclusion to be linked to) as well unexpressed as expressed. A syllogism of which only the conclusion and one premise are expressed is called by logicians, of course, an enthymeme. Most of the syllogisms we use in arguing, then, are enthymemes, and the unexpressed premise is usually the major.

But we must not go too far: we must not say that to express the major is never worth while. The assertion to be supported, is, let us say, *You should not vote for Smith.* Your minor is, *Smith was given the nomination by Williams.* In this case it might be important not only to express the major but even to emphasize and to support it. Three times out of four the major need not be expressed; the fourth time it needs to be expressed and perhaps emphasized and supported.

This may at first seem inconsistent with the conception of the major represented by the figure above. Not so, however: it is true that the major must be in the reader's mind before the minor, the argument *par excellence,* can do its work, but it is equally true that the major may be put there only a second before it serves its purpose. In other words, a major premise may be established in the reader's mind in order to be used a moment later to hang a conclusion to by the link of a corresponding minor. In such a case what is the major in the second argument is the conclusion in the first. All this can be represented graphically. It is not until 3, in the figure below, is linked to 5, so that it is logically part of the hearer's mind, that 1 can be linked to 3 by 2. But as soon as 3 is linked to 5, it is a part of the hearer's beliefs, that is, held fast to the circle *M* and ready to serve as the ring for 1 to be linked to. The words to the right of the figure express the meanings of the several parts they stand opposite.

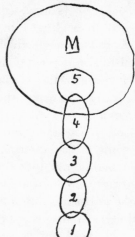

(Mind of the hearer.)

You should not do anything that tends to perpetuate the power of a bad "machine."

Voting for men given the nomination by Williams tends to perpetuate the power of a bad machine.

You should not vote for men given the nomination by Williams.

Smith was given the nomination by Williams.

You should not vote for Smith.

In regard especially to supporting the major one further word is necessary. Though sometimes, as we have seen, a writer should support a major premise, he does well to ask himself, before doing so, whether it is not possible to cut out that major and the corresponding minor altogether and link the conclusion directly to some generalization already in the hearer's mind, closely allied to that to which the dropped major would have had to be linked. Why hang a thing to a ring that must itself be hung to the ceiling if you can as well hang it to the ceiling directly? If the proposition is, *The city should own its street railways,* why say as an argument on the negative, *Municipal ownership of the street railways would be socialistic?* The major to which this argument would link the proposition, *The city should not do anything socialistic,* would be at least as hard to support as the original proposition—unless, of course, the readers were blindly antagonistic to socialism —and supporting it would mean linking it to the very generalizations already in the hearer's mind to which the original proposition could have been linked directly.

Considering now the minor, we may reasonably ask whether to it also apply these principles just explained in regard to the major. They do not: well-chosen minors that support directly the conclusion of an argument, that is, those I define below as "primary arguments," nearly always need support. The minors mentioned in the last few pages above will serve as examples. *Municipal ownership and operation of the street railways of Chicago will result in economic benefit to the people:* unsupported itself, that argument is worthless; supported successfully it does about half of all that is needed to convince the hearer of the truth of the original proposition. *Smith was given the nomination by Williams:* if we suppose

the major that corresponds to it established, that argument
is strong provided it is itself believed; not believed, it is
of course worthless.

One of the commonest faults in arguing is failure to
support duly minor premises that would go far towards establishing a proposition if themselves accepted but that
are not likely to be accepted unless supported with the
utmost thoroughness and skill. If a minor will do little
or no good if believed, it should be thrown out altogether
and the space devoted to arguments that will do good. If
it will do good if believed, it should be thoroughly established in the reader's mind even at the cost of considerable space. Propositions are not established by the number
of arguments which directly support the proposition but
by two or three arguments that settle the question if supported successfully and that are supported successfully.
Often a writer should spend half his space or more in
establishing a single minor.

How much support a minor needs and what will support
it, those clearly are questions quite distinct from the question how much support a minor, if believed itself, will
give the original proposition. They should be considered,
therefore, separately. It is largely because it makes these
questions distinct in the writer's mind and leads to his
considering them separately that a mastery of the logic
of argument is important.

How are minors supported? Exactly as original propositions are supported. And what if these supporting
arguments need support themselves? Then they should
be given support until they need it no more. And so the
process should go on until the arguments needed to establish the proposition are themselves established firmly.
Whether or not any specific argument will be accepted

without support can be decided, of course, by no rules but only by the common sense of the writer.

The arguments that support the original proposition directly are no more important logically than their own supporters or than the supporters of their own supporters down to the last arguments used. Yet, because they determine the division of the matter of the whole discourse, as will be explained, they are often called the "principal" arguments. For convenience I shall call them the primary arguments; those that support them, the secondary arguments; those that support the secondary, the tertiary arguments, etc. Two or more arguments of the same one of these orders, that is, two or more primary or two or more secondary arguments, I shall call, in respect to their relation to each other, co-ordinate.

When we thus support a primary argument, we are making what may be called a chain of argument. Such chains form the logical skeletons—to mix metaphors—of all extended arguments.

A chain of arguments of the less common sort in which a major is supported was represented graphically on page 20. One of the common sort, in which only minors are expressed, is represented in this figure:

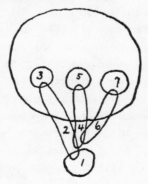

1 is the proposition. *You should not vote for B——*
for Governor.

2 is the first minor, the last link used by the reader
in reasoning to the proposition. It links 1 to 3. It would
be expressed in the argument. *B—— accepted a bribe*
while in the Legislature.

3 is the major to which 2 links 1. It would not be
expressed in the argument. *You should not vote for any-*
body who has accepted a bribe.

4 is the minor linking 2, which is found to need support, to 5. *L—— says he saw B—— accept a bribe*
while in the Legislature.

5 is the major to which 4 links 2. It would probably
not be expressed in the argument. *What L—— says he*
saw, he saw.

6 is the minor linking 4, which is found to need support,
to 7. *The Daily Herald quotes L—— as saying in a*
speech last week that he saw B—— accept a bribe, etc.

7 is the major to which 6 links 4. It would probably
not be expressed in the argument. *What the Daily Herald*
quotes L—— as saying, he said.

The common use of the words "a perfect chain of reasoning" suggests the idea that in a perfectly constructed argument there is but one such chain. Usually, however, there
are several. If it is possible to link the original proposition to the hearer's mind directly by two or more arguments, it is best to do so; and, of course, each such argument connecting the proposition directly with the hearer's
mind starts a separate chain. Could the proposition supported by the chain in the figure above be supported thus
directly by another minor besides 2? Doubtless it could.
If the issue covered by the question were that made by

the rise of the better citizens in a reform movement to put down a corrupt "machine," a good argument connecting 1 directly with the hearer's mind would, perhaps, be this: *Voting for B—— tends to strengthen the "machine."* That argument is evidently coordinate with 2 and starts a second chain.

Experience shows that the number of separate chains of arguments, in support of such propositions as are subjects of public discussion, is seldom more than three or four and seldom fewer than two. *Should Chicago buy and operate her street railways?* What principles or generalizations will cover that case? Analysis reveals a generalization in regard to economy that covers it: *Whatever will result in economic benefit to the people should be done.* Analysis reveals, too, a generalization in regard to politics that covers it: *Whatever will tend to strengthen the cause of good government should be done.* Perhaps you can think of one other generalization that can be shown to cover the proposition; possibly you can think of two others; but to more than three or four in all you evidently cannot reasonably connect the proposition directly. More than three or four chains of arguments, accordingly, you cannot reasonably make. When a writer supports his proposition directly by as many as eight or ten arguments, he does so simply because he fails to discard weak or trivial arguments and fails to distinguish between arguments that should be made "primary" and those that should be made "secondary," in other words, between those that should be made to support the conclusion directly and those that should support the supporters.

There is an interesting point to be noticed in regard to two or more coordinate arguments which support a single argument. The moment you put one of them, in almost any case, into syllogistic form, you notice that the major premise is not true independently of the other coordinate majors. Consider, an example. The conclusion, let us suppose, is this, *Chicago should buy and operate her street railways.* One argument to be used is this, *Municipal ownership and operation of the railways will result in economic benefit to the people of Chicago.* Now the major to which that argument links the conclusion, though surely held to be true, in a sense, by almost all readers, is not held true without reservation. The major in question, is, of course, this: *Whatever will result in economic benefit to the people of Chicago should be done.* Now that is obviously true, of course, but only with the reservation which we sometimes cover by the words *"other things being equal;"* that a thing is economically beneficial is a reason accepted almost universally for doing it, but only in the absence of counterbalancing objections. To steal may sometimes seem to a man beneficial economically, but he does not necessarily conclude to steal: he may be inhibited by a still stronger argument on the other side.

This interdependence of coordinate premises supporting the same proposition should be covered by our analysis of the logical structure of argument. What is, then, the principle that covers it, and how can it be represented graphically in our diagram? A little thought reveals the fact that rigid logic would require all coordinate majors supporting the same proposition to be combined into a compound major to each of the several parts of which a minor would correspond and link the proposition to be supported. To illustrate this we may suppose that the proposition is this, *Life imprisonment should be substituted for capital punishment in Pennsylvania.* The minors supporting it are, let us say, these: the first, *Life imprisonment is more effective than capital punishment as a preventive of murder;* the second, *Life imprisonment is more humane than capital punishment;* the third, *Life imprisonment is less likely than capital punishment to result in injustice that cannot be remedied.* Now, as we have seen, readers cannot be expected to hold true, sweepingly, without regard to any other considerations whatever, the major which must be held true by them if the first of these arguments is to be of any service, namely, *Any punishment that is more effective as a preventive of murder than capital punishment should be substituted for capital punishment in Pennsylvania:* one might grant, for example, that life-long torture would be more effective as a preventive without granting that it should be substituted for capital punishment. It is only if the punishment proposed is granted also to be at least as satisfactory in all other essential respects that the argument in question, the first minor above, is valid. And the same is equally true of the second and the third minors above. In other words, not one of the three majors to which these three arguments link the proposition is accepted independently of the other considerations. If, however, we combine the majors into one compound major, we have sound logic. The compound major might read: *Any punishment that is more effective as a preventive of murder than capital punishment, more humane, and less likely to result in injustice that cannot be remedied, should be substituted for capital punishment in Pennsylvania;* or it might read, *more effective as a preventive, as humane, and not more likely,* etc.; or it might read in any other such way that would suit the facts and make the combination of arguments used really conclusive.

Pursuing this line of thought farther, it becomes clear that the number of parts required by rigid logic in each such compound major would be indefinitely large, for all things in the universe are bound together and interrelated with all other things. Before so appalling a requirement of rigid logic, however, we may well recoil and fall all the way back to common sense: we may suppose the words "other things being equal" to be always understood and not compound our majors at all unless the case seems especially to require it, as it would in the support of the proposition about life imprisonment, and as, indeed, it often does.

To represent the compounding of majors graphically is easy: all that is necessary is to elongate the loop that stands for the major and to link to it every minor that corresponds to one of its parts.

If we now change the first of the three arguments above on the life imprisonment question to a form which it might just as reasonably have assumed, namely, *Life imprisonment is as effective,* etc., or *not less effective,* etc., we have an example of a rebuttal argument, that is, an argument of negative rather than positive service. Such a rebuttal argument must be worked into our logical scheme. Evidently such a rebuttal argument is merely one whose absolute dependence upon other coordinate arguments is obvious. So a rebuttal argument not only may but must appear in a graphic representation of the logic of argument as linking what it supports to a compound major. In the figure below I is the rebuttal argument; it is shown as linking the proposition it supports to a compound major to which II, an argument coordinate with I, links to the same proposition.

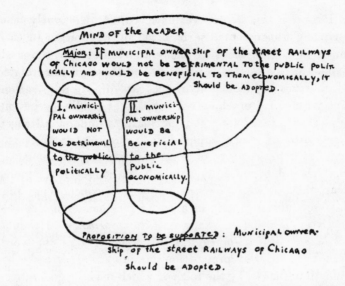

MIND OF the READER

MAJOR: IF MUNICIPAL OWNERSHIP of the street RAILWAYS of CHICAGO WOULD not be DETRIMENTAL TO the PUBLIC POLITICALLY AND WOULD be BENEFICIAL TO THem ECONOMICALLY, IT Should be ADOPTED.

I. MUNICIPAL OWNERSHIP WOULD NOT be DETRIMENTAL to the public POLITICALLY

II. MUNICIPAL OWNERSHIP WOULD Be BENEFICIAL to the PUBLIC ECONOMICALLY.

PROPOSITION TO be SUPPORTED: MUNICIPAL OWNERSHIP of the street RAILWAYS of CHICAGO should be ADOPTED.

I must now consider a point on which the acute reader has perhaps for some time been wanting to raise an objection. I have apparently wholly accounted for the logical structure of argument without bringing in inductive arguments at all. Surely inductive arguments must play a part. They do indeed usually play a part, often by far the most important part so far as weight of evidence is concerned; and yet in respect to the mere structure of the discourse, which is what we have been considering, their part in arguments on subjects of public discussion and academic debate is nearly always secondary to that played by deductive arguments.[3]

Structurally the whole argument is dominated by the arguments that stand logically next to the original prop-

<hr />

[3]Compare here the view of Baker and Huntington expressed on pages 91 and 92 of their *Principles of Argumentation.* I have quoted the passage above, pages 6 and 7.

osition, that is, those we have called arbitrarily the
"primary." arguments, such as I and II on page 33:
for it is on the basis of these arguments that the first
division of the matter is made.   And these primary arguments must be deductive in the case of, literally, quite
ninety-nine of every hundred subjects of public discussion
or of academic debate.   It is not hard to understand why:
ninety-nine of every hundred such subjects are propositions involving the idea of what is desirable, what is good,
what should be, and, as a minute's thought must make
clear, the last step in reasoning to such conclusions, and
therefore the first step in arguing for them, must be deductive.   Take as an example, *Life imprisonment should
not be substituted for capital punishment*—note the word
should.   Can that proposition be supported directly by
induction, that is, by the facts of which it is the generalization?   Certainly not, for it is not the generalization of
facts at all.   The only arguments that can conceivably be
given for it are links connecting it with generalizations
in the mind which themselves include the *should be* idea,
the idea of what is desirable or good or right; and of
course all such links are deductive arguments.   In ninety-
nine arguments out of a hundred, then, of the class we are
considering, it is only after the primary arguments have
divided the material that inductive arguments may appear.
And even then, though often they are by no means less
important than deductive arguments, they are in most
debates less frequent.   In nearly every discourse, on a
question of public discussion, therefore, the arguments
that determine the main structural lines and most of those
that determine subordinate structural lines are deductive.
Only in the field of experimental natural science are the
main structural lines of discourses often determined by
inductive arguments.

Nearly all the kinds of argument or evidence commonly designated by special names, such as "argument from authority," "direct testimony," "expert testimony," "argument from sign," and "argument from example," are deductive, but they are not explicitly classed as such in the current text-books. Apparently, indeed, their logical nature has actually not been fully thought out by the writers of these books. Professor Alden, for example, in his *Art of Debate*,[4] makes "processes of reasoning" a "class of proof" coordinate with the "testimony of witnesses" and with "expert testimony and authority." And Professors Baker and Huntington, in their *Principles of Argumentation,* though they give much space to certain kinds of deductive arguments under these special names, dismiss deductive argument with the passage I have quoted above from pages 91 and 92 of their book, which suggests no relation between it and the kinds of evidence to which they give the special names. Yet the logic of these kinds of evidence or argument is clear. In "argument from authority," for instance, the assertion that the authoritative person or book says so-and-so is a minor premise, and the major to which it links the conclusion is the assertion that whatever that authority says on the subject is true. In the cases of the other kinds of evidence, deductive logic is involved just as obviously. For our present purpose it is therefore unnecessary to illustrate every one of these specially named arguments in syllogistic form.

Inductive arguments we use whenever we can, and that means whenever the assertion needing support is a generalization the particulars covered by which can be adduced satisfactorily. Suppose the proposition is, *Life imprison-*

ment should not be substituted for capital punishment.
The arguments supporting that proposition immediately
must of course be deductive because the proposition
is not a generalization of facts at all. One of them
will be, say, *Life imprisonment is less effective as
a preventive of crime than capital punishment.* This argument is good if it is accepted as true itself, for there is
a ring (major) it can link to, namely, *Any penalty less
effective as a preventive of crime than capital punishment
should not be substituted for capital punishment;* but it
needs to be supported itself. Can it be supported inductively? Yes. In what does the inductive argument
consist? In the facts called statistics of which it is the
generalization. Can it be supported also deductively?
Yes. In what does the deductive argument consist? In
these assertions: *Any punishment less feared than capital
punishment is less effective as a preventive of crime than
capital punishment* (the major or ring), and *Life imprisonment is less feared than capital punishment* (the
minor or link). Of these two assertions the first will
surely be held true without even being mentioned and
therefore the second will be a good argument if only it
is itself accepted. It needs, perhaps, some support. Can
it be supported inductively? Yes. Can it be supported
deductively? Yes, conceivably, but it can be supported
best inductively.—These cases are typical of the part induction sometimes plays in argument.

To get a clearer view of all these logical relations let
us set down the original proposition with the arguments
under it in such a way as to represent lógical coordina-
tion and subordination. Let the primary arguments, those
that support the original proposition directly, be designated I, II, etc., and let them stand under each other.

Let the secondary arguments, those that support I, II, etc., be designated 1, 2, 3, etc., and let them stand under each other but farther indented than I, II, and III. Let the tertiary arguments, those that support 1, 2, 3, etc., be designated a, b, c, etc., and let them stand under each other but indented farther still. Give a major and a minor that work together the same designation followed by the word major or the word minor.

Proposition: *Life imprisonment should not be substituted for capital punishment.*

I (major) *Any punishment less effective as a preventive of crime than capital punishment should not be substituted for it.*

I (minor) *Life imprisonment is less effective as a preventive of crime than capital punishment.*

   1 (major) *Any punishment less feared than capital punishment is less effective as a preventive of crime than capital punishment.*

   1 (minor) *Life imprisonment is less feared than capital punishment.*

     (a) *It is less feared by Smith.*
     It is less feared by Jones, etc., etc.

   2 *Life imprisonment has been less effective in Massachusetts (in the form of statistics).*

   Life imprisonment has been less effective in Pennsylvania (in the form of statistics).

   Etc., etc.

II *(major).* *Any punishment less humane than capital punishment should not be substituted for it.*

II *(minor)* *Life imprisonment is less humane than capital punishment.*

Here the original proposition is supported deductively by the linking of it by "I (minor)" to "I (major)." Then "I (minor)" is supported deductively by the linking of it by "1 (minor)" to "1 (major)" and also inductively by the assertions under "2." Finally "1 (minor)" is supported inductively by the assertions under "(a)."

The wide-spread prejudice that inductive reasoning, and consequently inductive argument, is more valid than deductive is due to an imperfect understanding of the basis of logic. Really, of course, at least if we except from consideration deduction based on generalizations concerning what is desirable, what should be, in other words, deduction of which the major premise is in the ethical instead of the material world,—if, I say, we except these cases of deduction as involving problems of philosophy which cannot be treated here, the two kinds of reasoning rest on the same basis, that is, the constancy of what we call the "laws of nature." I have as good grounds for the conclusion, reached by deduction, that a particular stone left unsupported will fall, as for the conclusion, reached by induction, that all stones left unsupported fall and will fall; and I have no better. Both conclusions rest ultimately on my faith that the "laws of nature," this is, the concurrence or succession of events noted as constant in the past, will remain constant in the future. Leaving out of consideration the cases I have spoken of, induction is simply making, on the basis of observation of natural phenomena, a generalization covering the concurrence or succession of natural phenomena in the future as well as the past; deduction is applying a generalization to any case covered by it.

And not only are inductive and deductive arguments exactly equal in their strength: they are also exactly equal in their weakness. Though, as methods of reasoning, both are perfect in their validity so long as nature remains constant and therefore makes any reasoning valid at all, yet both are limited by the degree of constancy in the observed concurrences and successions of events in the several fields of nature, so to speak, in which we attempt to apply them. Since it is possible to distinguish in parts of the field of physics, for instance, concurrences and successions of phenomena so constant as to be called by us laws of nature, it is possible there to make generalizations or to predict according to them, that is, to reason either inductively or deductively, with what we may call almost absolute validity. But in fields like politics, economics, and sociology, in which most of our arguments on questions of public discussion and academic debate lie, we cannot distinguish concurrences and successions of such constancy, and therefore we cannot reason or argue either inductively or deductively with the same degree of validity. Usually, it is true, to take a typical example, men "buy in the cheapest market available," but they do not do so always. Hence our reasoning to that generalization from the facts it covers (induction) is reasoning to a tendency only, and our reasoning from that generalization to a case under it (deduction) is reasoning to a probability only.

Since usually in our arguments we are thus dealing with tendencies or probabilities instead of "laws," anything like absolute proof is usually out of the question. It is only the beginner, for example the inexperienced academic debater, who supposes that not to accept what he has "proved" is a sign of the hearer's insanity or stupidity; and it is, indeed, only the beginner who habitually uses such strong words as "proved" and "proof" in regard to the support of propositions that are subjects of public discussion. It is absurd to speak of "proving" that life imprisonment should be substituted for capital punishment or of "proving" that the tariff should be revised.

This misconception of the validity of logic is as fatal to good argument as sheer ignorance of logic. The writer who is ignorant of the logic of argument may fail, to be sure, to construct his discourse so that the bearing of each argument on every other argument and on the original proposition will be clear. But the writer who misconceives the validity of his logic, failing to realize that he is dealing throughout only with tendencies and probabilities, will fail to use all available means of making the tendencies seem as strong as possible and the probabilities as great as possible. The discourse of the former will lack logical structure; that of the latter will lack something not less necessary. What the latter lacks, however, should be discussed not under the present title but under that of the Rhetoric of Argument.

ON MILTON'S KNOWLEDGE OF MUSIC .

By Sigmund Gottfried Spaeth, A.M.

ON MILTON'S KNOWLEDGE OF MUSIC.

Even a casual reading of Milton's works, both poetical and prose, brings to light the fact that that extraordinary genius possessed, as a part of his great fund of general information, a most detailed and technical knowledge of music,—a knowledge which, in his case, inspired a reverence for the art and an idealization of its mystic sublimity which no other poet, before or since, has exhibited.

The many editors of Milton's works have commented largely upon this very evident musical appreciation, yet their explanations and interpretations of particular passages have been surprisingly at variance with one another, and have all shown a tendency toward seeking a general or allegorical rather than a particular, concrete meaning. The fact remains, also, that many of Milton's musical references, occurring here and there with no very evident connection, have either been very much slighted or else entirely overlooked. In view of this surprising neglect, therefore, the selection, classification and separate dissection of the musical terms in Milton furnish a most interesting study. The limits of the present article, however, necessarily confine the treatment of the subject to a few scattered notes embodying a discussion of the most important allusions. Some of the points mentioned will naturally be rather obvious, but so far as possible these will be dismissed with a mere passing reference.

It is not a very difficult matter to find natural causes for Milton's musical taste. Aside from the spirit of the age, which was a distinctly musical one, we must take into account the great influences of heredity and personal environment. The statement that the spirit of the age was "distinctly musical" may well be questioned by some who have in mind only the closing of the theatres, the war upon street minstrels, and the fanatical attacks of certain misguided Puritans upon the implements and accessories of church service. It must be remembered, however, that these acts by no means represented the "spirit of the time." Statistics show that there was an uninterrupted flow of musical publications during the Commonwealth, and that, at the very time when the theatres were closed, operas were being prepared for the stage, masques rehearsed, and countless themes composed for instrument and voice. During this period such musicians as the brothers Lawes, "Captain" Cooke, and Dr. Colman flourished, while the works of their predecessors, Coperario, Orlando Gibbons, Morley and Hilton, found a ready market.

The Puritans themselves can hardly be accused of any decided distaste for music. The prevailing impression that they were quite devoid of aesthetic sensibility is absolutely unfounded. Some fanatics there were, whose zealous following of the ascetic life left no room for any pleasure whatsoever. Some there were, who thought themselves the servants of God when engaged in smashing cathedral windows, destroying valuable organs, and burning choirbooks. But these individuals hardly represent the spirit of the entire body. At the worst, the hostility of the Puritans was directed against *church* music only, not secular music, and the latter, except for the closing of the theatres, was allowed to continue its way, uninterrupted. More positive testimony in regard to the Puritans' attitude toward music may be derived from the lives of such representative men as Cromwell, Bunyan and Colonel

Hutchinson. All of the Protector's biographers mention his love of music, his introduction of the "state concerts" and his employment of a private musician, John Hingston, who also acted as instructor to his daughters. John Bunyan's writings show a lively interest in music, which is amply supported by the popular story of the flute cut out of the leg of a prison chair. Colonel Hutchinson, that stern old regicide, is described in his wife's memoirs as one who "could dance admirably well," and "had a great love to music, and often diverted himself with a viol on which he play'd masterly." Aside from such individual cases, the spirit of the time is best illustrated by such quotations as the following from an anonymous "Short Treatise against Stage-Playes" (1625). A list of "natural recreations," such as change of occupation, sleep, etc., concludes with the words: "Musicke is a chearefull recreation to the minde that hath been blunted with serious meditations. These and such like are holy and good recreations, both comfortable and profitable." It is even possible to quote in this connection from Prynne's "Histriomastix," —that celebrated attack upon all light amusements, which proved so costly to its author. He begins his remarks on music with the following words: "That musicke of itselfe is lawfull, usefull and commendable, no man, no Christian, dares denie, since the Scriptures, fathers, and generally all Christian, all Pagan authors extant, do with one consent averre it."

The prevalence of music in all classes of society and under all conditions is pointed out by Chappell, when he says: "Tinkers sang catches; milkmaids sang ballads; carters whistled; each trade and even the beggars, had their special songs; the base-viol hung in the drawing-room for the amusement of waiting visitors, and the lute, cittern and virginals, for the amusement of waiting customers, were the necessary furniture of the barber's shop. They had music at dinner, music at supper, music at weddings, music at funerals, music at night, music at dawn, music at work, music at play."

A passage in Morley's "Plaine and Easie Introduction to Practicall Musicke" (1597) gives sufficient ground for the assertion that a knowledge of music was considered indispensable to the training of a gentleman. In the dialogue between Polymathes and Philomathes, the former says: "I pray you repeat some of the discourses which you had yesternight at Master Sophobulus his banket, for commonly he is not without both wise and learned guestes." Philomathes answers: "It is true indeed, and yesternight there were a number of excellent schollers, both gentlemen and others; but all the propose which was then discoursed upon was musicke."

Polymathes: "I trust you were contented to suffer others to speake of that matter."

Philomathes: "I would that had been the worst; for I was compelled to discover mine own ignorance, and confesse that I knew nothing at all in it."

Polymathes: "How so?"

Philomathes: "Among the rest of the guestes by chance Master Aphron came thither also, who falling to discourse of musicke, was in an argument so quickly taken up and hotly pursued by Eudoxus and Calergus, two kinsmen of Master Sophobulus, as in his own art he was overthrowne, but he still sticking in his opinion, the two gentlemen requested me to examine his reasons and confute them, but I refusing, and pretending ignorance, the whole company condemned me of discourtesie, being fully persuaded that I had been as skilfull in that art as they took mee to be learned in others; but supper being ended, and musicke bookes, according to the custome, being brought to the table, the mistress of the house presented me with a part, earnestly requesting me to sing, but when, after many excuses, I protested unfainedly that I could not, everie one began to wonder, yea some whispered to others, demanding how I was brought up; so that upon shame of mine ignorance I goe nowe to seek out mine old friende Master Gnorimus to make myself his scholar."

It is of interest to compare with this a passage in Peacham's "Compleat Gentleman," in which he says: "I desire no more in you than to sing your part sure and at the first sight; withal to play the same upon your Viol, or the exercise of the Lute, privately to yourself."

Such passages as these show beyond question that English music was enjoying its greatest vogue from the Elizabethan period down to the end of the seventeenth century. While the productions of this time were rarely of sufficient importance to be regarded as "classical," yet their number was so great and their popularity so widespread that they made England a "musically understanding" country. For the structure of these compositions was almost invariably contrapuntal in the extreme, and demanded a knowledge of theory and harmony on the part of both performer and listener. Intricate arrangements and complex elaborations were of more consequence than melodious themes. It was the age of the madrigal, the glee, the "round," the complex "mottect" of sacred music. Cavalier and Puritan alike, soldier, statesman and peasant, all had their part in the universal love of music,—music not merely as an amusement but as a science.

A poet born into such a world as this, and passing his entire life in such an atmosphere, could hardly escape a touch of the general passion. But add to this the more vital influences of heredity, education and personal environment, and the materials for the development of a master musician are complete. Milton's father was a well-known composer of the old school, and some of his work has survived to the present day. He was one of twenty-three contributors to "The Triumphs of Oriana," a collection of madrigals written in honor of Queen Elizabeth, and considered the most successful and representative music book of the time. When the names of other contributors, such as Morley, Wilbye, Bennet and Ellis Gibbons, are mentioned, the prominence of the elder Milton becomes apparent. Edward Philips records that he composed a forty-voiced "In Nomine," for a Polish prince, who rewarded him with a gold chain and medal. Such a feat, by the way, was not at all unusual in those days of elaborate counterpoint. Hawkins and Burney, in their histories of music, both quote compositions of the elder Milton with favorable comment, and one of his psalm tunes, known by the, title of "York," is still in use. The poet's estimate of his father as a musician is exhibited in his Latin elegy, "Ad Patrem," when in the course of his argument in support of his pursuit of literature he says:—

> "Nor thou persist, I pray thee, still to slight
> The sacred Nine, and to imagine vain
> And useless, powers by whom inspired thyself,
> Art skilful to associate verse with airs
> Harmonious, and to give the human voice
> A thousand modulations, heir by right
> Indisputable of Arion's fame.
> Now say, what wonder is it, if a son
> Of thine delight in verse, if so conjoined
> In close affinity, we sympathize
> In social arts and kindred studies sweet?"
>
> (Cowper's Translation.)

If the influences of heredity tended to make Milton a musician, those of education and personal environment certainly played their part in the development of the tendency.   Autobiographical passages scattered all through his works show how thorough was his early training both in practical and theoretical music, undoubtedly at the hands of his able father.   Later he came into contact with many skilled musicians, notably Henry Lawes, immortalized in the "Comus" and the flattering Sonnet XIII.

It would be difficult to estimate the exact extent of Milton's practical ability as a musician.   That he possessed a thorough knowledge of the current systems of harmony and counterpoint must remain undisputed, not only from the clearness and technical correctness of his allusions, but also from the fact that the poet never undertook a study of any kind without obtaining a complete grasp of the subject.   This would not, however, affect his skill as a performer, which can be gauged in no way except by the reports of his biographers.   Aubrey says "He had a delicate, tuneable voice and had good skill.   His father instructed him."   "He had an organ in his house, he played on that most."   One of his biographers reports that he played the viol also, but I can find no foundation for this statement.   All his biographers agree, however, that Milton was an organist of some ability.   The organ mentioned by Aubrey may have been the property of his father before him.   In his youth the poet probably heard the great organ at St. Paul's, and during his University days there was undoubtedly an organ at Christ's College, Cambridge.   Milton's knowledge of the organ, even in its structure and mechanism, appears to be so intimate, and his love for the instrument so great, that his references must here be given some particular comment.   It is inter esting to note that while the poet mentions a wealth of musical instruments, such as the lute, the lyre, the viol, the trumpet, he treats them all in conventional fashion, and it is only when he deals with the organ that he exhibits special partiality and personal affection. It is worth noting that it is the only instrument alluded to in his "Commonplace Book." ("Organa primum in Gallia, Les Ambassadeurs de Constantin emperour Grec apporterent a roy Pepin des Orgues, qu'on n'avoit pas encore veuës en France. Girard, Hist. France, l. 3, p. 138.") When the poet tells us in the "Second Defence of the People of England" that, during his life at Horton, he "occasionally visited the metropolis . . . for the sake of learning something new in mathematics or music," in which he, at that time, "found a source of pleasure and amusement," he may refer to regular organ or singing lessons, although it is more likely that his practical education had by this time been completed and that his trips to London were rather for the sake of *hearing* some new music or possibly buying some recent publications. It is often claimed that Henry Lawes acted as Milton's music teacher, but such a statement has no foundation other than their friendship and mutual regard.

Milton's love for the organ continued all through his life. That he was acquainted with its structure as well as with its manipulation, is shown by the famous passage in the first book of Paradise Lost, describing the building of Pandemonium,—(702-709)

> "A second multitude
> With wondrous art found out the massy ore,
> Severing each kind, and scumm'd the bullion dross;
> A third as soon had form'd within the ground

A various mould, and from the boiling cells
By strange conveyance fill'd each hollow nook,
As in an organ from one blast of wind
To many a row of pipes the sound-board breathes."

The accuracy of this simile has often been remarked upon. Keightley (Life, p. 433) gives the following explanation: "The wind produced by the bellows is driven into a reservoir, called the wind chest (above which is placed the sound-board) and then by intricate contrivances conveyed to each row of pipes. When a stop is drawn, the supply of wind is prepared for every pipe in it and it is admitted when the organist presses the key he wishes to speak."

The structure of the organ and the character of its sounds are often reflected in passages ordinarily considered devoid of musical significance as, for instance, in the use of the word "exhalation," a favorite with Milton, or when, in the "Second Defence" he "can hardly refrain from assuming a more lofty and swelling tone." Such an expression as the latter inevitably suggests the poet sitting at his organ, improvising in simple and "harmonious measures," but with now and then the temptation to draw out a stop and thunder his indignation "fortissimo." The frequent allusions to "pipes" may also have been inspired by the sound of organ-pipes rather than of the primitive instruments, which, to the poet, of course could have been nothing more than a name.

The sublimity of the organ in Milton's estimation is clearly attested by several passages relating to mystic and divine music. In the "Hymn on the Morning of Christ's Nativity," after describing the song of the angels and summoning, as it were, all the forces of Nature to join

in that triumphant chorus, he reaches a musical climax
in the lines—(125-132)

> "Ring out ye crystal spheres,
> Once bless our human ears,
> (If ye have power to touch our senses so,)
> And let your silver chime
> Move in melodious time;
> And let the *bass of Heaven's deep organ blow.*
> And with your ninefold harmony
> Make up full consort to th' angelic symphony."

Here the foundation of the spiritual music is the *organ,*
an instrument most naïvely introduced into this peculiarly Christian interpretation of a pagan conception.

On the hallowed seventh day, the music of Heaven was
by no means silent.   (P. L. VII, 594-599.)

> "the harp
> Had work and rested not, the solemn *pipe,*
> And *dulcimer*, all *organs* of sweet stop,
> All sounds on fret by string or golden wire,
> Tempered soft tunings, intermixt with voice,
> Choral or unison."

The figure here is a different one in the fact that the
inhabitants of Heaven evidently possess separate "organs
of sweet stop" with which they accompany the celestial
choruses.

A most interesting description of the organ in a mystic
setting occurs in the eleventh book of Paradise Lost,
(lines 556 to 563).   Michael is showing Adam in a vision
the future races of men.

> "He look'd and saw a spacious plain, whereon
> Were tents of various hue; by some were herds
> Of cattle grazing; others whence the sound
> Of instruments that made melodious chime
> Was heard, of harp and organ; and who mov'd
> Their stops and chords was seen; his volant touch
> Instinct, through all proportions low and high
> Fled and pursu'd transverse the resonant fugue."

The full force of this picture has never been satisfactorily explained. The passage is fairly teeming with technical terms, and Professor Taylor can hardly be blamed for suggesting that "its pregnant meaning can be fully appreciated only by a musician." Strangely enough, however, even musicians disagree as to the exact significance of such words as "volant," "instinct," "proportions low and high," "transverse" and "resonant." Commentators in general have made no effort to give these terms any definite meaning, and the definitions found in Miss Lockwood's "Dictionary" (the latest authority on the subject) are in most cases unsatisfactory from a musical standpoint. "Volant touch" should present no great difficulty. It can hardly mean anything but a light, fleeting touch, such as a supernatural organist might be assumed to possess. "Instinct," I take it, means that the performer was improvising—playing without notes, but instinctively finding correct harmonies and following the accurate structure of a fugue. What, then, are "proportions low and high?" Joannes Tinctor, who published the first musical dictionary in 1474, said "Proportio est duorum numerorum habitudo," thus making Proportion practically synonymous with Ratio (the arithmetical term), a usage which has continued to the present day. Strictly speaking, however, a true proportion should contain (mathematically) three terms, which is hardly ever true in music. "Of the three principal kinds of Proportion known to mathematicians, two only—the arithmetical and geometrical species—are extensively used in music; the former in connection with differences of pitch and rhythm, the later in the construction of the time table, the scale of organ pipes, and other matters of importance." (Grove's Dictionary of Music.) Milton's reference is obviously to proportions of pitch and rhythm. He probably possessed a table constructed by Thomas Morley (and published in his treatise) in which all the different kinds of proportion then in general use were exhibited. The Octave, for instance, was represented by the Proportion called Dupla, the Perfect Fifth by Sesquialtera, the Perfect Fourth by Sesquitertia. Such simple proportions as these would naturally be called "low," while the more complicated combinations would be termed "high." These words do not, therefore, as I take it, refer to differences of *pitch,* but to degrees of complexity, both in intervals and in time. (Cf. "well-proportioned melodies,"—Second Defence; "disproportioned sin,"—Solemn Music 19; "sounding disproportion to the whole gospel,"—Tetrachordon; "these two proportioned ill, drove me transverse,"—Samson Agonistes, 209.) The words "fled and pursu'd" are here peculiarly apt, when one considers the etymology of the word "fugue" (Lat. fugare)—a *flight* of themes, one chasing the other. "Transverse" can hardly be taken to mean "across the keys," as defined by Miss Lockwood. It refers rather to the themes, crossing and re-crossing, and this meaning is completed by the term "resonant," which must be taken literally as "sounding again and again." The grammatical structure of the sentence presents one more difficulty. Are we to consider "touch" as the subject, making both "fled" and "pursu'd" transitive verbs, with "fugue" as the object? In view of Milton's free use of verbs, transitive and intransitive, such a construction seems permissible and almost necessary. But there is a possibility of considering "his volant touch instinct" as a mere subordinate phrase, making "fugue" the subject of the real sentence, with "fled" and "pursu'd" both used intransitively. Roughly paraphrased, the sentence would then read about as follows: "His light, fleeting touch being instinctive, the fugue, sounding its themes again and again, crossing and recrossing, now fled now pursued, through all kinds of harmonies, simple and complex." The awkwardness of the word-order, although by no means unusual in Milton, would seem to make this interpretation rather far-fetched. In either case, however, the picture is made more distinct and vivid by the substitution of definite, concrete terms for vague, allegorical allusions.

The organ appears also in the musical climax of Il Penseroso (161-166):

> "There let the pealing organ blow
> To the full voic'd quire below,
> In service high, and anthems clear,
> As may with sweetness, through mine ear,
> Dissolve me into ecstasies,
> And bring all Heav'n before mine eyes."

Curiously inconsistent with this is the passage in "Eikonoklastes" in which Milton rails at the follies and hypocrisies of the "King's Chapel." "In his prayer he remembers what 'voices of joy and gladness' there were in his chapel, 'God's house,' in his opinion, between the singing men and the organs; and this was 'unity of spirit in the bond of peace;' the vanity, superstition, and misdevotion of which place was a scandal far and near." It must be admitted, however, that it is the misuse of the organ, rather than the organ itself which is here attacked. Moreover, Milton is speaking for his party, not for himself, and may well be excused for publicly attacking conditions which his private opinion might easily have tolerated.

It is interesting to compare with this a passage in the

little tractate "On Education," in which a very personal
and sincere opinion of music is given. The organ again
figures prominently, "The interim . . . before meat,
may, both with profit and delight, be taken up in recreat-
ing and composing their travailed spirits with the solemn
and divine harmonies of music, heard or learned, either
whilst the skilful organist plies his grave and fancied
descant in lofty fuges, or the whole symphony with artful
and unimaginable touches adorn and grace the well-
studied chords of some choice composer; sometimes the
lute or soft organ-stop waiting on elegant voices, either to
religious, martial, or civil ditties; which, if wise men and
prophets be not extremely out, have a great power over
dispositions and manners, to smooth and make them
gentle from rustic harshness and distempered passions."
The picture here given of the actual organist may well
be compared with that of the visionary one in P. L. XI,
560 ff. In this instance he "plies his grave and fancied
descant in lofty fuges," a performance certainly similar
to that in which the organist instinctively, "through all
proportions low and high, fled and pursu'd transverse
the resonant fugue." Morley defines "descant" (or "dis-
cant") as "singing a part extempore on a playne-song."
The force here is evidently that of improvisation on some
set theme, the words "grave" and "fancied" having much
the same significance as "proportions low and high."
In other words, the organist improvises, probably on well-
known themes, at first in single chords and harmonies,
and then more *fancifully,* with elaborations and complex
"proportions." The care and technical correctness with
which Milton uses the word "descant" is illustrated by
his description of the nightingale who "all night long her
amorous *descant* sung." (P. L. IV, 603.) The aptness

of the word in this connection is obvious, for, of all bird-songs, that of the nightingale probably comes nearest to an actual improvisation.

Granting that the organ was Milton's favorite instrument, it becomes difficult to find any others treated with particular partiality. While the allusions are always technically correct, they are usually also merely conventional, and the instrument seems generally to be selected to fit the situation, rather than the situation the instrument.

In "Areopagitica" a satirical passage, comparing the possible licensing of musical instruments with that of books, makes particular mention of "the lutes, the violins and the guitars in every house," besides "the bagpipe and the rebec" of the villages. The names appearing here are, of course, no indication of the author's taste or preference. (The fact that they are "in every house" furnishes another interesting clue to the prevalence of music in Milton's time.) The rebec (rebeck) has been defined as a kind of fiddle, and seems to be the symbol, in the poet's mind, of village music, as is shown by the well-known lines in L'Allegro, (93-96),

> "When the merry bells ring round,
> And the jocund rebecks sound
> - To many a youth, and many a maid
> Dancing in the chequer'd shade."

In his many descriptions of *sacred* music, Milton naturally refers most often to the harp and the trumpet, the conventional instruments of the angelic hosts. It is significant that when such descriptions are most vivid, a realistic touch is added by the introduction of such instruments as the lute, the lyre, the dulcimer and the organ. The harp is mentioned altogether sixteen times and the trumpet fifteen times in the poetical works. This would seem to indicate that these instruments were the favorites of the poet. This impression, however, is proved false by the fact that the pipe and reed (which occur ten and nine times respectively) stand next in the order of preference, both of them instruments which had no actual existence for Milton. When we realize that, compared with these four (the harp, the trumpet, the pipe and the reed), the actual instruments of the time and of Milton's personal acquaintance receive, with the single exception of the organ, a mere passing mention, then the truth of the matter becomes obvious enough. Milton's instrumental references are in most cases purely *conventional,* and a majority of them necessarily concern either the harp and trumpet, the conventional instruments of the Bible, or the pipe and reed, the conventional instruments of pagan mythology. When we consider how greatly Milton was indebted to these two sources, the prevalence of their conventional instruments is not remarkable. Wherever a more detailed knowledge or a more intimate acquaintance is needed, however, it will be observed that Milton never wanders very far from the *organ,* which is his own instrument, the one which he knows most thoroughly.

The inference which naturally arises from such statistics as the foregoing is that Milton was, in general, more interested and better versed in *vocal* than in *instrumental* music. Several facts may be cited to prove that this is correct. In the age in which he lived, vocal music was, on the whole, much more popular than instrumental. Madrigals, airs, dialogues and rounds were still the commonest forms, while masques, such as "Comus," were pre-

paring the way for the flood of opera which was soon to
follow. Out of forty-five "music books" (*i. e.* collections) published between 1627 and 1659, twenty-eight
were entirely vocal as against nine of an instrumental
character, the rest being a mixture of the two, often inter-
spersed with remarks on theory and harmony. It must
be remembered, also, that Milton's father wrote almost
entirely vocal music, as did Henry Lawes and other
musical friends of the poet. Of Milton's own abilities we
have ample testimony from his biographers. Aubrey has
already been quoted as referring to his "delicate, tuneable
voice." The same biographer makes particular mention
of Milton's singing to keep up his spirits during his
attacks of gout late in life. Further evidence lies in the
fact that he taught his nephews to sing. But the most
convincing proof is found in Milton's writings. In his
Paradise Lost alone, some variation of the verb "sing,"
or the noun "song" occurs no less than sixty-one times,
while reference is made to the human voice in a musical
way, no less than forty-three times. Other poems, and
particularly the prose works, are full of allusions. Whenever the poet wishes to express some general musical idea,
he almost invariably uses the figure of singing. Of course
his use of the term is again in most cases purely conventional. His intimacy with classical poetry and his dependence on its figures of speech would naturally lead to
such a use. At times it is employed as a synonym for
the writing of verse. At other times an actual chant is
implied, in the manner of the ancient bards. But often
the word is to be taken quite literally, as when in the
description of the fallen angels (P. L. II, 553), "Their
song was *partial,* but the harmony (what could it less
when spirits immortal sing?) Suspended Hell, and took

with ravishment the thronging audience." (The word "partial," in this passage, is usually explained as meaning "prejudiced—*i. e.,* "partial to themselves," "sung from their own point of view only." Such a usage seems weak and colloquial for a man of Milton's careful choice of words. Could it not be given a musical significance, in the sense that they were singing very different parts of the same story, each one for himself, yet producing ravishing harmony in *spite* of the "partial" character of the song?)

The commonest forms of vocal music were evidently very familiar to Milton and allusions to them appear frequently in his writings. He naturally gives the preference again to sacred forms, the hymn and the anthem being his favorites. Of the popular and complicated "mottects" (sacred part-songs with instrumental accompaniments) he makes no mention whatever, probably because the word was an extremely unpoetical one, and its meaning could easily be included in the general term "anthem." Airs (ayres) and madrigals were the popular forms of secular song. The latter may be defined as part-songs, written in counterpoint, without instrumental accompaniment, and often set to words of little or no meaning. Airs differed from them in possessing a regular accompaniment and in lacking counterpoint and complex harmonies. This distinction, however, was not always closely observed, and the forms were often confused after the middle of the seventeenth century, when the madrigal was gradually losing its popularity. It may easily be surmised that a form of part-song in which the words were of little moment but the accuracy of harmony all-important, would soon give way to instrumental forms based on the same structure. This was actually the

case, and the "fantasies" and "little consorts" of Milton's
own time are really only madrigals in instrumental form.
There are several allusions to "airs," on the part of Milton,
which may usually be interpreted in the conventional way,
but must in one or two instances be given the technical
force, as when in "Areopagitica" he mentions the combination of "airs and madrigals that whisper softness in
chambers," and when in Sonnet XIII, Henry Lawes is
described as the one "that with smooth *airs*" could "humor
best our tongue." The technical force of the word might
also be applied in such lines as "harmonious *airs* were
heard," P. R. II, 362; "lap me in soft Lydian *airs,*"
L'Allegro, 136; "me softer *airs* befit, and softer strings,"
The Passion, 27.

The waning popularity of the madrigal may account
for the fact that, aside from the passage in "Areopagitica"
mentioned above, Milton makes only one allusion to the
form, where in "Comus" (495) he speaks of "Thyrsis,
whose artful strains have oft delay'd the huddling brook
to hear his *madrigal.*" It will be remembered that the
part of Thyrsis was played by Henry Lawes, a famous
writer of madrigals. This would point to the fact that
the word is here used in its technical sense, as a slight
compliment to the composer, not, as most editors take it,
in the conventional meaning of "pastoral song."

The friendship between Henry Lawes and Milton will
always continue to be of interest to lovers of music and
literature alike. It is doubtful whether Lawes would ever
have attained the fame which he now possesses had it not
been for the enthusiastic eulogies of Milton, not only in
the famous sonnet, but also in the personal passages of
the "Comus." (It should be stated that the poets Waller
and Herrick gave public expression to opinions of

Lawes as flattering as those of Milton.) Henry Lawes
was considerably older than Milton. Their friendship
may have continued up to the time of the composer's death
in 1662. But it is extremely doubtful whether the relations of teacher and pupil ever existed between them.
The inspiration for "Comus" certainly came from Lawes.
(It has been suggested that he may also have been responsible for the "Arcades.") The masque of "Comus"
was written for the occasion of the Earl of Bridgewater's
appointment to the Lord Presidency of Wales and the
Marches, and was performed at Ludlow Castle. Lawes
had consented to supply the music for the celebration.
Being desirous that it should take the popular form of
a masque, he persuaded the young Milton to write the
words of "Comus," which he himself then set to music.
The part of "the Lady" was played by Lady Alice Eger-
ton, a daughter of the Earl, and a pupil of Lawes. The
latter himself took the part of the "Attendant Spirit"
(afterward "Thyrsis"). The performance seems to have
been most successful, and the author was evidently as
much pleased with the music as was the composer with
the lines. Five songs have survived in their original setting, namely "From the Heavens," "Sweet Echo," "Sa-
brina Faïr," "Back Shepherds," and "Now My Task."
The historian Burney, in quoting the song "Sweet Echo,"
points out a number of "inaccuracies of musical accen-
tuations," and refers to one interval in the music as "one
of the most disagreeable notes in melody that the scale
could furnish." He adds, "I should be glad, indeed,
to be informed by the most exclusive admirer of old
ditties, what is the *musical merit* of this song, except
insipid simplicity, and its having been set for a single
voice instead of being mangled by the many-headed mon-

ster madrigal." In view of this severe criticism from a skilled musician, the elaborate praise of Milton's thirteenth sonnet may seem rather artificial. I quote in full: "To Mr. H. Lawes, on the Publishing his Airs."

> "Harry whose tuneful and well measur'd song
> First taught our English music how to span
> Words with just note and accent, not to scan
> With Midas' ears committing short and long;
> Thy worth and skill exempts thee from the throng,
> With praise enough for envy to look wan;
> To after age thou shalt be writ the man,
> That with smooth air could'st humour best our tongue.
> Thou honour'st Verse, and Verse must lend her wing,
> To honour thee, the priest of Phœbus' quire.
> That turn'st their happiest lines in hymn or story.
> Dante shall give Fame leave to set thee higher
> Than his Cassella, whom he woo'd to sing,
> Met in the milder shades of Purgatory."

("Various readings" are of interest from a musical standpoint in line 4, "*misjoining* short and long" and in line 6, "and gives thee praise above the pipe of Pan.") Veiled compliments to the musician are also implied in such lines of the "Comus" as the following (86-88),

> "Who with his soft pipe and smooth-dittied song
> Well knows to still the wild winds when they roar,
> And hush the waving woods."

And the lines (494 ff.) quoted above, "Thyrsis, whose artful strains," etc. And again in lines 623-625,

> "He lov'd me well, and oft would beg me sing,
> Which when I did, he on the tender grass
> Would sit and hearken even to ecstasy."

Milton evidently felt that Lawes' settings were more in harmony with the *words* than those of other musicians, who overpowered the beauty of the lines by the force of

their own melodies.   In this connection Burney's opinion
is again interesting.   He says "The notes set by Lawes
to the song of 'Sweet Echo,' neither constitute an air nor
melody, and, indeed, they are even too frequently pro-
longed for recitative.   It is difficult to give a name, from
the copious technica with which the art of music is furnished, to such a series of unmeaning sounds." As a matter
of fact, this style of musical setting is generally known
as "aria parlante,"—implying a preservation of the accent and rhythm of the spoken words, without sufficient
melody to direct the attention from them.   It is only
natural that such a style should have been popular with
the poets who supplied the words.   Lawes was content
to subordinate his music to his lines.   His reward was
an immortal characterization from the pen of one of the
world's greatest poets.   (It is worth noting that Lawes
made a change in the lines of "Sweet Echo," which
undoubtedly detracted from their beauty but was evidently
countenanced by the poet.   The words "and give *resound-
ing grace* to all heaven's harmonies," become in the Lawes
setting "and *hold a counter-point* to all heaven's harmonies,"—technical but not particularly graceful.)   In 1637
Lawes, in answer to a general demand, published the
"Comus" (without music) probably with the consent of
the author, and in the following year he obtained for
Milton his passport for continental travel.   After this
time there is no evidence of continued friendship on the
part of the musician and the poet, although Milton's
eulogistic Sonnet appeared with other tributes of a similar
character in the first edition of Lawes' "Ayres and Dialogues" (1653).

The influence of Milton's Italian journey upon his
musical taste and knowledge must be considered as ex-

tremely important. We have a record in one of his letters
of a "musical entertainment" which he attended, and he
surely must have come into contact with many musicians
both in Florence and in Rome. That his interest in music
at this time was unabated is shown by the fact that he
"sent home a chest or two of choice musick-books of the
best masters flourishing about that time in Italy." (Life,
by Edward Philips.) It is very probable that Milton
acquired his knowledge of "fugue" in Italy, for that style
of organ music had just been perfected by the great Frescobaldi (not to be confused with the Florentine academ-
ician, Pietro Frescobaldi, mentioned by Milton in his
letters.) The influence of the Italian phraseology is apparent in many of the poet's later musical terms. He
had always, however, shown a fondness for words of Italian
origin, as appears from his frequent use of "concent"
(concento), "symphony" (sinfonia), "serenate" (sere-
nata), etc. "Concento" is the technical term for the striking of all the notes in a chord of unison (the opposite of
arpeggio). Its musical force becomes evident in such
lines as "that undisturbéd song of pure *concent.*" (Solemn
Music, 6.) (Browne retains "content" as in the edition
of 1645. Some editors spell "consent," which is obviously
out of place.) (Cf. a line from the Prolusion "Utrum
Dies an Nox præstantior sit?" "Cum vel ipsæ volucres
nequeant suum celare gaudium, quin egressæ nidulis,
ubi primum diluculavit, aut in verticibus arborum *con-
centu suavissimo* deliniant omnia, aut sursum lib-
rantes se, et quam possunt prope solem volitent, redeunti
gratulaturæ luci." Cf. also "audi argutos auvium *con-
centus* et leves apum susurros," occurring in a Prolusion
"Mane citus lectum fuge," presumed to be by Milton.)
The word "symphony" is often used as if synonymous

with "harmony," but must sometimes be given a more technical meaning. For instance, when, in the tractate "On Education," "the whole symphony with artful and unimaginable touches adorn and grace the well-studied chords of some choice composer," the meaning is evidently that of a choir or orchestra, playing some set piece, full of art, and of scientific, well-studied construction. At times, the word must be taken literally as a certain style of composition. In this sense it appears in P. L. V, 162—"and choral *symphonies,* day without night," and in the Hymn on the Nativity, 132—"make up full consort to the angelic symphony." The word is also used as the name of a mediæval musical *instrument* (sinfonia) of the pipe family, and it may possibly be interpreted in this sense in P. L. 1, 712—"the sound of dulcet *symphonies* and voices sweet." (The modern "symphony" as a musical form, had, of course, not yet appeared in Milton's time.)

Such facts as the foregoing are sufficient to prove the technical correctness of Milton's musical knowledge. He never used musical terms in a slip-shod manner, and it is a mistake to interpret them loosely. He never was guilty of such mistakes as appear even in Shakespeare, when in the one hundred and twenty-eighth sonnet he speaks of virginal keys which "kiss the tender inward of thy hand." (Other notable examples of musical errors are Browning's description of a fugue in "Master Hugues of Saxe Gotha," —interesting, but incorrect; Coleridge's *"loud* bassoon" in the "Ancient Mariner;" and Tennyson's agonizing combination of "violin, flute and bassoon" as a band in "Maud.") Such errors as these were impossible with a man of Milton's training and thoroughness. But it is to be noted that he did not allow his technical knowledge to keep him from idealizing the art and surrounding it with a mystic glamor which placed it among the most sacred things of the universe. To him, music was an element, a principle, something inherent in Nature, universal, and, in its essence, incomprehensible to mankind. He accepted the "sphere-music" of the ancients as an important part of his remarkable cosmography, and he Christianized the pagan superstition by making his Heaven a musical one, with troops of singing angels, and with a perpetual, supernatural harmony. The great "Hymn on the Morning of Christ's Nativity" might almost be called a "study in sounds," so full is it of melody, not only in suggestion but reality. The song of the angels is pictured in ideal fashion—

> "When such music sweet,
> Their hearts and ears did greet,
> As never was by mortal finger strook;
> Divinely-warbled voice,
> Answering the stringed noise,
> As all their souls in blissful rapture took;
> The air such pleasure loth to lose,
> With thousand echoes still prolongs each heav'nly
>   close." (93-100)

> . . . . . .

> "Such music (as 'tis said)
> Before was never made,
> But when of old the sons of morning sung,
> While the Creator great,
> His constellations set,
> And the well-balanc't world on hinges hung,
> And cast the dark foundations deep,
> And bid the weltring waves their oozy channel keep."

> "Ring out ye crystal spheres,
> Once bless our human ears,
> (If ye have power to touch our senses so)
> And let your silver chime
> Move in melodious time;
> And let the bass of Heaven's deep organ blow;
> And with your ninefold harmony
> Make up full consort to th' angelic symphony."
>   (117-132.)

I have already remarked on the addition of the "bass" of "Heaven's deep organ" to the "sphere-music" in this passage. It is only one of many instances in which a pagan myth is given by Milton a Christian interpretation. The music which "the sons of morning sung" seems to be described in P. L. VII, 252-260:

> "Nor past uncelebrated, nor unsung,
> By the celestial quires, when orient light
> Exhaling first from darkness they beheld;
> Birthday of heav'n and earth; with joy and shout
> The hollow universal orb they fill'd,
> And touch't their golden harps, and hymning prais'd
> God and his works, Creator him they sung,
> Both when first ev'ning was, and when first morn."

Again in 449:

> "The sixth, and of creation last, arose
> With ev'ning harps and matin."

And on the seventh day (594-599)

>   "the harp
> Had work and rested not, the solemn pipe,
> And dulcimer, all organs of sweet stop,
> All sounds on fret by string or golden wire,
> Tempered soft tunings, intermixt with voice
> Choral or unison."

In connection with the heavenly music, I cannot refrain from quoting entire the lines entitled "At a Solemn Music":

> "Blest pair of Sirens, pledges of Heav'ns joy,
> Sphere-born harmonious sisters, Voice and Verse,
> Wed your divine sounds; and mixt power employ
> Dead things with inbreath'd sense able to pierce;
> And to our high-rais'd phantasy present
> That undisturbéd song of pure concent,
> Aye sung before the sapphire-colour'd throne
> To him that sits thereon

With saintly shout and solemn jubilee ;.
Where the bright seraphim in burning row
Their loud up-lifted angel trumpets blow,
And the cherubic host in thousand quires
Touch their immortal harps of golden wires,
With those just spirits that wear victorious palms,
Hymns devout and holy psalms
Singing everlastingly :
That we on Earth with undiscording voice
May rightly answer that melodious noise ;
As once we did, till disproportion'd sin
Jarr'd against nature's chime, and with harsh din
Broke the fair music that all creatures made
To their great Lord ; whose love their motion sway'd
In perfect diapason, whilst they stood
In first obedience, and their state of good.
O may we soon again renew that song,
And keep in tune with Heav'n, till God ere long
To His celestial consort us unite,
To live with Him, and sing in endless morn of light."

("Various readings" are again interesting in line 11, "loud symphony of silver trumpets blow," and line 18, "by leaving out those harsh, ill-sounding [chromatic] jars Of clamorous sin that all our music mars.")

A curious musical interpretation of the connection between heaven and earth, sin, man and eternal life, is evident in these lines. The inhabitants of Heaven are perfect in their music, which continues everlastingly in praise of the Creator, whereas the inhabitants of earth are out of tune and unable to comprehend the higher music. Evidently there was harmony between heaven and earth before "disproportion'd sin jarr'd against Nature's chime" and caused eternal discord. (According to the myth, the music of the spheres was always beyond the reach of human ears. This Christian conception is infinitely more reasonable and interesting.) The use of the word "diapason" is important. It is the mediæval term for the

interval of the octave, and it is only natural to suppose
that Milton had in mind a harmony in which the earth
was tuned, as it were, an octave lower than heaven, thus
singing in perfect accord with the "celestial consort" (in
this case used in the sense of "band, orchestra.")   The
prayer of the closing lines is naturally to the effect that
humanity may at some time return to that primitive state
of harmony when all the universe joined in one great song
to the Creator.   A hint as to the nature of this instinctive
harmony, before the days of sin, may be found in the
description of the orisons of Adam and Eve (P. L. V, 144-
152.)

> "Lowly they bow'd adoring, and began
> Their orisons, each morning duly paid
> In various style, for neither various style
> Nor holy rapture wanted they to praise
> Their Maker, in fit strains pronounc't or sung
> Unmeditated, such prompt eloquence
> Flow'd from their lips, in prose or numerous verse,
> More tuneable than needed lute or harp
> To add more sweetness."

A passage in the "Arcades" (62-73) gives the most con-
cise account of Milton's conception of sphere-music.

> "Then listen I
> To the celestial Sirens' harmony,
> That sit upon the nine infolded Spheres,
> And sing to those that hold the vital shears
> And turn the adamantine spindle round,
> On which the fate of gods and men is wound.
> Such sweet compulsion doth in music lie,
> To lull the daughters of Necessity,
> And keep unsteady Nature to her law,
> And the low world in measured motion draw
> After the heavenly tune, which none can hear
> Of human mould with gross unpurgéd ear."

The uniformity of conception in these passages is really remarkable. I may include also some lines from the elegy "Ad Patrem" (34-43, *Cowper's Translation*).

> "We, too, ourselves, what time we seek again
> Our native skies, and one eternal now
> Shall be the only measure of our being,
> Crowned all with gold, and chaunting to the lyre
> Harmonious verse, shall range the courts above,
> And make the starry firmament resound;
> And, even now, the fiery spirit pure
> That wheels yon circling orbs, directs, himself,
> Their mazy dance with melody of verse
> Unutterable, immortal."

It becomes evident from the citations above, that Milton's musical references may be roughly divided into three great classes, which I shall call the technical, the conventional (or historical) and the idealistic. The first is in many ways the most important, for without the technical knowledge as a foundation it is doubtful whether the ideal treatment could exist. To the second class belong all historical references, and that multitude of allusions which are inspired by the conventional usages of mythology. Often it is almost impossible to distinguish between the musical reference introduced for its own sake, and the necessary insertion of some musical term in a conventional description. Classification is, accordingly, extremely difficult, but it is safe to say that in a majority of cases the *music* and not the mythology was uppermost in Milton's mind. Finally we have the idealistic class of references, without which Milton's music would be dry and uninteresting to all but technical scholars. With his mystic idealization, his deep-seated theory of universal harmony, music takes on new life. Its subtle force is applied in all directions. It breathes through the sounds of Nature, winds whisper it, waves echo it, it reappears in the song of birds. It holds the universe together and it is essential to the existence of an ideal Heaven. It is no exaggeration to say that, in spite of the multitude of technical references, at the existence of which these scattered notes have merely hinted, in spite of the many interesting echoes of musical mythology and of musical history, the subject could not possibly be a living one to the student of Milton, were it not for the insight which it gives into the mystical temperament of the poet,—the temperament which rejoiced in a sacred veneration, a glorification, an idealization of the art of music. It is summed up in the beautiful lines which mark the climax of "L'Allegro" (135-144):

> "And ever against eating cares,
> Lap me in soft Lydian airs,
> Married to immortal verse;
> Such as the meeting soul may pierce,
> In notes with many a winding bout
> Of linkèd sweetness long drawn out;
> With wanton heed, and giddy cunning,
> The melting voice through mazes running;
> Untwisting all the chains that tie
> The hidden soul of harmony."

GEORGE HERBERT: AN INTERPRETATION.

By Walter S. Hinchman, A.M.

GEORGE HERBERT: AN INTERPRETATION

I. THE PLACE.

"Delay, they say, begetteth peril; but it is rather this itch of doing that undoes men."—*(Stevenson, "Black Arrow.")*

Every summer a few visit with knowledge and deep regard the last earthly home of George Herbert; many others stop at Bemerton because they have a vague remembrance of a poet clergyman who sometime lived and died there. Both these classes, however, are far outnumbered by those who fly head-in-air past the little Wiltshire parish. Yet those who make little visits to the verse of Herbert, or to Bemerton—and in truth those who know them never think of the one without the other—feel themselves ever richly rewarded.

If, then, you have unhorsed *atra cura,* and have no longer fear of "the perils of delay," you will be able to linger quietly in Salisbury, with the prospect of mornings and evenings—and, let us hope, a Sunday—ahead. Salisbury is the Cathedral: for though you make the town your headquarters for excursions to Old Sarum and Stonehenge and Wilton—and, this time, Bemerton—the object you see first from the train, the point that catches your eye when far off on Sarum Plain, or the old road to Wilton, is the spire of the Cathedral; the first thing you go to see in Salisbury is the Cathedral; and in the long English twilights you wander about the "close"—perhaps the finest in all England—or read a bit of Sidney or Herbert under the old tall trees, until the grayness draws on, and only the spire, dark against the sky, is still distinct. Then you need neither to read nor to wander; you are

at peace and joining in the great silent service of God's
temple.   That is the influence of Salisbury, and that is
the simple charm of the Cathedral.   Of course you will
study the interior, note the perfect example of "early
English" architecture, admire the tomb of that fine old
Crusader, William Longsword, learn the history of the
so-called Boy-Bishop, loiter in the beautiful cloisters, and
condemn the ruthless restorations of Wyatt; and on Sunday you will enjoy the simple dignity of the service in an
old graysided English Cathedral.   But if you have not
been alone in silent service under the tall trees, at the
time when English evening is at its loveliest, and if you
do not go home to bed with a gentle hymn at your heart,
you will not know Salisbury or the Cathedral there.

   With such an evening behind you, you may wander
the next afternoon out on the old Wilton road, shaded by
arching elms which in their day have perhaps looked upon
the proud charger of Sir Philip Sidney, as he rode to
Pembroke Castle.   About a mile and a half on the way,
you will find a turning to the left, running between high
hedges down to the village of Bemerton.   If you ask the
passer-by to point out the village church, he will show you
a large new edifice on the hill towards Wilton, and if
you should ask him of George Herbert, he would probably
look as if he did not speak the language.   But if you
keep to the left for about one hundred yards, you will
find, at a fork in the road, a little ivy-hidden chapel behind
a wall of climbing roses.   In this little building, which
can scarce seat fifty people, are the simple letters "G. H.,"
cut in the stone on the left side of the chancel, and under-
neath, "1632."   One or two things in the church are
interesting, especially the porch and the little window
behind the reading-desk.   The building dates perhaps two

centuries before Herbert, but Wyatt has been here as well as at Salisbury, so the whole east end is a result of his "itch of doing."

Outside the church, the little graveyard should not be hastily passed by; not that it is interesting as a graveyard, but lying as it does about the old church, holding as it does the bones of those who link you through the centuries to the poet clergyman, it is perhaps the best place to drink in the quiet loveliness that is Bemerton, that is George Herbert.   By this time the sun will be low in the west—striking long yellow shafts through the tall trees.   There is no sound but that of the wind, soft in the highest tops, the distant call of a rook, black across the light, or the sharp note of the swifts, out for the evening insects.   A proud robin hops before you, as if he had done a good day's work, and were out in his "Sunday best" for a promenade.   Then hark! those are the bells of Salisbury Cathedral, and if you turn you will see its tall spire over a house and a hill of golden grain, bright in the light of the setting sun—the same spire that George Herbert saw through the summer evenings, the same bells that perhaps called him from meditation by the very grave where you are standing.

And so, as the long twilight draws almost imperceptibly on, you stroll along, past green places by running waters, to Wilton.   You will carry with you, too, the spirit of gentleness and loveliness of Bemerton—the delight in tall trees and green grass and dark running waters and an old world chapel—the spirit of the beauty and gentleness of George Herbert.   And if you are up betimes the next morning, you will hear the lark against the morn, and see the dew on the rose, and feel the wonder of an English lane.

What, after all, is significant in these things? Why should one speak of the Cathedral spire, the evening under the trees, the old road to Wilton, the graveyard, and the robin on the grass? Did you never look over a bridge at running water? And as you looked, did your thoughts never flow with the leaf in the current, over bright shallows and in dark eddies, on past village and town to the sea? Well, as you lie along the banks of the full, fresh-flowing Nadder, a "strange mysterious dream of lively portraiture" will "wave at his wings" before your eyes, and Salisbury and Bemerton and Wilton will suggest these things—the distant spire, and the little church by the graveyard, and the tall trees—and ever the hymn at the heart.

You, however, are only a passer-by. *You* may drink never so deep of this spirit, *you* are, nevertheless, off in a few days for London and its proud sights. But that lark you heard in the dawning—it lives in this spirit, it rises every morning to all this glory, it knows well the Cathedral spire, it has ever the hymn at the heart. And so in the days of King Charles, when London's tumult of modern machinery was supplied by the clash of arms, and by visits to the Tower that cost far more than your sixpence, there lived a gentle soul, George Herbert, who, like the lark, took inspiration from this spire, from these trees and meadows and waters. If you think of Bemerton, it is to think of "G. H. 1632" cut in the little church wall, and then you are carried on again down the stream past village and town to the sea.

II. THE MAN.

"Only a sweete and vertuous soul,
Like season'd timber, never gives."
(George Herbert, "Temple.")

The note of the Wiltshire landscape is the chief note in the life and verse of George Herbert.   True, a proportionately short period of his life was spent at Bemerton, but his early years prepared him peculiarly for his final earthly home—as did the Wiltshire parish for his heavenly resting place— so that the two years actually passed as Rector of Bemerton were relatively great in significance. Born in Wales, educated at Cambridge, government officer in London—George Herbert lacked, until he came to Bemerton, the final chord that should make the melody of his life complete.   It was here that his gentle spirit first took an unwavering course; it was here that the song of his life first struck a permanent note.   Wiltshire ever sings its song—in the shade of the tall trees, in the glad sunlit downs, in the melody of the flowing waters, in the skyward pointing spire—sings it, too, in the life and verse of George Herbert.

George Herbert, the fifth son of Richard Herbert and Magdalen Newport, and brother of Edward, Baron Herbert of Cherbury, was born on the 3d of April, 1593—in the family castle of Montgomery, Wales.   His mother seems to have had a strong and beautiful influence over her sons; for after the father's death in 1597, she gave herself up, says Grosart in his memorial-introduction to Herbert's Poetical Works, "with a fine enthusiasm of consecration to the training and general education of her fatherless family, in their castled home and at Oxford." This affection had such a lasting influence that up to her death in 1627, George always consulted her wishes.

About his twelfth year—just after King James had ascended the throne—George was sent to Westminster school, his family having meanwhile moved to Oxford. In his fifteenth year he was elected King's scholar for Trinity College, Cambridge. Both at school and at college he speedily made a name for himself by his scholarship, oratory, and Latin verses. In 1616, he received the degree of A.M., and the following year became "sublector quartae classis." In 1619, he was made public orator—the *sinecure,* says Isaac Walton, "that Queen Elizabeth had formerly given to her favorite, Sir Philip Sidney, and valued to be worth an hundred and twenty pounds." His chief duty was to write letters to the government. This office brought George Herbert in contact with the court, and with many prominent men, among whom may be numbered Bacon, Lennox, Richmond, Hamilton, and Pembroke. That this acquaintance was more than official is attested by the later liberality of the Earl of Pembroke, in rebuilding Layton Church, and by "the affectionate dedication by Bacon to him of his versification of certain Psalms." Soon after the death of James, however, the Buckingham-Charles policy, sickness, and religious reflections caused Herbert to resign his position, and "betake himself to a retreat from London to a friend in Kent, where he lived very privately, and was such a lover of solitariness as was judged to impair his health more than his study had done." "In this time of retirement," continues Walton, "he had many conflicts with himself, whether he should return to the painted pleasures of a court life, or betake himself to a study of divinity, and enter into sacred orders, to which his dear mother had often persuaded him. These were such conflicts as they only can know that have endured them; for ambitious desires and the outward glory of the world are not easily laid aside; but at last God inclined him to put on a resolution to serve at His Altar."

This conflict is an important point in George Herbert's life; for "the resolution to serve at His Altar" was not made without a struggle.   It was indeed a *resolution,* not the passive submissiveness of unearned piety.   Witness "The Collar," one of Herbert's best poems; in it are both the struggle and the resolution—the beautiful answer that such a nature as his could at last gladly give:—

> "I struck the board and cry'd, 'No more; I will abroad.'
> What! Shall I ever sigh and pine?
> My lines and life are free, free as the road,
> Loose as the winds, as large as store.
>   Shall I be still in suit?
> Have I no harvest but a thorn
> To let me bloud, and not restore
> What I have lost with cordiall fruit?
>   Sure there was wine
> Before my sighs did drie it; there was corn
> Before my tears did drown it;
> Is the yeare onely lost to me?
> Have I no bayes to crown it?
> No flowers, no garlands gay? All blasted, all wasted?
> Not so, my heart; but there is fruit,
>   And thou hast hands.
>
> *   *   *   *   *   *   *   *
>
> But as I raved and grew more fierce and wild
>   At every word,
> Methought I heard one calling, 'Childe;'
>   And I reply'd, 'My Lord.'"

The last six years, then, from his thirty-fourth year to his fortieth, were the period spent in the church.   In 1626, Herbert was made Prebend of Layton Ecclesia, in the Diocese of Lincoln; which, with the help of London friends, he recovered from a dilapidated condition.   In 1629, "he was seized with a sharp quotidian ague," the effects of which never left him, "for he brought upon himself a disposition to rheums and other weaknesses, and a supposed consumption." He seems to have recovered sufficiently, however, to marry rather suddenly Jane Danvers. The romantic story told by quaint Isaac Walton—though highly improbable—is well worth while. It seems that Mr. Charles Danvers entertained so high an esteem for George Herbert "that he often and publicly declared a desire that Mr. Herbert would marry any one of his nine daughters—for he had so many—but rather his daughter Jane than any other, because Jane was his beloved daughter." Mr. Danvers, in short, "so much commended Mr. Herbert to her, that Jane became so much a platonic as to fall in love with Mr. Herbert unseen. This was a fair preparation for marriage; but, alas! her father died before Mr. Herbert's retirement to Dauntsey;[1] yet some friends to both parties procured their meeting; at which time a mutual affection entered into both their hearts, as a conqueror enters into a surprised city; and love, having got such possession, governed, and made there such laws and resolutions as neither party was able to resist; insomuch, that she changed her name into Herbert the third day after this first interview." Considering that Charles Danvers' "profound esteem" was the result of "long and familiar knowledge of Mr. Herbert" and that Sir John Danvers, a near relative, had been for sixteen years the second husband of George Herbert's mother, it is improbable that Jane and George had not met frequently before— but no matter!

On April 26, 1630, Dr. Davenant, Bishop of Salisbury, "inducted" George Herbert into the parsonage of Bemer-

---

[1] Herbert retired to Dauntsey in Wiltshire (where Mr. Danvers lived) to recover from his consumption.

ion.   As the biographer Grosart has well said: "It were
to violate the sanctities of reverence to retell the story of
the 'ministry' at Bemerton and its all too premature close"
—"an almost incredible story," says Isaac Walton, "of
the great sanctity of the short remainder of his holy life:
a life so full of charity, humility, and all Christian virtues
that it deserves the eloquence of St. Chrysostom to com-
mend and declare it."   Here, beloved of all, he went his
daily round, filling two short years "full of charity,
humility, and all Christian virtues."   It is said that "some
of the meaner sort of his parish did so love and reverence
Mr. Herbert, that they would let their plough rest when
Mr. Herbert's Saint's-bell rang to prayers, that they might
also offer their devotions to God with him; and would
then return back to their plough."

But the end soon came.   "The sharp sword of the ever
active spirit wore out its fragile sheath, the body."   On
the 3d of March, 1632 (o. s.), George Herbert was bur-
ied in Bemerton Church.   There you may read "G. H.
1632" scratched on the northern wall.   Walton tells
touchingly the story of his death: "He called for one of
his instruments, took it into his hand, and said,

> 'My God, my God,
> My musick shall find Thee
>   And every string
> Shall have His attribute to sing;

and having tuned it, he played and sung:

> 'The Sundaies of man's life,
> Thredded together on Time's string,
> Make bracelets to adorn the wife
> Of the eternall glorious King:
> On Sunday, Heaven's dore stands ope,
> Blessings are plentifull and rife
>   More plentifull than hope.'

Thus he sang on earth such hymns and anthems as the angels and he and Mr. Farrer now sing in heaven." "He not merely *walked* down 'the valley of the shadow of death,' says Grosart—knowing no 'fear' and making no 'haste'—but sang." Just before his death, he consigned his unprinted verses, "The Temple," to Mr. Duncon, to be delivered to his "dear brother Farrer." "Desire him to read it," he said, "and then, if he can think it may turn to the advantage of any dejected, poor soul, let it be made public; if not, let him burn it; for I and it are less than the least of God's mercies."

Brother Farrer had the good sense to make public the verses. They are inseparably linked with Bemerton and George Herbert; they are the expression of the man when his life was attuned to the spirit of the place. Let us, then, sit down for a few moments under the "immemorial elms," with the Nadder whispering at the bend, and glance at some of these old religious lyrics, with their quaint seventeenth century conceits, their flashes of spontaneity, their strong individual note—their melody of the waters of Wiltshire.

Professor Palmer, in his recent careful analysis of Herbert's verse, has given a thorough survey of the religious lyric in the 17th century. Perhaps a word, however—for the sake of continuity—is justifiable. The lyrics of the century are famous; were one to mention only the rulers of verse—Shakespeare, Jonson, Milton, Herrick—proof would be complete. Outside of the better known poets, however, there were countless lyricists of varying merit; in fact, the English lyric has never flourished so luxuriantly as in the seventeenth century. The breadth of imagination, the spontaneity and originality of thought, the unerring felicity of phrase which had characterized the Elizabethans were not quite banished, but rather imprisoned by the conscious art, the perfected form of the Jacobeans. The consequence was lyrics of every conceivable form with spontaneity as well as with *finesse*—lyrics strangled rudely in their prime by Puritanism.

The poems of the period, moreover, fall, roughly speaking, into two convenient classes—*religious* and so-called *cavalier*. Milton's life shows that it is indeed difficult to make this distinction rigid, that a Puritan could be either Churchman or Dissenter, that a man could write verse which evinced a love for ecclesiastical pomp and yet, politically, be strong for Parliament. It is fair to say, however, that lyric poets, with a few exceptions, tended to confine themselves to one class or other, so that by the outbreak of war—1642—almost no writer of lyrics dealt with both kinds, religious and cavalier. Those who did invariably felt uncomfortable in the unaccustomed attire. It must be admitted, for instance, that Herrick was in spirit a cavalier poet, that 'the more pagan the better' is strikingly true of him, and that when he prayed the Lord in his "Noble Numbers" that his hen might meet with daily success in egg-laying he was quite at his worst. As a clergyman, he felt the necessity of writing something *religious;* there was a growing gulf between that and *cavalier*—so he climbed down from his Pegasus, and, forgetting that he must mount a spiritual steed, wrote standing right in his barnyard. Milton frankly took to prose. It was among such poetical possibilities that Herbert wrote. Yet, before him, few had been able to write religious verse quite freed from the trappings of sexual passion. In this sense he was one of the first to write completely religious lyrics, a form of verse which has become so well known to-day.

The bearing of Herbert's education and environment
on his lyrical impulses was important.   Both had their
tap-root in the church, though superficial roots may
have fed on a soil of gay cavalier pageantry.   But this
soil must have been very superficial; what of worldly
picturesqueness he did see—at least by the time he began
to write his verses—went down before him as "vain
pleasures;" the spirit of "boot, saddle, to horse
and away" was the antithesis of this gentle soul.
His gentleness, moreover, was backed up by resolutions
and quaintly conscious art, in support of his Master.   It
is most probable that the fine sensibilities of his lady
mother, together with the rich sonorous music of the
church, left a lasting influence; while the phase of his
London environment which may have burned most strongly
into his character—especially by virtue of his intimate
acquaintance with court extravagance—was the great
movement for purity and simplicity.   All this is the
more probable since the mental attitude of a man is half
the force of what determines *his* influences—the liquid
metal is as necessary to the mould as the mould to the
liquid metal.

Much of Herbert's verse, it must be admitted, is of a
not very high order.   In the first place, he is dwarfed by
his contemporaries; his voice is small beside that of "deep-
chested Chapman" or "firm-footed Ben."   In the second
place, the quaintness often renders it dull to anyone who
is not particularly interested in seventeenth century lyrics.
There is, on the other hand, much of genuine worth; and
one finds, if one considers always the man and the place
together with the verse, true touches that could have come
from none of the great contemporaries.   Everywhere is
met the gentle soul, "full of all Christian virtues," regard-

ing with almost Puritanic disfavor the gilded glories of the court, speaking ever of the "beauty of holiness," and taking up, finally, his instrument on his deathbed to sing once more a hymn of praise.

Herbert's verse is indeed moral—sometimes unattractively so. The same impulse that had led Milton to "scorn delights and live laborious days"—the vanity and frailty of mankind—had, as we have seen, guided Herbert to Layton and Bemerton. This didacticism, with its Puritanic touch, not infrequently kills rudely the charm of the verse; for example:

> "Summe up at night what thou has done by day,
> And in the morning what thou hast to do;
> Dresse and undresse thy soul; mark the decay
> And growth of it; if with thy watch that too
> Be down; then wind up both: since we shall be
> Most surely judged, make thy accounts agree."

Admirable advice—but the artist stops in the middle of the next to last line.

Herbert constantly impresses one, however, with the sanity of his didacticism. He clings to the beautiful forms of the English church; he finds in the "via media" room for both mystical worship and moral instruction. The poem on "Constancie" expresses well this sanity:

> "Who is the honest man?
> He that doth still and strongly good pursue,
>   *   *   *   *   *   *   *   *
> Who rides his sure and even trot,
> While the world now rides by, now lags behind."

The old sense of honesty is preserved in these lines; "moderation," "sanity" are there too.

But if one is wearied for a moment with the didacticism, one soon forgets it for the chief charm of the poems— gentleness, fullness of song, spontaneity of thought—after all, the characteristics of the man. There lacks the ingenuous enthusiasm of the Renaissance, but there is wanting, too, the shallow apotheosis of form of the Augustans. One finds, however—naturally enough, too, if one recalls the date—a suggestion of the imaginativeness and fine splendour of Shakespeare's England, the compact thought of Jonson's age, and the skill in polishing to which all the lyricists of the time aspired. Indeed this perfection in trifles often breaks out in quaint conceits. One poem is in the form of an altar; another of Easter wings; a third bears the title "Ana (Mary) (Army) gram;" a fourth has the line:

> "Shall Thy strokes be my stroking?"

—devices dictatorially condemned by Addison. The studied art, however, does not often, as in Quarles, obscure to modern eyes, or, as in Crashaw, provoke irrelevant mirth. Beneath the extravagant figures descriptive of "Prayer," for example, one feels the final touch of a master:

> "Prayer, the churche's banquet, Angels' age,
> God's breath in man returning to his birth,
> The soul in paraphrase, heart in pilgrimage,
> The Christian plummet sounding heav'n and earth;
> *   *   *   *   *   *   *   *
> Church-bells beyond the stars heard, the soul's blood,
> The land of spices, something understood."

This man's face was turned upwards. In little expressions, running like a glimpse of the fresh Wiltshire morning through the poems, in lines like:

> "I made a posie while the day ran by"

—one catches, too, the note of a "sweete singer." Though Herbert never attains to the occasional felicity—the "deep-sea stirrings," as Professor Schelling puts it—of Henry

Vaughan, yet he strikes, at his best, a quite individual note
that is true and of a fine melody—

> "Chase brave employment with a naked sword
> Throughout the world. Fool not, for all may have,
> If they dare choose, a glorious life or grave."

This is of a different and higher order than anything
already quoted.   No room for conceits here; it is truth—
gleam of naked sword. An "Easter Song" sums up in
four of its lines the main theme of Herbert's verse and
life:

> "I got me flowers to straw Thy way,
> I got me boughs off many a tree;
> But Thou wast up by break of day,
> And brought'st Thy sweets along with Thee."

There is the "life of charity, humility, and all Christian
virtues;" there is Bemerton Church and the evening light;
there are the tall trees, the Cathedral spire, and the gentle
hymn at the heart.

III.   THE MEDLAR-TREE.

> "Those trees for evermore bear fruit
> And evermore do spring:
> There evermore the angels are,
> And evermore do sing."
>
> "O Mother dear, Jerusalem." *Anon.*

We have followed, then, George Herbert down to his
little parish of Bemerton, and we have lingered under the
old elms long enough to catch at least a glimpse of the rest
and cheerfulness that pervades all. We have looked,
moreover, at a poem or two, and, while we find much that
is mediocre and some that is bad, we are, nevertheless,
pleased with the acquaintance; for, losing for a moment
our stern and terrible faculty of criticism, we delight in

the little poems, not so much because they are good or bad or something else, but because we delight in Bemerton and George Herbert, and we find it hard, under these old trees, to answer the searching question: which is it that you really like—Bemerton, or Herbert, or his verse? For *before* all is said and done to show this virtue or that defect of the poems, we must first listen to the harmony. That which delights is the gentle spirit of loveliness pervading the three—place, man, and poems; it is like the song of the lark we heard in the early morning; it is like the deep shadows and long beams of light in the churchyard at Bemerton. You can explain and criticise it when you can analyze the odour of the flower.

Whether or not George Herbert did the vigorous thing in going to Bemerton, in running away from the strife, suggests the contrast of the country and the city. At Bemerton the rich experience of sensations came from the hills, the sunset, the light on the Cathedral spire; there, in London, was the press of mankind, working, loving, hating, fighting. At Bemerton one was half with man, half with nature; in London was the "mighty heart," throbbing in deeds by day, throbbing in sleep by night. Here the intercourse was spiritual, gently intellectual; there it was of all kinds—brutal, avaricious, passionately emotional and intellectual—the white light of intellect! The man in the country has a kind of religious sureness: the sky and the stars and the morning sun are ever a sign and a wonder for him. But, be it never so deep, it is a child-like sureness—emotional, not intellectual. What, on the other hand, shall the man in the city take for a sign? Doubt, discouragement, pallid pleasures, where the "desire outruns the delight"—what shall he make of the glittering, tinseled, pagan monster? He no

longer sees through a glass darkly, but now face to face.
What shall he see?   God or No-God?

This is ever a fundamental contrast.   Shall your life
be simple and sweet in the country; shall it be seared,
yet strong, in the city?   "I bear them and *yet* I triumph"
—how this word must ring in the ears of the man at
work among men!   And then comes perhaps the sound
of the swift-running water and the light of the sun on
the everlasting hills—"O Paradise, O Paradise, who doth
not crave for rest!"—and the sin-sick soul, George Herbert
if you like, goes back to his woods and fields and sky.
The suggestion of such an action is a tremendous challenge
to vigorous souls that

> "Dare look the omnipotent tyrant in his everlasting face,
> And tell him that his evil is not good."

They put the slug-horn to their lips, they sing, they whistle,
they cry:

> "Speed, fight on, fare ever there as here!"

Thus stood "Milton, like a seraph strong."

To a man, then, in 1630, who, still churchman, felt a
need for simplicity and purity, there were two courses
open: stay and fight for them, or go seek them in unfre-
quented places.   That many bravely stayed is true.   That
many, on the other hand, perhaps wisely avoided London
and the broil, is also true.   Nicholas Farrer had shut
himself up in monastic seclusion, at Little Gidding, to
escape "the furie of Protestantism."   Gentle Isaak Walton found enjoyment, at this martial time, in fishing and
meditation, along the winding waterways of Wiltshire.
George Herbert would, no doubt, have floundered sadly in
the hard steel accoutrements of that day—for the contest
was like to be physical—but he could live purely and

kindly and sing sweetly by the banks of the Nadder.
Something in him, strong and restful as the voice of the
woods to the hunter, drew him there.

It was not a vigorous step. Was it hence an unworthy
action? Listen to his own resolutions: "And I now can
behold the court with an impartial eye, and see plainly
that it is made up of fraud and titles, and flattery, and
many other such empty, imaginary, and painted pleasures;
pleasures that are so empty as not to satisfy when they
are enjoyed. But in God, and His service, is a fulness
of joy and pleasure, and no satiety." Exactly! cries the
vigorous soul, and the true service is in the thick of the
fight. Not so for George Herbert. After all, the sincerity, not the conviction, is what counts. In London,
the church, with Laud already in full charge, with anonymous accusation and vituperation, with extravagance and
corruption—an easy-going secularism on the one hand,
and a run-down Romanism on the other—did not exactly
suggest restfulness and religious meditation. The needless strife, the priests of God soiling their robes with
political intrigue, civil war in the air—these were to
George Herbert a note inexpressibly harsh; they were
absolute contradiction to *his* idea of the "beauty of holiness." He did not gird his buckler on; he fled from the
wrath to come. And as we look back through nearly three
centuries, and can see a little of right on both sides, we
find much consolation in Herbert's retreat—we find a
lesson in Bemerton as well as in London.

In his little garden at Bemerton, George Herbert one
day planted a medlar-tree. That tree flourishes to-day—
only a tree, to be sure, but one more memorial to come
back to mind when we think of the two letters, "G. H.,"
scratched on the church wall. It is a memorial, moreover,

peculiarly proper to Herbert. He has given long life, in his gentleness, to a little tree, growing quietly out of the common bustle and noise of the world, as he would have spread his gentle influence over his parish, as he himself, in fact, lived in simple beneficence. To live simply, to do our little well and kindly is an old and commonplace lesson, no doubt, but it is nevertheless a hard one—perhaps much harder than that of the big work in London-town, before the eyes of the world. In Westminster stand memorials to great men of every age. As one walks past the spirit of Kings and councillors, or stands silent before the "souls of poets dead and gone," an awe for the great dead creeps over him. The lesson of Westminster is written for all men and is daily learned in various ways by the great and the small. But let us turn for a space to the medlar-tree at Bemerton. Does it not teach its lesson, too? And do the lessons of Westminster, be they never so grand, go more deeply or truly to the heart? Does this medlar-tree not bring back the river of thoughts with the bright scenes by the way—the churchyard with its holy light, the old tall trees, the birds and the yellow grain on the hill, the Cathedral spire, and the gentle hymn at the heart?

THE YOUNGER WORDSWORTH.

By Charles H. Burr, A.M.

THE YOUNGER WORDSWORTH.

There is an almost universal disposition to adopt as the common conception of men great in literature the impression made by their personalities in the closing years of their lives. The image of the old Goethe, serene, Olympian, has long overlaid the intensely passionate youth of the author of "Werther;" nor will any ever know how far the accustomed judgment of Keats as a poet voicing only warm and sensuous youth is due to his early death. It is the man as it knew him last, the world remembers. The causes which bring this about are natural. After fame has come to a man, it is then that his every day words and doings take on importance, and impressions of personality are gained by many among whom in younger days he would have moved unnoted. These many then bequeath to the future the impressions thus formed. It is around a man's later years that the mass of reminiscence, anecdote and recollection gathers.

Wordsworth is a marked example of this tendency, a peculiarly strong illustration of its danger to the critic. His detractors and admirers alike will recognize the fact that the great mass of his literary work is not poetry at all. The heavy verse which fills the printed volumes of his poems has held aloof innumerable readers, and dulled the enthusiasm of all but a small remnant. Matthew Arnold, appreciating this unfortunate condition, endeavored to meet it by a carefully excised edition of his poems. But this is only to provide a method of temporary escape for his admirers. The world will never accept a condensation as a man's real work. It is a difficulty in the way of common enjoyment of Wordsworth which must be faced and overcome. But how? By the only possible method: by complete understanding of the causes and the consequent correct estimation of the results. To explain from the course of Wordsworth's outward and inner life whence came the poetical impulse out of which was created his great poetical work, and how and wherefore the mass of valueless verse came from the same man, is the object of this brief essay.

That Wordsworth affords an illustration of the generalization we have allowed ourselves in the opening paragraph, would seem apparent; still it will be best to consider the facts. Wordsworth died in 1850 at the age of eighty years. For at least a quarter of a century fame had set her seal upon him. One cannot question the solemn depth, so to speak, of Wordsworth's character, nor the rare elevation of his spirit in the later years of his life; and universal respect and honor came to him as his rightful due. To his home in the late country traveled daily the admiring and the curious. They saw a man of great personal dignity living a calm, simple life; but they did not see the gentleness and largeness of view, which would seem to belong of right to the old age of a poet. Emerson, fresh from the beginnings of that life-long friendship with Carlyle, was "surprised by the hard limits of his thought." "To judge from a simple conversation," he wrote, "he made the impression of a narrow and very English mind." And Harriet Martineau recounts the lack of sensitiveness with which he received her. These expressions were only too accurate: Wordsworth had become a placid adherent of Church and the established order of things, a talkative old man with a mind firmly closed against the entrance of new ideas. His own letters confirm the observation of his visitors beyond appeal. Writing to an American friend, he contentedly observes: "The reception given me "by the Queen at her ball was most gracious. Mrs. "Everett, the wife of your minister, among many others, "was a witness to it. It moved her to the shedding of "tears to see a gray-haired man of seventy-five years of "age, kneeling down in a large assembly to kiss the hand "of a young woman." Of Shakespere, he fatuously remarks: "He had serious defects and not those only pro-"ceeding from carelessness. For instance, in his delinea-"tions of character he does not assign as large a place to "religious sentiment as enters into the constitution of "human nature under normal circumstances. If his "dramas had more religion in them, they would be truer "representations of man, as well as more elevated, and of "a *more searching interest.*"

It is not from a man who so thinks and feels that great poetry comes, and many years had indeed passed since the period when the diverse qualities of Wordsworth's poetic nature were in harmonious accord. True it was that year upon year Wordsworth had lived close to nature, but now that old age was upon him the very closeness and absorption of his devotion had its perilous event. The old Goethe had likewise left far behind him the passionate emotions of youth, but he stands in the pages of Eckermann the one great critic of modern life. Largeness of view, breadth of sympathy, world-wide reachings after knowl-edge, glorify the old age of Goethe. But they were not given to Wordsworth to compensate for failing delicacy and keenness of vision. And indeed, so fleetingly evan-escent is that rare union of qualities resulting in sensitive-ness to beauty, openness to truth, which go to make up a poet's genius, that one stands before the old Wordsworth and marvels whence could have come that vibrating response of his poetry to the speech of nature and the voice of humanity. It is not however in the study of the old Wordsworth that one may come upon the secret. Long ago it was observed that none of Wordsworth's really valuable poetry was written before he was twenty-eight years of age, very little after he was thirty-eight. It is the man who then lived we should seek to know and understand.

Wordsworth's boyhood lived in the country had been, as he always afterwards pictured it "a time of pleasure "lying upon the unfolding intellect plenteously as morn-"ing dew-drops,—of knowledge inhaled insensibly like a "fragrance,—of dispositions stealing into the spirit like "music from unknown quarters." But when, just before his coming of age, Wordsworth received his degree from Cambridge University, he went to London and within a few months passed over into France. The influence of his relatives and friends had been strongly exerted to induce him to choose a vocation, but for over four years he lived as he might, hoping for some chance escape from the thraldom of regular work, until in 1795 a legacy from an admiring friend rendered possible, with the exercise of exceeding frugality, that life given to poetry to which he had destined himself with pure and unchangeable devotion. In after years, looking back upon these days of choice, and the disapprobation he had braved, Wordsworth paused to explain his motives, and perhaps in some measure idealized them. "Youth," he said in one of his finest of prose passages, "has its own wealth and inde-"pendence; it is rich in health of body and animal spirits, "in its sensibility to the impressions of the natural uni-"verse, in the conscious growth of knowledge, in lively

"sympathy and familiar communion with the generous
"actions recorded in history, and with the high passions
"of poetry; and above all, youth is rich in the possession
"of time, and the accompanying consciousness of freedom
"and power. * * * Hence, in the happy confidence
"of his feelings, and in the elasticity of his spirit, neither
"worldly ambition, nor the love of praise, nor dread of
"censure, nor the necessity of worldly maintenance, nor
"any of those causes which tempt or compel the mind
"habitually to look out of itself for support, * * *
"have power to preside over the choice of the young."

How salutary to exchange for our memory of the older
man this image of Wordsworth in the vitality of youth,
with its idealism and its freshness of promise!

It was in the early days of the French Revolution
that Wordsworth came to Paris. To the eye of eager
youth

"appeared
"A glorious opening, the unlooked-for dawn,
"That promised everlasting joy to France!"

In its inception an intellectual movement, the French
Revolution had knit up with its own destiny the hopes and
dreams of the young thought of Europe. All that was
progressive, all that was ardent, all that was aspiring was
enrolled under its banner.

"Europe at that time was thrilled with joy,
"France standing on the top of golden hours,
"And human nature seeming born again."

This was the one great modern *a priori* effort to solve the
problems of social and political life. No one alive just
before the beginnings of the Revolution who preserved
his powers of perception and clear thinking but felt
through and through that the conditions of existence were

intolerable to the multitude throughout Europe. And above the moan of pain had been heard and still echoed the voice of Rousseau, reminding his hearers of a time long past of innocence, happiness and equality; urging a return to nature and these conditions. It mattered not that the ideal of Rousseau and of the Europe which followed him never existed nor could exist, that it was an *a priori* proposition incapable of surviving dispassionate examination. The intense and powerful influence of Rousseau was due solely to the fact that his time demanded and welcomed eagerly an ideal with which their imagination might be fired and to which their sympathies might respond. Much was promised, and fed upon rash hopes, all that was best and aspiring rushed blindly onward, till there came the Reign of Terror and the still more disillusioning years which succeeded.

The mind and heart of the young Wordsworth in Paris went wholly with this movement. "Bliss was it that dawn to be alive," he exclaimed, "but to be young was heaven!" He remained over a year in France, coming into vital contact with the forces there at work, and when he returned unwillingly to England in December, 1792, he had made the cause of the Revolution, as he conceived it, his own.

In the lives of most men of genius there has early come the longing for experience, the longing to handle and taste life for themselves in all its possibilities of intensity, whether of pain or of joy. Genius in men of emotion seems to involve the capacity, the necessity of passionate sensation. To feel, has been the cry of their youth; to know, the desire of their mature manhood. And as poetry is above all a matter of emotion, so have the world's greatest poets most passionately suffered, most intensely lived. For thirteen months Wordsworth felt and lived, for the balance of eighty years he thought and reflected. In the significance of this fact lies the key to the understanding of Wordsworth and of his poetry.

The deposition of the King and the September massacres had not served to weaken Wordsworth's faith, but on his return he found it otherwise in England. Many at first had sympathized excitedly and loudly, but by the end of 1792 the excesses of the Revolution and its threat to vested interests had roused a strong and general reaction. Wordsworth burned to throw his whole force against the current. His long letter to the Bishop of Landaff signed "A Republican" glows with white heat of indignation against monarchy and "the baleful influence of aristocracy and nobility upon happiness and virtue." Lacking a publisher and a hearing, Wordsworth was thrown back upon himself, and passed through days and years of almost morbid dejection, out of which came "The Borderers" and "Guilt and Sorrow," early and valueless poems. He had seen his bright dreams for the quick advance of humanity shattered; and, more than this, his healthy mind had come to perceive the hollowness of the ideas on which he had builded, the falsity of the theories he had grasped as revelations. The emotion and high idealism with which his young imagination had touched the Revolution vanished before the attack of France upon Switzerland. Wordsworth was then under twenty-five, and the shock was bitter, the blow went deep. He himself felt that he had been "tossed about in whirlwind," but he had kept grip upon himself; when it was over he possessed himself utterly. He wrought his way out of the storm roused within him by a return upon his younger self, developed and broadened in some measure by the experience through which he had passed, but yet in all reality the same self. It is significant that before beginning "to construct," to use his words, "a literary work that might live," he composed "The Prelude" as a "review of his own mind," attempted to examine what he had acquired from nature and education, seemingly without thought of development through entering into new regions of feeling and experience. From that day onward (and he was not yet thirty) life, as signifying sensation, passion, was a thing unknown. The history of these years does not present the gradual attaining to clearer vision and a serener outlook worked out in a man by new ideas transforming his character and life, but the resolute taking up again of the old self and life, the transformation of which by the ideas so lately abandoned appear as an illusion. Around this thought must gather any real understanding of Wordsworth's development and life; it alone explains the vital enthusiasm and spirited energy toward progress manifest in the young man, the contented acceptance of conservative conventions in the middle-aged and older man.

By 1798 Wordsworth's life had taken the course from which it never afterwards varied, passed as it was in his quiet home with his sister and wife. Dorothy Wordsworth was a woman of the most delicate originality. Her diary, her letters, every trace she has left, show her great gifts, her sensitive, beautiful, and yet strong nature. She gave herself wholly to her brother, and effaced herself; that his indebtedness to her was great indeed is clear, how great can never be known. His wife was not comparable to her as an influence or as a character. Wordsworth judged her, when, thinking to praise, he wrote of her: "Peace settles where the intellect is meek."

These two women were his daily companions, and his

whole life became one of self-absorbed reflection and contemplation. It was within, that he found the springs of poetic impulse, and the subject of his interpretation was nature as she lay around him. The lines composed above Tintern Abbey are dated in the year 1798, and mark the beginning of his fruitful period. It is the man who then lived and wrote, not the older Wordsworth, who has most to give the world of encouragement and delight, and whom we must seek to understand.

When Wordsworth turned in the Prelude to examine his faculties and powers, he looked upon a nature of great depth and strength. It was necessarily a character of fundamental stability which, after the ardent dreams known in France, could face the bitterness of the awakening, and resolutely and withal joyously, take up again the eventful succession of days his country life meant to him. Such conduct, however, was not that of the sensitive, passionate lover of mankind. Keats was more highly sensitive than he, Shelley more swiftly imaginative, Byron, perhaps, had more force at the moment of contact; but among literary men of the century none had a nature so firmly rooted in itself. To find such another, one must go back to Milton. An all-sufficing self-mastery, a noble dignity in purpose and in the achievement was the distinctive mark of Milton's genius, and among moderns is found in Wordsworth alone. If by the magic color of his verse Keats is, as Arnold said, with Shakespere, so by the solidity and substance of his poetry is Wordsworth with Milton.

One is accustomed to think of the riches, the wealth of a poet's gifts from nature: of Spenser, let us say, or Keats, or the young Goethe. But in studying Wordsworth, one thinks rather of strength and steadfastness.

Strong affections, strong imaginative insight, strong faith in reality, touched to finest beauty by an abiding spirit of joyousness, made the man a poet. The Lucy poems are intense in their strength of emotion, and reveal the nature of Wordsworth, as his last sonnet likewise reveals Keats. Wordsworth lacked emotionally the ease and unreserve which would have allowed him to give himself with effusion; deep as were his affections, though they had the intensity of strong feeling, they lacked always the intensity of sensuousness, of passion. His use of this last word is curious: with him it is the equivalent of "emotion;" its meaning is heightened by words such as "holy" and "pure;" never does it become the "breathing human passion" of Keats: never would Wordsworth have hailed the bending lover: "Forever shalt thou kiss and she be fair," but again never would love as he conceived it have brought "a morn high-sorrowful and cloyed, a burning forehead and a parching tongue."

To some again Wordsworth may lack the lightness, the fire, the uplift of Shelley in his lines to a Skylark; or the melancholy tenderness of his lament over Keats:

> "Alas! that all we loved of him should be,
> "But for our grief, as if it had not been,
> "And grief itself be mortal! Woe is me!
> "Whence are we, and why are we? Of what scene
> "The actors or spectators?"

Wordsworth, it is true, walked close to nature and stepped firmly upon this earth. And one may venture to think that the very stability of his footing gives to his words a greater healing power:

> "Though nothing can bring back the hour
> "Of splendor in the grass, of glory in the flower;
> "We will grieve not, rather find
> "Strength in what remains behind:

"In the soothing thoughts that spring
"Out of human suffering;
"In the faith that looks through death,
"In years that bring the philosophic mind."

Sensitiveness and delicacy of perception are to be found in strong, deep natures as often as in those richly and vehemently emotional; and the greatest possession of Wordsworth was his rarely penetrative imagination. None ever so highly conceived the office of this faculty,

"   but another name for absolute power
"And clearest insight, amplitude of mind,
"And reason in her most exalted mood";

none ever glorified it so highly

"The gleam,
"The light that never was on sea or land
"The consecration and the poet's dream."

This it meant to him, this it became in his hands. And with it there went along a purity of sensibility till he became

"as sensitive as waters are
"To the sky's influence";

and felt in his love for nature

"Those hallowed and pure motions of the sense
"Which seem, in their simplicity, to own
"An intellectual charm."

The imagination in Wordsworth was penetrative, not constructive; it never mastered him, took the pen from his fingers, and wrote of things greater than he knew. To the eyes of Wordsworth's imagination never appeared

"Magic casements opening on the foam
"Of perilous seas, in fairy lands forlorn."

But working with his sense of joy, it carried him into the heart of things and revealed to his deep nature the deepest and most fundamental facts of life.

That which gives Wordsworth pre-eminent distinction is his vital faith in the "deep power of joy." The first half of this century was not a time when the need for joy was generally either accepted or recognized. The bitter words of Carlyle to Goethe strike the more popular note of feeling: "I have learned that what I once called "happiness is not only not to be attained on earth, but not "even to be desired." But Wordsworth, looking upon man, perceived "the grand elementary principle of pleasure, by "which he knows, and feels, and lives and moves." It meant to him, not the fleeting exhilaration of the senses nor light-hearted immunity from the pains and sorrows of life, but that normal, healthy sense of happiness and delight which comes to a man when his faculties and activities are all in harmony with the conditions of his life. Joy, then, is the child of health, health of mind and soul as well as of body; and it is in reality that one shall seek and find it, not by building impossible dreams out of beautiful imaginings, but by living close to the heart of nature, and treading in the fragrant footing of duty. Then will nature appear to man "as a teacher of truth, "through joy and through gladness, and as a creatress of "the faculties by a process of smoothness and delight;" he will say of duty:

> "Nor know we anything so fair
> "As is the smile upon thy face."

"The joy of elevated thoughts" will be his, and under "the deep power of joy" he will "see into the life of things." Out of the real facts of existence into the common life of man Wordsworth wished to bring joy, carrying inevitably with it into that life perceptions of truth and sensitiveness to beauty.

It was in nature that Wordsworth found "a never-failing principle of joy."

> "The ever-living universe,
> "Turn where I might, was opening out its glories,
> "And the independent spirit of pure youth
> "Called forth, at every season, new delights
> "Spread round my steps like sunshine o'er green fields."

Nature became to him, therefore, "a strong and holy passion," "strong," because of his deep memories of delight in her, "holy," because he felt he perceived in her forms of beauty the revelations of the spirit of the universe,

> "Whose dwelling is the light of setting suns,
> "And the round ocean, and the living air,
> "And the blue sky, and in the mind of man
> "A motion and a spirit, that impels
> "All thinking things, all objects of all thought,
> "And rolls through all things."

Wordsworth—

> "Felt the sentiment of Being spread
> "O'er all that moves and all that seemeth still;
> "O'er all that, lost beyond the reach of thought
> "And human knowledge, to the human eye
> "Invisible, yet liveth to the heart;
> "O'er all that leaps and runs, and shouts and sings,
> "Or beats the gladsome air."

Tenderly, therefore, reverentially even, did he approach nature; sacred to him were her moods and words. Intimately and closely he lived near her and studied her, and her slightest motion he perceived and stored in memory. To her influence he left his nature open and sensitive, that he might receive what she had to give; he felt her to be infinitely greater than himself, and into her moods he never forced his own. Impossible to him was a demand like Shelley's to the West Wind:

> "Be thou, spirit fierce,
> "My spirit! Be thou me, impetuous one!
> "Drive my dead thoughts over the universe,
> "Like withered leaves, to quicken a new birth!"

To Wordsworth that would have been to reverse his whole relation to nature. Equally impossible to him was the conception of her as fruitful and teeming; the "Ode to Autumn" breathes a feeling he never shared. The intoxicating and magical in nature, her fecundity, Wordsworth never felt; to him she was bright and beautiful, pure and majestic.

In this noble and elevated attitude toward nature, we may unreservedly follow and learn from Wordsworth. What is elemental in man, what is in him born of the traditions of his origin, what unites him to the universe about him and gives him his place therein—all this Wordsworth alone among moderns has firmly grasped, and the "Ode of Duty" and the "Lines composed above Tintern Abbey" come to us with the authority of the seer. There is nothing more tonic in English Literature than that invocation to the "Stern Daughter of the Voice of God!"

> "Thou dost preserve the stars from wrong
> "And the most ancient heavens, through Thee, are fresh and strong."

Again we venture to repeat that deep and powerful was the nature which returned upon itself and, while Europe was doing penance for her dreams, built up so sane an outlook upon human life.

But Wordsworth, though he saw life steadily, saw it not whole. Turning back even to the days of Shakespere, how far removed is that world in which Hamlet lives to our imagination, from the life of nature of which Wordsworth sang! Man in society with its inherent complexity, its subtle heightening of life, its broader capacities and wider possibilities for pain and joy, its graver dangers, its brighter promises to the spirit of man—all this was not within the scope of Wordsworth's vision. There is an accent in the greatest poetry, an abiding sense of the struggle and distress of mankind upon this sorrowful earth alien to Wordsworth's thought. Homer long ago voiced it in Zeus' address to the horses who were immortal:

"O, unhappy pair! why gave we you to Peleus, the King, a mortal? * * * Was it that with man born to misery, ye might know sorrow?"

It informs the verse of Shakespeare:

"We are such stuff as dreams are made of, and
"Our little life is rounded by a sleep."

It is known to Goethe:

"Soul of man,
"How like to the water!
"Future of man,
"How like to the wind!"

But this is only to say that Wordsworth is not one of the greatest of the world's immortals, and to mark the limits of his genius as poet. And the very comparisons he challenges place him far beyond the reach of envious fame. To the first flush of youth, the poetry of others— of Keats and Shelley, perhaps—may appeal as Wordsworth's cannot. Their work was the work of youth, for Keats died at twenty-five, Shelley at twenty-nine; at nearly the age when Wordsworth's really valuable work began. Let a few years pass over one, and in the best verse of Wordsworth is felt a deeper knowledge and a richer wisdom, it sounds upon one's ears with an authority soon

honored and beloved; it appeals to a more matured imagination, to the man in whom the early all-importance of
sensuous emotion each day grows less, and whom more and
more moral and intellectual questions engage. Not for
one moment be the suggestion made that the treatment
of moral and intellectual questions in verse will constitute
great poetry; often, as in Wordsworth's later verse, they
operate to deprive it of all real poetry; but his best
work came from a man whose mind and heart were alive
to these questions, and in it he informed them with emotion
and with beauty. The measure and health of his poetry,
its reality, its high idealism, have a wonderful power of
engaging and sustaining us. He gives us emotion, emotion
chastened but unequalled in intensity. What in Keats or
in Shelley can we lay beside the Lucy poems ? He makes
us think, and where shall we find such depth of thought
clothed in rarest beauty as in the "Lines composed above
Tintern Abbey ?" He is spiritual, and it is an elevating,
vitalizing, effectual spirituality, never ethereal and trans-
cendental. What can be sounder, more applicable to daily
lives than the sonnet "The world is too much with us ?"
And if in the feeling of some pure beauty is the one
thing demanded of poetry, what more beautiful than the
images which came to him as he lay and courted sleep ?

"A flock of sheep that leisurely pass by
"One after one; the sound of rain, and bees
"Murmuring; the fall of rivers, winds and seas,
"Smooth fields, white sheets of water, and pure sky."

In the lives of too many of us there comes a time when
we cease to draw each day new vitality from real contact
with life and nature, and with unenlightened steps walk
the path marked out by habit. That time came to Wordsworth. A young man, he had warmed his whole nature

with generous dreams of lofty purpose; and then returning to his country home, he drew upon the stored-up treasures of his young days for the inspiration of his earlier verse; and full and rich was the response. But he had severed himself from the sources of inspiration, from contact with real vitalizing life among men; he had failed in persistent effort to gather to himself new ideas, to widen the bounds of his intellectual self, and broaden the possibilities of sympathy; and the sterility of his later life was the certain and sad consequence.

Yet one may wonder if in the man himself there was not inherently something which made him not so much narrow as limited. Even in his best poetry—and certainly in his best years when "Peter Bell" and "The Idiot Boy" were written—there was much in the world even of nature, and especially of mankind, seemingly cut off from his perception and knowledge. The ethereal imaginative sweep of Shelley, the warm richness and color of Keats, the melodious finish of Tennyson, one will not find in Wordsworth's poetry. Yet how much of greatness about the man remains, must always remain. On the poetry of whom else among moderns can one rest with equal sense of stability and happiness? Who other speaks so clearly and with such authority to what is most fundamental in us, what most deeply concerns our lives?

There is one all-important fact one must grasp if one would come fully to know Wordsworth, the secret of his youth and his old age. It is that his best work is not the fresh and spontaneous outgiving of a man whose whole self is daily renewed and made fruitful, but is a result of a return upon his younger self. Happy for the world and for Wordsworth that such return was made upon a youth so worthily lived, so stored with beautiful and joyous

memories! And, when all is said and one tries to call
up the image of Wordsworth as he will dwell in the
memory of the world, there must vanish wholly the recollection of the older uninspired man, and remain only the
bright picture of that young spirit of health and joyousness
who speaks to us out of his earlier verse, and brings us
to say with him: "Poetry is the breath and finer spirit
"of knowledge—it is as immortal as the heart of man."

VITA NUOVA, CHAPTERS 24-28.

By A. G. H. SPIERS, A.M.

VITA NUOVA, CHAPTERS 24-28.

Most critics see in the second Canzone the pinnacle of the Vita Nuova. Prof. Grandgent, writing in 1901, said: "Now in this carefully planned Vita Nuova there is, in one place, a formidable gap: a poem is lacking in the very spot where one is most needed. At the real conclusion of the young poet's history, the death of Beatrice, we find nothing but plain prose. It seems incredible that Dante, with his tendency to put all his psychic experiences into verse, did not at once attempt a poem on his bereavement; if he did so, his composition evidently did not suit him, either because he had not yet attained sufficient power to treat such a theme, or because the very keenness of his grief benumbed his inspiration. When he came to construct his New Life, artist as he was, he certainly felt this lack and *adroitly shifted the centre of interest to a different part of the narrative, the premonition of his lady's death, told in the second Canzone.*"[1]

Prof. Norton had already suggested this; while John Earle had based upon the same opinion an argument for the allegorical interpretation of the whole book.[2] Nor

---

[1] Romania, XXXI (Jan., 1902), pp. 17, 18.

[2] —"So that this translation of B. (not her natural death, but her Heavenly translation) crowns the highest pinnacle of the whole structure, and likewise pervades it to its uttermost extremities" (*i. e.*, the first and last sonnets.) "If we consider that the natural death of B. is put by, as a matter not to the purpose, while her removal to another sphere stands first, middle, and last, can we think the 'Vita Nuova' to be in the nature of a literal memoir, or to be anything but a work of imaginative art and an allegory?" (Anonymously, in the Quarterly Review, July, 1896).

do the majority of Italian scholars themselves hold a different view.[3]

Now if we consider only the arrangement of the poems, only the design laid down by the verse compositions, the importance of the second Canzone cannot be contested.[4] There is, however, something else to be weighed. Besides poem-grouping there is content. In addition to the interrelation of the verse, there is the broader and palmary consideration of the matter as a whole—not merely the story itself, but the manner in which, through both prose and verse, it is presented to us in the finished production of the artist.

Dante has stressed, we believe, a totally different point of the Vita Nuova. This other stress receives too little recognition, being hidden by our different habits of composition and shadowed especially, perhaps, by the discoveries of Rossetti and Prof. Norton.[5] Yet our text suggests it; and a study of the methods of procedure in the work of the Provençal and early Italian poets supports this suggestion. While space does not permit us to indicate here the place occupied in this early lyric by the tendency which we shall cite in support of our views, the present paper will, however, attempt to indicate briefly the presence of this tendency in Dante's writing in general and then show how its use, coupled with certain

[3] *e. g.*, Cesareo, who, reviewing G. Melodia's: La V. N. di D. Alighieri (Milan, 1906), looks upon the vision of Chapter 23 as "un pretesto di D. per collocare, nel bel mezzo della V. N., la canzone del transito dove B. di donna ridiventa cittadina del cielo." Zeitschrift f. rom. phil., XXX, p. 685.

[4] For discussion and bibliography of this question v. Kenneth McKenzie's Symmetrical Structure of Dante's V. N. (Public. of Mod. Lang., Ass. XVIII, p. 341).

[5] v. McKenzie ibid, p. 342.

peculiarities of the Vita Nuova itself, makes of Chapters 24-28 a studied preparation for an important climax—a climax coincident with the death of Beatrice.

Dante had a feeling for mass and progression. It is a fundamental principle of his style.

This general feeling can be traced even in his prose. The introduction to Canzone I of the Vita Nuova gives remarkable evidences of this. The incident to be given there contains two salient points, viz. the ladies' question and their final comment. Accordingly the story is divided into two parts. A leisurely preparation, rich with pretty details, prepares the way for each of these; but their entry is short and terse. The second, however, is the really startling point of the two. Dante has answered simply, giving what—without stopping to reflect—he believed to be the truth. Then suddenly, almost brutally, the blow falls. Introduced only by the words "Ed ella rispose," the lady shows him that his whole attitude toward Beatrice has been wrong. This second part, pausing for a moment, slowly develops, enwrapping the crest of the first as it proceeds, overtops it, and falls with the accumulated weight of both in the pregnant utterance: "Se tu ne dicessi vero, quelle parole che tu n'hai dette, notificando la tua condizione, avresti tu operate con altro intendimento."

A natural consequence of this feeling is a solicitude for the excellence of concluding passages, being, as they are, the terminus ad quem of the whole composition.[6]

* It must be noted, however, that in many cases Dante's concluding lines do not represent the culmination of the thought developed in the sonnet or stanza. They partake often of the nature of an embellishment, as in the case of the first stanza of "Amor dacchè convien," or the third stanza to "Io sento sì d'Amor." v. note 10.

Dante has openly confessed an interest in these. In Convivio IV-XXX, he says: "And here it must be known especially that every good poet should ennoble and beautify the end of his work as much as in him lies, so that it may leave his hands more worthy and more excellent." While, speaking of the final lines to the opening stanza of Canzone VI, he explicitly states that the reference to the star is made in order to catch the ear of those whom he is addressing. In a third case, his own commentary emphasizes his adherence to this principle: "Oh quanto e come bello adornamento è questo che nell'ultimo di questa Canzone si da ad essa, chiamandola amica di quella, la cui propria magione è nel secretissimo della divina Mente."[7]

In the separate Canzone-stanzas and in the sonnets, this solicitude takes the form of particular attention paid to the effect of final lines. Indeed "Dante's stanza or sonnet in nearly every case closes with a certain fillip to the mind or to the feelings."[8] Among the most striking examples are Sonnets 18 and 23 of the Vita Nuova, and the fourth stanza of "O patria degna———." Of a different nature, though similar in strength, is the ending to "Guido vorrei———." The two lines which end the first stanza of "Tre donne———" (lines very much admired by Carducci[9]), the pathetic addition of "Purchè la vita tanto si difenda" to the third stanza of "Io sento

---

[7] Convivio IV, XXX. All references are to Moore's Tutte le opere di Dante Alighieri. Third edition, Oxford, 1904.

[8] This statement, which space will not allow us to prove here, is drawn from "Character and Effectiveness of Final Lines in Dante's Lyric" (A. G. H. Spiers), a dissertation accepted at Harvard University as part fulfilment of the requirements for the degree of Ph.D. v. our note 10 below.

[9] Studi Lett. Second edition, p. 221.

sì d'Amor————," the final line to Sonnet 3: "Che donna fu di sì gaia sembianza," etc. Even the metre is made at times to minister to the effect of the stanza-ending.[10]

But of the many forms taken by this constant solicitude for the final passages, one is of special significance to our study.

This may, for lack of a better term, be styled "use of contrast." That Dante appreciated the force of contrast in general, the close of Sonnet 2 will testify:

> "Sicchè, volendo far come coloro
> Che per vergogna celan lor mancanza,
> Di fuor mostro allegranza,
> E dentro dallo cor mi struggo e ploro."

[10] G. Lisio (L'Arte del Periode nelle opere volg. di D.A. e del secolo XIII. Bologna, 1902), while paying no particular attention to final lines, has incidentally brought corroboration to our statements, as when he notes (p. 162) the strength, through unusual word-order, of "Morta è la donna tua che era sì bella" (Canzone II, IV), or when writing (p. 105) of Sonnet 21, he says: "Così nel sonetto XXI, L'Amaro lagrimar che voi faceste, tutto il discorso intimo del cuor di Dante termina per periodo al verso 13°, dove a punto non vorremmo fermarci per compiere il suono: e l'improvvisa sosta e la cortezza sintattica danno quindi all'ultimo verso 'Così dice il mio core, e poi sospira,' tale efficacia, che noi restiamo lungamente sospesi innanzi ad esso." Or when, again, he says (p. 205): "Altro effetto si ottiene, specie in fine di composizione, con un construtto che par come una sospensione indefinita di desiderio o di altra sospirata fantasia. Così mi sembra avvenga per questi tre versi in fine di sonetto (Sonnets XI, XII and XV): Sì è novo miracolo e gentile: Che il cor mi trema di vederne tanto: E va dicendo all'anima: sospira." It is pleasing to find a born Italian's appreciation, somewhat subjective though it may be, coinciding unwittingly with our own views. When we deal with final lines alone, however, far more conclusive reasons may be adduced to prove that Dante used his metre, as well as his matter, in such a way as to emphasize the last lines. v. Note 8.

as might also the conclusion:

> "Che da sera e da mane
> Hai ragunato e stretto ad ambe mano
> Ciò che sì tosto ti si fa lontano."[11]

Considerable power is derived from this procedure in the closing lines of

> "Ch'Amor, quando sì presso a voi mi trova,
> Prende baldanza e tanta sicurtate,
> Che fiere tra' miei spirti paurosi
> E quale ancide, e qual caccia di fuora,
> Sicch'ei solo rimane a veder vui:
> Ond'io mi cangio in figura d'altrui;
> Ma non sì ch'io non senta bene allora
> Gli guai degli scacciati tormentosi."[12].

Similarly there is an effective contrast between the attitude of mind provoked by the preceding lines and the message of the final statement when the poet sings:

> "Quando l'imaginar mi tien ben fiso,
> Giungemi tanta pena d'ogni parte,
> Ch'io mi riscuoto per dolor ch'io sento;
> E sì fatto divento,
> Che dalle genti vergogna mi parte.
> Poscia piangendo, sol nel mio lamento
> Chiamo Beatrice; e dico: Or se'tu morta!
> E mentre ch'io la chiamo, mi conforta."[13]

A more sudden shock is given in "Poschia ch'Amor——," where eighteen lines, explaining the behavior of a man who is really noble, are followed by the brief:

> "Color che vivon fanno tutti contra,"

[11] "Doglia mi reca * * *" Stanza IV.

[12] V. N. Sonnet 7. Moore and Fraticelli do not, we think, clearly bring out the function of the last lines here: they use a simple comma after "altrui." Surely D'Ancona's semi-colon is preferable. Dante's preference for the independent construction and the effect to be obtained therefrom is briefly indicated by Lisio ibid, p. 185.

[13] V. N. Canzone III, Stanza IV; cf., also Stanza V.

as closing words of the whole canzone. But most effective of all perhaps is the surprise in Vita Nuova Sonnet 20—all the more worthy of notice in that the prose does not suggest it:

> "Io non posso tener gli occhi distrutti
> Che non riguardin voi molte fiate,
> Pel desiderio di pianger ch'egli hanno:
> E voi crescete sì lor volontate,
> Che della voglia si consuman tutti;
> Ma lagrimar dinanzi a voi non sanno."

Having noted this general tendency in Dante's work and recognized particular manifestations of this tendency (and one especially, that of contrast), let us now turn to Chapters 24-28.

Perhaps the most striking peculiarity of this group of chapters, regarded as a whole, is the pause in the story's advance. From the beginning to Chapter 24, prose and verse lead the mind on continually; each is a step in a progression, and each contains, to a certain degree, the seed of its successor while presenting in itself the development of that which has preceded. In Chapters 24-28, this is not so. Even a casual perusal of the ideas in verse and prose shows this. Here the poet omits those episodes introduced elsewhere, as Cesareo has said, "per comporre il suo romanzo che, intimo e spirituale quanto si voglia, dovea pur esser variato di qualche azione accessoria."[14] If, before, we have been ascending a gradually rising slope, we ascend no further here: a sort of plateau lies before us, and not until Chapter 29 are we to rise or descend again.

The individual poems themselves deserve comment.

[14] Zeitschrift f. rom. phil., XXX, pp. 687-8.

Of the four verse compositions, the three sonnets seem to have little real connection with the Vita Nuova. Rather they belong to other surroundings, and perhaps even to a different inspiration.

Two patent peculiarities distinguish the first. One is the oft-noted use of the name "Bice," while elsewhere in the verse of the Vita Nuova Dante's lady is never mentioned by name until after her death, and even then only the full form "Beatrice" is used. The second is the extreme irregularity of structure. Thoroughly in keeping with these, is the expression of an almost careless joy (we are speaking of the Sonnet considered apart from the prose) of the kind found in the pastorals. Adding to these points the mention of Giovanna, we have every right to believe, as some critics do, that this poem was written under the direct influence of Cavalcanti, and is closely related to "Guido vorrei——————."

The two following sonnets present two peculiarities. As a rule, Dante's sonnets are distinguished, as we have said, by the careful development of each part from the preceding part, at least through the first tercet.[16] It must prick our attention, therefore, to find looseness of construction in these two sonnets. These poems present ideas as a series rather than as a development, as a catalogue rather than as a progression; that is, they are an attempt to combine into a sonnet certain separate expressions of praise. Sonnet 16 especially presents this peculiarity—to such an extent, indeed, that, in spite of Dante's own analysis in the "divisione," we feel that it lacks unity of point of view.

[16] cf. Note 6 above.

The second peculiarity lies in the final lines. Sonnet 15 ends with:

> "E par che della sua labbia si mova
> Un spirito soave d'Amore
> Che va dicendo a l'anima 'sospira'"

and Sonnet 16 with:

> "Ed è negli atti suoi tanto gentile
> Che nessun la si può recare a mente
> Che non sospiri in dolcezza d'amore."

It is useless to recall to the student of early lyric how frequently the sigh figures in the verse of the troubadours and how it later became incorporated in the system of the dolce stil nuovo. Now Dante was fond of this idea.[16] Appreciating its delicate power, and with that feeling for the importance of final lines which everywhere characterizes his lyric, Dante used it, as he did other cherished ideas,[17] to heighten the effect of his conclusions. Two other sonnets, besides Sonnet 15, end with "sospira" as the last word of the whole composition, while two canzone-

---

[16] As shown, for instance, by " * * * Ne alcuno era lo quale potesse mirar lei, che nel principio non gli convenisse sospirare. Queste e più mirabili cose da lei procedeano virtuosamente" (V. N., Chapter 26).

[17] Interesting in this particular is Dante's use, in conclusions, of the exclamatory summary, as in Sonnet 14: " * * *sì mi somiglia," and in the Canzone "Quantunque volte * * *" which ends with " * * * tanto è gentile." This trait which, save for one possible exception—Guinizelli's " * * * e quest'è la cagione" (Casini: Le Rime dei Poeti Bolognesi del secolo, XIII, Bologna, 1881, p. 42), does not appear in the works of Cavalcanti or of the "Maximus Guido," Dante developed from a similar but less pronounced use of the same, found among the Provençaux. In Dante's lyrics this summary occurs as often in the final position as in all other positions put together: e. g., S., 11; S., 14; Canzoni V. II; XI. XIII; XV. II; Sestina I. I.

stanzas give "sospiri" the same prominent position.[18]
Whence it is evident that such conclusions were not
unpremeditated, and that the final words of our sonnet
received special attention—a point further emphasized
by the direct quotation, in the use of which our poet was
careful.[19] In Sonnet 16 Dante has undertaken even
more. Not content with the sigh, with "dolcezza" or with
"Amore" alone, all favorite ideas,[20] he heaps them
together, including them all in the one last line.

Admitting, therefore, the great care which Dante
bestowed on these last lines, and noting in the sonnets a
looseness of construction unusual in his verse, as well as
no references connecting them especially with incidents of
the Vita Nuova, we may be allowed to believe that they
may have been mere exercises, that Dante was practising
his conclusions. The fact that the construction is worse

[18] Sonnets 21 and 39; Canzoni VI. II, and VII. II; compare the
interestingly parallel use in Rambaut di Vaqueiras:

>   *   *   *   tals vira
>   sentira
>   mos dans, qui. ls vos grazira,
>   que us mira
>   consira
>   cuidans, don cors sospira.
>   (Appel's Provenzalische Chrestomathie,
>   Leipzig, 1902, No. 52).

[19] Not to enter upon a long discussion here, we simply indicate
the fact that in what are perhaps Dante's two finest canzoni, "Donna
pietosa * * *" and "Voi che intendendo * * *" every stanza,
save the first, ends with a direct quotation. In the latter, Stanzas
II and III have it at the end of the pedes as well (that point at
which this canzone makes its main pause); while in Stanza IV
the final quotation is double.

[20] "Amor" is the last word of two poems, Ballad X and Sonnet 27.
It occupies the same position in the first stanza of Canzone VII;
while the verb is similarly used in Canzone VIII. I, and Canzone
XIII. II.

in that poem which undertakes the most in its conclusion supports this supposition.

It would seem then that the three sonnets of the chapters under discussion had originally no real connection with the Vita Nuova. That on Monna Vanna and Monna Bice was plainly out of harmony with the general tone of the "libello," and Dante felt that it was unsuitable, as the efforts of the preceding prose to bring it into line readily show.

To be sure, this very prose indicates a possible difference to be made between these sonnets and those before Canzone II, by suggesting a more unearthly character for Beatrice, whereby the "loda di questa gentilissima" might resemble the prevailing manner of praising saints;[21]

[21] It would be possible to go still further than Salvadori (Sulla Vita Giovanile di Dante, Rome, 1907, p. 88): "quello che più importa è che per essa (this new "poesia di lode") abbiamo la manifestazione della bellezza dell'umiltà. L'umiltà si presentò ai nostri antichi poeti velata sotto il dolce riso femminile, etc." We might recall the frequent use of "humilitas" as applied to the saints. Folquet de Marselha presents an interesting use of the equivalent in the vulgar tongue, applying it to the divinity:

> "Aias de mi bos chauzimens
> car ieu soi ples de tot peccat
> E tu, senher, d'umilitat."
>
> Mahn. Werke, I, p. 335.

v. also Salvadori's own interesting notice (pp. 168-9) on the parallel treatment of Beatrice and St. Margaret as identified with Christ (an identification which, it will be noted, is emphasized strongly in the first of our set of chapters). "Ma il massimo dono concesso dal Salvatore a Margherita fu che la vita di lui in lei si rappresentasse per la conformità, etc."

Nevertheless, it must be remembered that, after all, this attitude need in no way be the result of a special phase of Dante's love for Beatrice at this point of his story; for all the poets of the *dolce stil nuovo* stood, as Bertoni puts it (Studi Medievali, 1907, p. 368), in relation to their ladies as the great doctors did to Mary Virgin.

and in that case, we should understand their being introduced.   It would be logical, then, to agree with Salvadori
who, referring to the fragment immediately following,
writes: "L'ultimo termine di quest' amore poteva essere
l'abbandono senza resistenza alla sua signoria sentita come
soave, la dolcezza dell'estasi.   Allora non rimangono che
sospiri, e un intimo contento di trovarsi in quella condizione, così profonda, che l'uomo non può quasi più
muoversi nè parlare, rapito fuor di sè.   È questo lo stato
descritto nell'ultima canzone composta Beatrice viva,
rimasta interrotta."[22]   This can hardly be so, however, as
we shall see by considering the "fragment"—the only poem
of our set of chapters not yet examined.

We shall not insist upon the tone of this "fragment,"
which might well arouse a suspicion of exaggeration,
exposing, as it does, an absolute lack of personal reaction
that can be found in no other of Dante's poems.   Such an
observation is too weak a foundation for what we would
demonstrate.   We shall, however, lay stress on three other
peculiarities, on three strong indications that this poem
is not the transcription of a real state.   The first is that
Dante insists upon the incompleteness of a composition
which seems to us, as to very many critics, to be complete
as it stands.   Casini, for instance, maintains that the
ideas which Dante meant to put forward are completely
expressed, and that this stanza formed originally a separate
composition,[23] and all those, who, with Prof. Norton,
regard it almost as a sonnet, doubtless share this view.
The second indication shows us that the "divisione" to
this poem is entirely lacking: and yet it is mentioned

---

[22] Sulla Vita Giovanile di Dante. Rome, 1907, p. 89.

[23] La V. N. di D. Al. con intr., commento e glossario. Florence,
1890.

at least (if not developed) for every other poem in the book; nor can this omission be due to the "fragmentary" nature of the present verse, since the four lines of an unsatisfactory beginning to Sonnet 18 are explained with care.[24] The third indication draws our attention to a still more significant fact. This canzone is broken off by the cry of the prophet: "Quomodo sedet sola civitas plena populo————." This lament breaks in upon the song with absolutely no warning. Nor is this all. Conscious planning, plainly discernible already, becomes still more obvious when we note that this Latin quotation is displaced. The natural sequel to the poem was the words: "Io era nel proponimento ancora di questa canzone, etc." But, instead, the Latin citation is thrust in before them, although its bearing on the narrative is explained only two chapters later and, even then, its presence is not by any means clearly justified.

These three facts—insistence upon the fragmentary nature of a poem in all probability complete, unique omission of the disturbing "divisione," displacement of the Latin quotation—all can mean but one thing: Dante sought to emphasize very vigorously the interruption of the song by the cry of lament.

Summing up, then, what reason can we find for including Chapters 24-28 in the Vita Nuova? We have seen that the narrative does not progress through them, as a whole. The first sonnet was clearly out of keeping with the tone which our poet wished to stamp upon the finished work. The two following sonnets are in no way definitely con-

[24] It is needless to remind the student that Dante was fully aware of the interruption which an inserted "divisione" would cause; as is evident from the words, "Acciochè questa canzone paia rimanere viepiù vedova dopo il suo fine, la dividerò prima ch'io la scriva," prefixed to "Gli occhi dolenti *   *   *"

nected with the Vita Nuova, and originally indeed may have been nothing but exercises on climax. The fragment seems destined, with the aid of the following Latin, to fulfil some duty performed by the juxtaposition of the two. Why, then, did Dante insert these chapters?

Let us examine them from a different point of view.

After the preparatory vision of Canzone II, all is calm. Even those episodes destined to lend life and motion to the narrative, and which necessarily centred about the narrator's emotions, are withheld here. Our attention is turned away from the effects of Beatrice on the poet: his suffering and unrest vanish. Four of the five chapters, save perhaps a hint here and there, may be called entirely objective. Chapter 24 shows Beatrice superior to all women; Chapter 25 discusses a poetical usage; the two following are devoted to praise of Beatrice and her influence, not upon Dante particularly, but on all persons. Only in Chapter 28, the fragment, does the subjective element return; and, having at last appeared again, it emphasizes, as never elsewhere, the total loss of independence, of personal reaction. Beatrice is perfection, and whatever she may bring of pain or sorrow, the poet accepts with delight. Thereupon, in sudden, planned explosion, the personal note, the protest, bursts out once more. The voice of the individual cries aloud. After four chapters of repose, the climax of happiness is cut short by a wail of sorrow; the song of finally acquired peace is broken by an exclamation cherished throughout Christendom as an expression of deepest anguish.

To obtain this sudden turn, this shock, was Dante's aim. Its preparation extends backward as far as the end of Canzone II. If we accept, as we must, the idea that he prepared the finished work with the preoccupation of an artist, it is thus that we can account for the introduction of that apparently irrelevant chapter on the personifying of love. It is in this way, too, that we can understand the release of tension in general throughout this group of chapters. And the possible exaggeration of the fragment, as well as the evident preparation for the following prose, likewise find here a satisfactory explanation.

As we have seen, the Vita Nuova itself authorizes this form of appreciation: the peculiar character of the matter in Chapters 24-28 lends itself to this interpretation, while structural peculiarities almost require it. In addition, the analogy with the methods of procedure found elsewhere in Dante, especially the use of contrast, is only too plain. Just as, in spite of Salvadori, we are unable to find any real model for the Vita Nuova,[25] and are consequently forced to consider it as a development to a larger scale of a single canzone, so the method applied in this group of chapters seems to represent the expansion of a procedure found elsewhere in single canzone-stanzas. Of

[25] Salvadori (ibid. pp. 234-5) refers to Guittone d'Arezzo (with his series of Sonnets I-LXXIX, in the Pellegrini edition) and Cavalcanti (with the 61 sonnets in the Vatican Canzoniere) as the "antecedenti" of Dante: indeed he speaks of the Vatican collection as perhaps the "antecedente immediato, e *probabilmente l'esempio,* d'una raccolta di rime ordinata a contare un'intima storia d'amore, quale fu poi la Vita Nuova." A hasty perusal of Pellegrini will show how unfitted—for our subject at least—Guittone's work is to serve as a model; while the one-man authorship of the sonnets in Vatican 3793 seems to be about disproved. Bertoni, who gives the bibliography on this subject up to 1907 (in Studi Medievali, Vol. 2, fasc 3, pp. 363-366), writes: "Noi ci troviamo dinanzi ad un florilegio, di cui le parti costitutive possono anche risalire a poeti conosciuti per altri componimenti * * *"

course, the Latin quotation should be included in the same chapter as the fragment (or at least be severed from the succeeding chapter). It is part and parcel of Chapters 24-28, and more particularly attached to the last. Lacking it, this part of the book is as incomplete as though the final line were dropped from Cavalcanti's:

"Per gli occhi fere la sua claritate
Sì che quale mi vede
Dice: non guardi tu questa pietate,
Ch'è posta invece di persona morta
Per dimandar mercede?
E non si n'è madonna ancor accorta.
(Io non pensava * *)"

or Guinizelli's

"e poi direttamente
fiorisce e mena frutto,
però mi sento isdutto;
l'amor crescendo fiori e foglie ha messe
e ven la messe—e'l frutto non ricoglio."[26]

or any one of those passages from Dante quoted above, where the strength of the sonnet or stanza depends upon the contrast introduced by the final lines.

It is beyond our ability to determine the value of the stress planned for this point in the Vita Nuova, and to indicate its relation to the evident stress on Canzone II. But of one thing we may be sure: it certainly was considered as having great strength by Dante himself. And no interpretation of the book can, we believe, neglect a consideration of this well-marked emphasis.

[26] Casini: Le Rime dei Poeti Bolognesi del secolo XIII, Bologna, 1881, p. 13.

SOME FRANCO-SCOTTISH INFLUENCES ON THE EARLY ENGLISH DRAMA.

By John A. Lester, Ph.D.

SOME FRANCO-SCOTTISH INFLUENCES ON THE EARLY ENGLISH DRAMA.

From the treaty of Philip the Fair with John Baliol in 1295, down to the union of England and Scotland under one king, there runs an uninterrupted line of alliances between the two countries. Scotch troops fought continually with the French, and on more than one occasion French troops were landed in Scotland. Buchanan, for instance, served with the French force organized by Albany, which raided the English border in 1523. Intellectual relations necessarily followed the political. David Murray founded and endowed a Scots college in Paris in 1350, and before long schools for teaching French were started in Scotland. Rich youths aimed to go from St. Andrews to Paris, as Lindsay bears witness in making his purse-proud Abbot say: "I send my sonis to Paris to the scuillis."[1] Scottish ecclesiastics held French benefices, and a Frenchman was, early in the sixteenth century, regent of Scotland. William Dunbar, Alexander Barclay, and Lindsay were all representatives of their country in France, as were Alain Chartier, Ronsard, and Du Bartas in Scotland. These were all poets who must have carried from court to court the taste for that literature and those forms of entertainment which flourished in a court atmosphere.

The relation between the early drama of Scotland and that of France first shows itself in the fifteenth century,[2]

[1] *Satire of the Three Estates. Works* (ed. Chalmers), II, 91.

[2] Records of payments to French minstrels can be found in the *Calendar of State Papers for Scotland* as early as Feb. 3, 1303-4: "Datum per regem Morand le Taborier facienti menestralciam suam coram rege apud Dunfermelyn."

as is shown by the following records, which seem heretofore to have escaped notice. In the *Exchequer Rolls of Scotland,*[3] in the year 1436, there is record of the payment of £18 to three stage-players, who are hired at Bruges, and sent with their outfit to Scotland; and of £32 for a similar purpose, to some other stage-players. One of the said players, Martin Vanartyne, signs the receipt. The records read as follows:

"Et tribus mimis conductis per computantem et transmissis in Scociam, et preparando se ad mare, sub periculo computantis XVIII li. gr. Et quatuor aliis mimis secunda vice conductis versus Scotiam pro servicio domini regis per compotantem, ad parandum se ad iter, ut patet per literas domini regis sub signeto de precepto et cujusdem Martini Vanartyne, unius dictorum mimorum, sub sigillo suo de recepto, ostensas super compotum XXXII li. gr."[4]

There is a further payment for the dresses of these actors. :

"Et compotat transmisse domino regi in nave vocata Skippare Henry, cum Willelmo Wik, in vestimentis mimorum, et argento dicta bullioun pro eisdem vestimentis, et duobus mantellis pellium martrix dicti sabill, scripto particulariter examinato et remanente ut supra, sub periculo compotantis XXXIII li. VI s. gr."[5]

Flanders was at this time under the illustrious and cultured Dukes of Burgundy; and Bruges especially, where Philip the Good had frequently held his court, was a centre of commercial and literary activity. English merchants lived there in considerable numbers; and Cax-

---

[3] ed. Burnett, Edin., 1880.
[4] *Id.*, IV (1406-1436), p. 678.
[5] *Id.*, p. 680.

ton began his long residence there five years after these players were shipped. These mimi were perhaps professional court performers, accustomed to act before the Burgundian aristocracy. Two years later there is a record of a reward paid to one Martin, presumably Vanartyne. An. 1438; "Et Martino, mimo, et sociis ejusdem, tempore coronacionis regis, de mandato regine et consilii, sub periculo computantis VIII li. X s."[6]

At the end of the century French actors were still in demand, as appears from the following entry in the accounts of the Lord High Treasurer;[7] "1490, Item, on Fryda the XXIII Julii in Dunde, to the king to gif the Franschemen that playt, XX unicornis XVIII li." But it was in the sixteenth century[8] that early French dramatic forms most impressed themselves on Scotland. Influence of this sort was only a part of the refining process which Scotland was undergoing through contact with France. The Scotch court must have French builders, doctors, apothecaries, printers and tailors. French fashions in dress were indeed always a standing target for Scotch satirists. Buchanan, Knox and Lindsay[9] all protested

[6] *Id.*, V (1437-1454), p. 35.

[7] ed. T. Dickson (Edinburgh, 1877), p. 170.

[8] The play called "Haliblude," acted at Aberdeen May 13, 1440, by the so-called Abbots of Bonaccord (vid. E. Bain, *History of the Aberdeen Incorporated Trades*, Aberdeen, 1887), pp. 49, 51, 58, to judge from its name and its suppression because of "divers enormyities" in 1445, was a mock-religious burlesque. In view of the close relations between France and Scotland, "Haliblude" may well have been a reproduction in Scotland of the type of plays furnished by the "sociétés joyeuses"—burlesque dramatic societies which sprang up all over France at the end of the fourteenth and beginning of the fifteenth centuries. The Abbot of Bonaccord would correspond with the "prince des sots" of Paris, "la mère folle" of Dijon, or the "Abbé de la Liesse" of Arras.

[9] Cf. *Ane Supplication directit to the Kingis Grace in contemptioun of Syde Taillis*. *Works* (ed. Laing), I, 128.

against them. But it was in entertainments, courtly and popular, that French influence is most clearly seen. French musicians were hired by the Scotch court in the fifteenth century.[10] Henry IV of France sends to James VI "un tireur d'armes et un baladin de la capacité et fidélité duquel il respondra."[11] James IV had a French entertainer who combined the art of alchemy, astrology and morris-dancing. Mary Stuart had a French female comedian called La Jardinière, and a company of French puppets.[12]

The first case of a farce known to Collier[13] is the performance mentioned in a letter of February 1541/2 from Sir William Paget, English ambassador in the French court, to Henry VIII. But farces were played in French mysteries long before 1541. For instance, in the miracle-play called "La Vie de Sainct Fiacre,"[14] a farce occurs following the notice, "cy est interposé un farsse." What the Scotch writers call farces bear evidence of French influence. Robert Lindsay, writing of the marriage of James IV with Margaret, daughter of Henry VII of England, which took place at Holyrood on August 8, 1503, says: "The heill nobillitie and commons of the realme * * * everie one according to thair estait, maid hir sic bankattin feirceis and playes that nevir siclykk was seine in the realme of Scotland for the entres of na queine that was resawit afoirtyme in Scotland."[15]

[10] *Exchequer Rolls of Scotland*, an. 1467; *Lord High Treasurer's Accounts*, CCLXI.

[11] *Recueil des lettres missives de Henri IV*, VI, p. 181.

[•] Joseph Robertson, *Inventories of Mary Queen of Scots*, LX, LXXI.

[13] *Hist. of Eng. Drama. Poetry* (L. 1879), I, 71.

[14] Jubinal, *Mystères Inédits 15ᵐᵉ Siècle*, I, 332.

[15] Robert Lindsay, *The Historie and Chronicles of Scotland* (ed. Mackay, Sc. T. S., Edinburgh and London, 1899), I, 240. Vid. also his account of the marriage of James V with Madeleine of France on Jan. 1, 1537; I, 365.

Again describing the coronation of Mary Queen of Scots in 1543, the same chronicler relates: "Schone after this the lardis convenit at Stiruiling the XX day of August in the zeir of God 1543, and thair convenit the zoung quein with gret solempnitie, trieumphe, playis, phrassis and bankating, and great danceing befor the quene with greit lordis and frinche ladyis."[16]   Again at Mary's marriage with the Dauphin, in 1558, Lindsay says, there was "gret singing, playing, dansing and pheirsis."[17]   As early as 1530 Sir David Lindsay writes in the *Complaynt of the Papingo:*

"And in the courte, bene present, in thir dayes,
   That ballatis brevis[18] lustelie, and layis,
   Quhilkes till our prince daylie they do present.
   Quha can say mair, thou schir James Inglis sayis
   In ballatis, farsis and in plesand playis."[19]

Sir James Inglis was superintendent of court entertainments, and the Treasurer's accounts show payments to him as an actor: "Dec. 10, 1511, 12 ells of taffety and 12 ells of canvass were furnished at an expense of £8/8/0 and 14/ to be hyme and his collegis play-cotes."   About the end of 1526 is recorded, "Item, to Sir James Inglis to by play-coitis agane Yule, be the kingis precept £40."[20] His "farces" may be what some of this provision was made for.   In 1554 there is mention in the Edinburgh records of the performance of a "litill farsche and play, made be William   Lauder;"[21]   and   in   1561,   "triumphs   and

[16] Id. II, 15.
[17] Id. II, 125.
[18] Writes.
[19] *Works* (ed. Chalmers), I, 286, Stanza V.
[20] *Dunbar's Poems* (ed. Laing), II, 392-3.
[21] Dibdin, *Edinburgh Stage*, p. 9.

fairsais"[22] were played in the same town. We have the authority of Knox for saying that these farces were copied from the French.[23] Probably well before the middle of the century, but certainly by that time, the Scotch had made considerable progress in copying French triumphs, and those dramatic performances which were used on special public occasions.

The preceding considerations show an early connection between France and Scotland in things appertaining to the drama, which will not be considered superfluous when it is remembered that Scotch drama, if we may give it that name, with all its tendencies, preferences and precedents, was bodily transported to England and grafted on the national stock in 1603.

But a direct line of French influence seems to have reached England by way of Scotland through Sir David Lindsay. Lindsay's well-known *Satire of the Three*

[22] The Scotch writers are extremely careless in their use of the word farce. The earliest example of the word (missed by New England Dictionary) is in Lindsay's *Epistil to the Kingis Grace*, prefixed to his *Dreme*, which was written in 1528. The reference is to a time ten or twelve years earlier. He reminds James V that he used to amuse him by "sumtyme playand farsis on the flure;" *Works* (ed. Laing, Edinburgh, 1879), I, 1. "Farces" here seems to mean gambols such as might please a child; for James at the time referred to was a young boy. But Robert Lindsay (*Op. cit.* I, 379), describing the reception in Scotland of James V and his second French bride, Mary of Guise, in 1538, says, "Thair was maid to hir ane *trieumphant frais* [MSS I has "pheirs," *i. e.*, farce] be Schir David Lyndsay of the Mont." But the description which follows shows this to have been not a farce, nor a masque (as is stated by Dict. of Nat. Biog., James V, p. 157), but a triumph. It means this also in Robert Lindsay's account (*Op. cit.* I, 381) of the reception of James V and Mary of Guise in Edinburgh in 1538. They were received, he says, with "greit triumph phraisses." But cf. the instance in the text, where triumphs and farces are mentioned as distinct and separate performances.

[23] *Hist. of the Reformation* (Works, ed. Laing), II, 287.

Estates, was probably first played in 1540. It is a political morality denouncing and satirizing abuses in both church and state. Though political poems were perhaps even commoner in Scotland than in England during the time of the Reformation, the political morality was known in neither country before the time of Lindsay.

The Scotchman's play was trenchant and witty to a degree far surpassing contemporary English drama, and attacked abuses which did not exist alone north of the border, but were objects of satire in every country which felt the Reformation. It would, then, be strange if Ward's opinion,[24] that this work was without influence on contemporary English drama, were founded on fact.

The *Satire of the Three Estates* was very popular in Scotland, and was being played as late as 1554. Sir William Eure's letter to Cromwell, in which he says that after the Linlithgow performance of 1540 the king called upon Chancellor Dunbar and several of his bishops and bade them reform "their fashions and manners of living," or else he would send "six of the proudest of them to his uncle, of England,"[25] shows how it impressed contemporaries. Its influence appears first south of the border in Bale's *King John.*[26] R. Wever's *Lusty Juventus* (1550) seems to have caught the spirit of reformation controversy from Scotland, and in the *Respublica,*[27] a morality on the Catholic side, produced in 1553, there

[24] *History of Eng. Dram. Lit.* (3d ed.), 1899, I, 131.

[25] *Dict. of Nat. Biog.,* Sir David Lindsay.

[26] Cf. Herford *"Literary Relations of England and Germany,* p. 135. In dating the first performance 1539, Herford fails to correct for new style. The performance was on Epiphany 1539/40; *i. e.,* Jan. 6, 1540.

[27] Printed by Brandl, *Quellen and Forschungen,* Heft 80.

is again evident influence of Lindsay.[28] *Albion Knight,*
entered in 1565-6, shows a further step toward the freedom
and boldness of the Scot. Ward calls this a "political
morality,"[29] and Collier says it is part of a political play
which, so far as is at present known, has no parallel in
our language.[30] The part which survives shows us a
satire in Lindsay's manner, where the troubles of Albion
at the hands of Injuri and Division are expressed almost
as boldly and bitterly as those of John the Commonweale.
The same frequent use of Latin phrases occurs in both.
The unpublished morality of *"Somebody, Avarice and
Minister"* is, according to Brandl, modeled on Lindsay;[31]
and he thinks that several figures of G. Wapull's *Tyde
taryeth no Man* (published 1576), and Thomas Lupton's
All for Money (published 1578), correspond with characters in the *Three Estates.* Again, in Preston's *Cam-
bises,* licensed in 1569, a personification called Commons
Complaint[32] prefers charges of venality against the judge,
much as John the Commonweale does in Lindsay.

It was never possible for the English moralists of the
drama to speak out for political reform with the astonishing frankness of Lindsay, Buchanan and Alexander.[33]
The monarchy was stronger in England than in Scotland,
and in the northern monarchy court poets stood far closer
to the person of the king. James VI always had a school-
boy's dread of his austere tutor, and James V could take
plain words from the man who had once carried him in his

---

[28] Vid. Brandl LV.

[29] *Op. cit.* I, 139.

[30] Shakespeare Society Papers, Vol. I, p. 55.

[31] But the names of the characters point to a direct French source.

[32] Manly, Specimens of Pre-Shaksperean Drama, II, 176-7.

[33] Cf. Buchanan's *De Jure Regis,* and Alexander's *Paraenesis to
Prince Henry,* both of which advocate the murder of tyrants.

arms and sung him to sleep.[34] But Lindsay pointed the
way which English political satirists could endeavor to
follow; and what they accomplished between 1550 and
1580 was largely due to the example of the intrepid Scot.

The *Satire of the Three Estates* is clearly drawn from
French models. During the reign of Louis XII (1498-
1515) there sprang up in France the political morality,
unknown before, and again unknown soon after the acces-
sion of Francis I. Gringore, whose relation to Louis XII,
though far less familiar, is analogous to that of Lindsay
to James V, was the exponent of the new genre. He
was the leader of the Enfants-sans-Souci, one of the
French mediaeval fraternities of comedians. His *L'espoir
de paix,* 1510, attacks the Papacy for worldliness and corruption, as Lindsay attacks spirituality in his first part,
and the *Folles entreprises,* 1505, attacks princes and lords
who crush poor serfs and "vassoulx," as Lindsay attacks
Temporality in his second part. It was Gringore who
first in France applied the mediaeval drama to political
ends; and it seems to be from him that Lindsay took his
pattern. The work which directly gave him a model
appears to be Gringore's *Sottie.* This was played in Paris
on Mardi Gras, 1511. The play is a more open satire on
both church and state than any other work of the French
poet. Louis XII, the "prince des Sotz," is to hold his
court and mete out justice to all comers. Many characters
arrive, representing the multitudinous vices and follies of

[34] Cf. Lindsay's *Dreme: Epistill to the Kingis Grace,* composed
1528:

> "Quben thou wes young, I bure the in myne arme,
> Full tenderlye, till thou begouth to gang:
> And in thy bed, oft lappit the full warme,
> With lute in hand, syne, softlye to the sang."

mankind, Ignorance, La Paillardise (cf. Lindsay's Sensuality), La Seigneur Joye (cf. Lindsay's Wantonness), La Manque de zèle Apostolique. Then enters La Commune, representing the people, and lodges complaints against the oppression of the seigneurs and the clergy. Last of all comes in the Mère Sotte, clad in the robes of Papacy, supported by her adherents. She preaches to the Seigneurs and the Clergy, advocating treason and rebellion against the king. A quarrel is provoked, and, in the scuffle, below the garb of the Pope is found the face of the fool.

Here we have the main features of Lindsay's play, namely, a keen satire of the evils of church and state, under the figure of a court, presided over by the king himself, before which appear as plaintiff La Commune (Lindsay's John the Commonweale), and as defendants the seigneurs and the prelates (Lindsay's Temporality and Spirituality).[35] The parallel in detail is often striking. We have in Gringore, as in Lindsay, the call of the seigneurs and the clergy to the court,[36] a discussion about the relative limits of the jurisdiction of the spiritual and temporal powers,[37] an impeachment of the morality of the clergy,[38] a denunciation of plurality and sale of benefices,[39] complaints by the representative of the people of distraint and confiscation of property by the church,[40]

---

[35] A somewhat similar *mise en scène* is to be found in the first tale of *The Three Priests of Peebles*, dating perhaps from 1535. Cf. *Complaynt of Scotland*, ed. Murray, CXVI, 143.

[36] *Œuvres Complètes de Gringore* (ed. Hericault and Montaiglon, Paris, 1858), I, 206. Cf. Lindsay, I, 469.

[37] Gringore, 206, 229; cf. Lindsay, 73, 116.

[38] Gringore, 219; cf. Lindsay, 388, 433, etc.

[39] Gringore, 220; cf. Lindsay, 62.

[40] Gringore, 237; cf. Lindsay, 5-7.

satire against the abuse of pardons,[41] and the final abolition of the corrupt clergy.[42] Lindsay's character of Divine Correction, of which there is no example in this *Sottie,* seems to be modeled on the figure of Pugnicion Divine in Gringore's *Moralité.*[43] The speech with which this abstraction introduces itself, and tells of the powers and terrors with which it is armed, is of the same character in each play.[44] Lindsay's Good Counsel, not found in Gringore's *Sottie,* is perhaps taken from his play of *La Vie de Monseigneur Saint Loys.*[45] The character of People, not found in any English morality previous to Lindsay, occurs in both Gringore's *Moralité* and in his *Vie de Saint Loys.*[46]

It has been said that Gringore was the leader of one of the theatrical companies of Paris. This was the fraternity of the Enfants-sans-Souci, a band of amateur comedians, who affected to regard the earth as populated mainly by fools. Upon their stage the world was turned topsy-turvy. The mighty were put down from their seats, and the humble were exalted; but the change was nothing,

[41] Gringore, 234; cf. Lindsay, 9ff.

[42] Gringore, 241, cf. Lindsay, 108.

[43] *Œuvres Complètes,* I, 244-269.

[44] Gringore, I, 251-3; cf. Lindsay, I, 452.4.

[45] *Œuvres Complètes,* II, 29 ff.

[46] Gringore may have taken the idea of his *Sottie* from the *Quadrilogue Invectif* of Alain Chartier written in the third decade of the 15th century, and printed in the 1617 edition of his works, pp. 402-454. This however is not a satire but an appeal to the wearied patriotism of France to unite against the English invaders. Dr. Neilson has shown (*Journal of Germ. Phil.* I, 411ff.), that this is the source of the *Complaynt of Scotland,* which shows one or two striking resemblances to the *Three Estates.* These, and others of no significance, as for instance a parallel between a sentiment in the *Complaynt* and Lindsay's proverb, "Wo to the realme that hes ower young ane king," which last is a commonplace taken originally from Ecc. X, 16, are noticed by Leyden, *Complaynt* p. 47, 48.

for high and low were alike fools. Besides the farces and
sotties which constituted their stock in trade, there was the
sermon, a mock exhortation declaring that folly was everywhere, that motley was the only wear. Instead of a
Biblical text, the preacher took as his theme:

"Stultorum numerus est infinitus,"

which indeed was the motto of the fraternity. Lindsay's
figure of Folly plays the part of such a preacher, and the
sermon he delivers is modeled on the type of the Sermon
des Fous. In parts it is not unlike the *Sermon Joyeux,*
printed by Violet-le-Duc in his second volume,[47] as the
following lines show:

Lindsay II, 148. "Heir sall
Foly begin his sermon as followis:
"Stultorum numerus infinitus."
The number of fuilles ar infinite.
I think na schame, sa Christ me
    saife,
To be ane fuill, among the laife,
Howbeit, ane hundreth standis
    heir by
Perventure, als gret fuillis as I,"

Anc. Th. Fr. II, 214.
"Or ça, pro secunda parte
Je trouve, de quantitate,
Que numerus stultorum est
    infinitus.
A savoir mon, si toute arisme-
    tique
Sçauroit nombrer le sexe fola-
    tique
Je ditz que non: il est inestim-
    able.
*   *   *   *   *   *
S'il y a donc icy trois cens
Hommes, à les comprendre tous,
Je dy que les deux cens sont
    foulx."

p. 216.
Si bien nous cherchons, nous
    trouverons
Foulx à monceaux en toutes
    regions.
L'on a bien veu, par plusieurs
    foys,

I have of my genelogie,
Dwelland, in everie cuntrie

[47] *Ancien Théâtre Français* (Paris, 1854), II, 207 ff.

Erles, dukis, kingis and empri-
   ouris,
With mony guckit conquerouris:
Quhilk dois, in folie, perseveir,
And hes done sa this monie yeir.

*   *   *   *   *   *

De sotz papes et de sotz roys.
Sotz empereurs, cardinaux, arch-
   evesques,
L'on a veu, et de sotz evesques,
Abbez, curez, aussi chanoynes
Y a partout, et de sotz moynes,
Sotz gendarmes et chevaliers.

p. 219

Sum dois as thay suld never die,
Is nocht this folie, quhat say ye?
"Sapientia hujus mundi stultitia
   est apud Deum."

Vous aultres qui entendez latin,
Levés voz cueurs, ouyez que c'est:
Sapientia hujus mundi stultitia
   est, etc."

One of the classes of fools which Lindsay's Folly goes on to satirize is the class of cuckolds, and the French sermon runs on in the same strain:

> "Ilz ont femme honneste, gracieuse,
> Belle, plaisante, amoureuse,
> Mesnaigère fort diligente,
> Et de mal aussi innocente
> Que Judas de la mort Jesus."[48]

What was the direct channel by which Gringore's works reached Lindsay is not certain. The French satirist had, however, been made known in Scotland by Lindsay's predecessor, Barclay, who in 1506 published the *Castell of Laboure,* a translation of the Frenchman's *Le Chasteau de Labour,* 1499. Gringore did not die till 1544, and the Scot may have met him in France, when he was negotiating for James V in and after 1531. Gringore as court poet was succeeded by a new school of which Ronsard was the leader. With Ronsard, Lindsay was on intimate terms, for they sailed together to Scotland, when James returned with his second French bride in 1538, and Ronsard, on that occasion, remained three months at the Scotch court.

The political morality was not the only form of the

[48] *Op. cit.* p. 210.

early drama to flourish north of the Tweed. Early traces of the masque can be found. One of the elements of the masque, namely, the dance, was in Scotland borrowed very frequently from France. Early in the sixteenth century we have records of payments to Frenchmen for dancing the morris,[49] and among the popular sports which ended so boisterously at *Christis Kirk on the Grene,* it is related that

> "Auld Lightfute thair he did forleit
> And counterfuttet Franss;
> He used himself as man discreit
> And up tuke Moreiss danss
> Full loud
> At Christis Kirk on the Grene that day."[50]

To judge by the names of dances given in an old Scotch poem quoted by F. Michel,[51] one would conclude that the majority of Scotch dances in the sixteenth century were of French origin.[52] From other payments to entertainers it is clear that some of these dances were elaborate, and required special costumes. In 1494 there is a record, "Item, gevin to Pringill, be a precept of the Kingis, for a liffray to make a dans again Uphaly day * * IIII ellis

[49] March 5, 1507-8. "To the French menstrallis, that maid ane danss in the Abbey, be the King's command, 12 French crowns.

Dec. 5, 1512. Payit to Monsur lo Motés [the French ambassador's] servitouris that dansit ane Morris to the king 10 crowns of wecht.

Dec. 16. To Monsur le Motés servitouris that dansit an uthir Moriss to the king and Queen £5|8|0." Vid. *Dunbar* (ed. David Laing) II. 289.

[50] Ascribed to James I of Scotland. *Poetical Remains of James I,* (Edinburgh, 1783), p 170.

[51] *Rise and Progress of Civilization in Scotland,* p. 231. Cf. also the long list of dances, native and foreign in *Complaynt of Scotland,* ed. Murray, Early English Text Society, p. 66, and XCIV; also *Leland Collectanea,* IV, 291.

[52] Scotch dances in their turn found their way into France. Cf. Michel, *Ecossais en France,* etc. II. 3.

of taftays, price of ellen XVIII s."[53]   In some of these,
the dancers were masked,[54] as appears from the following
entries. In 1488, "Item in Lannerisk, to dansaris and
gysaris XXXVI s."[55] And in 1496, "Item, that samyn
nycht [Dec. 27th] giffin to the gysaris in Melros
XXXVI s."[56] And in 1504-5, Feb. 2, "To the Gysaris
that dansit to the king and queen, 7 French crowns."

The rapid development of masquerades in Scotland
during the last part of the sixteenth century was due in
large part to Mary Stuart. As early as 1536, however,
if we may trust one of the manuscripts of Robert Lindsay's
Chronicles, James V had indulged in masking at the French
court. He writes, "thair was nothing bot mirrienes,

[53] *Accounts of the Lord High Treasurer*, ed. T. Dickson, Edinburgh,
1877, p. 232.

[54] Cf. Edmonstone, *View of . . Zetland Islands* (Edin., 1809), II 64.
If Ward is right in his view that the "masque probably at
first differed from the mummings and disguisings customary before,
by nothing except the fanciful adjunct of a mask to the costume worn
by the participant" (*Op. cit.* I, 150), there is no reason to insist on the
Italian origin of the masque so strongly as he does. The actual
mask for the face is one of the oldest elements: (vid. Ducange
"larvae," "larvarium," "cervula"). Cf. Brotanek *Die Englischen
Maskenspiele* 1902, p. 3, and 4 n.; and the illustrations of masked
figures in Strutt, *Sports and Pastimes* (new ed. L. 1903), plates
opposite pp. 138, 202; and Ed. Fournier *Le Th. Fr. avant la Renaissance*, plate opposite p. 333. Cf. also Hugh Haliburton (pseudo. for
J. L. Robertson), *Furth in Field* (L. 1894), p. 26 s. v. Hogmanay.
The masks, even in early times, were sometimes human; vid. Brotanek
p. 6. Masquerades and plays ("larvales et theatrales jocos") were
forbidden in France by the Council of Bâle 1436; and the custom of
masking the face had gone so far in France before the earliest date
set for the Italian masque by Symonds, viz. 1474,   (*Shakspere's
Predecessors*, L. 1884, I. 321), that the society of Basochiens in Paris
used masks reproducing the features of well-known people.

[55] *Accounts of the Lord High Treasurer of Scotland*, ed. T. Dickson
I., (1473—1498) p. 93.

[56] *Id.*, p. 308.

bancatting and great cheir * * * with great musick
and playing on instruments and tryme[57] danceing be the
sound of instrumentis playand melodiouslie witht gallzart
dancing in messerie [MS. I. has 'maistrie' or 'maskrie;'
Freebairn reads 'masks'], and prattie frassis [I. has
'pheirsis' = farces] and pleyis."[58] Mary Queen of Scots
was greeted with a brilliant pageant at her wedding with
Francis II;[59] and, naturally, on her return to her own
country, she wished to emulate the splendor of the continent. She brought with her to Scotland such Frenchmen
as Ronsard, Guillaume Barclay, and James Crichton.
When she entered Edinburgh in 1561, there were various
dramatic entertainments modeled on those of France. To
quote the blunt words of Knox, "Great preparations war
maid for hir enteress in the town. In ferses, in masking
and in other prodigalities, faine wold fooles have counter-
footed France."[60] Before this time, pageants and public
spectacles with some dramatic action had been introduced
into Scotland. Lindsay was in Paris at the marriage
of King James V to Madeline, and must have seen the
devices so quaintly described by his namesake. He
profited by his experience in France to devise plays himself
in honor of Madeline after his return, and though she died
before the occasion for their production, he wrote a
Deploratioun of the death of Queen Magdalene,[61] a large

---

[57] Trim.

[58] *Op. cit.* I. 359.

[59] For a contemporary account of these "triumphes et mommeryes,"
vid. Teulet, *Papiers d' Etat relatifs à l'Histoire de l'Ecosse,* I. 300-303.

[60] *History of the Reformation,* (Works ed. Laing, Edin., 1848), II.
287. Calderwood, *History of the Kirk of Scotland* (Edin., 1843),
II. 154 (written in the first half of the 17th cent.), uses the same
expression, evidently borrowing it from Knox.

[61] *Works* (ed. Chalmers), II. 179-189.

part of which is merely a description of the plays and pageants he had devised to please her. The arrival of the new bride, Mary of Guise, gave him another chance. When the new queen landed in Scotland the king met her, "and ressaved her with great joy and mirrines, of fearssis and plays maid and prepared for her." Next day the queen "confessed to the king that shoe never saw in France so many pleasant fearsis in so little rowme, as shoe did that day in Scotland."[62]

But after the middle of the century masquerades no less than public pageants grew in elaborateness and in popularity in Scotland. If the masking of 1561, as Knox says, was in imitation of that of France, the pageantry with which Mary was actually welcomed in the streets was also French. The account of it, as given in the *Diurnall of Occurrents of Scotland,*[63] yields several points of resemblance with the fête given in honor of the court at Rouen in 1550. The years between 1561, when Mary entered Edinburgh, and 1567, when she married Bothwell, were full of masquerades of great splendor. In the Autumn of 1561 was played at Holyrood the masquerade of which the verses remain in Buchanan's "pompa," *Apollo et Musae Exules.* In November of the same year, there was an equestrian spectacle, probably accompanied by a masquerade.[64] The masquerade at the marriage of the Earl of Murray in the next year, noticed in the Diurnall of Occurrents,[65] gave Knox another opportunity for a

[62] Robert Lindsay, *Chronicles of Scotland* (Sc. T. S., Edin., 1899), II. 380.

[63] Ed. Thomson (Edinburgh, 1833), p. 67 ff.

[64] Buchanan, *Rerum Scot. Hist.* XVII cap. XI, mentions "luda et convivia," as part of the entertainment.

[65] p. 71.

sneer.[66] There was a masquerade of shepherds at mid-winter in 1563,[67] and at Shrovetide next year a masquerade of great magnificence, with verses by Buchanan. A three-day spectacle celebrated Mary's marriage with Darnley in 1565, with another equestrian performance;[68] and next year the Queen and her ladies appeared in the disguise of men in a masquerade at Holyrood.

These masquerades were often planned by Frenchmen in attendance on Scotch princes or lords. In 1566 the young prince James was baptized at Stirling. Court festivities were arranged for the occasion, and Buchanan wrote some Latin verses to be spoken by the participants.[69] But the planning of the action disguises and machinery was all done by a Frenchman called Bastien Pagez. The complexity of the masquerade is remarkable for so early a period, and recalls the masques of the early Stuarts. Hidden machinery was devised, which caused the feast to come in on moving tables. Before them marched a procession of rural gods, each of whom turned to the dais, where royalty sat, and recited his verses. Satyrs, naiads and oreads addressed the prince; nereids and fauns the queen. At this point the satyrs indiscreetly or impudently,—it does not appear which,—wagged their tails. The English embassy took offence, and the masquerade was interrupted. When quiet was restored, there was a sudden discharge of fireworks from a mimic fortress. This was a signal for the arrival of bands of "Moors, Highlanders, Centaurs, Lanzknechts and Fiends," who

[66] *Works*, II. 314. Vid. also 319.

[67] Vid. J. Robertson *Inventories of Mary Queen of Scots*, p. 136.

[68] For a figure from a similar French spectacle, the picture of the Duke of Guise commanding a quadrille of American savages, vid. Pongin, *Dictionnaire du Théâtre*, p. 147.

[69] These are extant: *Omnia Opera* (1725), II. 404-5.

strove for the possession of the fort.[70]   This performance
has the marks of the French renaissance court masquerades.   Satyrs had, it is true, appeared in early Scotch
religious drama,[71] but not in company with fauns, oreads
and the rest.   It is not more complex than many other
Scotch masquerades of the same time, and attracted the
attention of chroniclers,[72] not because it surpassed others,
but because it vexed the English, and caused a disturbance
which nearly resulted in bloodshed.

When Mary left Scotland, and her household of foreign
servants and attendants was dispersed, the Holyrood
masquerade, as we should expect, declined.   It still
existed, however.   "It may haply fall out," writes Robert
Bower to Walsingham, on Feb. 7, 1580-1, "that * * *
some strange mask may be seen in this Lent in Holyrood
House."[73]   And the splendor to which it had already
attained in Scotland must be taken into consideration

---

[70] Robertson, *Innventories of Queen Mary*, LXXXXI.

[71] In a mystery of 1442 in Aberdeen. Vid. Joseph Robertson, *Book
of Bon-Accord*, p. 236.   A. S. wudu-wasa is satirus (Prompt. Parv. p.
531).   This is M. E. wodwos, (Gaw. and Gr. Kn. 721; Alex, 1540),
wodewese or woodwose.   This is popularized into woodhouse or
woodman.   The Scotch form, wodmen, in the mystery above referred
to, (pointing to A. S. wód-wasa), is much earlier than the first
appearance of the "salvadge man," (at Christmas, 1514-15, vid.
Collier, I. 69; Sp. hombre salvaje), which is the form often taken by
the satyr in continental and English renaissance drama.   Thorndike
in *Pub. of Mod. Lang. Ass.* Vol. XV, p. 118, attempts to fix an early
limit for the *Winter's Tale* from its antimasque of satyrs, which
he conjectures was suggested by the similar masque in Jonson's
Masque of Oberon, Jan. 1, 1611.   It should be noted, however, that
the satyr is one of the commonest characters in masquerades; and
that satyr-dances were known in the French "mascarades" as early
as 1581. Vid Lacroix, *Ballets et Mascarades de Cour* (Genève,
1868), I. 53, 56.

[72] Such as Sir James Melvil, *Mémoires* 3rd ed., Glas., 1751, p. 150.

[73] *Calendar of State Papers* (1907), V. 619.

when an explanation is sought for the great development of the masque after the two crowns had been united. As soon as James I came to the throne, the masque developed rapidly.[74] Of all English courts, that of James was most attached to this form of dramatic entertainment. This was due to his love of pageantry,[75] and to the passion for a certain aspect of classicism, caught from his tutors, whose minds were furnished with all the classical apparatus of French scholar-poets. The royal taste for the classics was a narrow one, and the dramatic form which best satisfied it was one which showed most strikingly the figures of Greek and Roman mythology. This could best be done in the way in which Ben Jonson and her assistants did it, namely, by bringing to the aid of poetry cast in dramatic form, and written in this quasi-classical manner, striking scenery and novel machinery.

James' queen, Anne of Denmark, was an ardent lover of masques. Her love of splendid entertainments and pageantry had been fostered by such spectacles as those of 1590, when she was received by the citizens of Edinburgh with pantomimes and pageants at a greater cost than had ever been bestowed on any English or Scotch queen.[76] At the English court her love of such festivities soon obtained full gratification, and she displayed her great skill in dancing in masques prepared by Jonson and Daniel. Jonson, indeed, often refers to the queen as the prime mover in deciding the nature which his masques were to take. Thus he says, in the introduction to the

[74] Cf. Johnson's Encyclopedia, article *Masque* by G. P. Baker.

[75] Vid. the account of the pageant at his entry into Edinburgh, Oct. 17, 1579. Calderwood *History of the Kirk of Scotland* (Edin., 1843), p 458.

[76] *Queens of Scotland*, Strickland (1851), V. 40.

Masque of Blackness:[77] "Hence (because it was her majesty's will to have them, [*i. e.,* the daughters of Niger] blackmoors at first) the invention was derived by me." And again, in the introduction to the *Masque of Queens,* "Her majesty (best knowing that a principal part of life, in these spectacles, lay in their variety), had commanded me to think on some dance or show that might precede hers, and have the place of a foil or false masque."[78] Gifford says that Queen Anne had been regaled in Scotland with nothing better than "one goodly ballad called Philotas" or the ribaldry of the Lion King, as his countrymen delight to call Sir David Lindsay, in the interminable "Satyre of the Three Eistatis."[79] Queen Anne would have been badly off indeed if this had been all her entertainment in Scotland. She could never have seen Lindsay's *Satire* acted, for the last recorded performance was at Greenside, in 1554; and it is extremely doubtful if *Philotas* was ever performed at all. But her knowledge and love of the masque may not improbably be referred to the court pageants and masquerades performed during her thirteen years of residence at the Scotch court.

In conclusion it may be noted that the vital element in the development of the masque, namely, dialogue, first appearing, according to Soergel,[80] in 1604-5, and according to Brotanek, in conjunction with the other elements, in 1595, is to be found forty years before in the remnants of Buchanan's *pompae,* consisting of Latin verses written for the Holyrood masqueraders.

[77] *Works* (ed. Cunningham), VII, 6.
[78] *Works,* VIII, 107.
[79] *Ben Jonson's Works* (L. 1816), VI, 468.
[80] *Die Englischen Maskenspiele,* p. 27.

In the *Pompa Deorum,* played at Mary's wedding with
Darnley, Diana begins with a complaint that love and
marriage are claiming one of her five Maries. Juno and
Venus reply to her, ridiculing her grief, for as for them
love and wedlock is their care. Pallas, Saturn and other
gods answer Diana in the same strain, and Jupiter replies
that the five maids are worthy of marriage, and dismisses
the complaint.[81]

The limits of this paper forbid the tracing further of
indirect influences in this channel on the early English
drama. But enough has been said to show the close relation between political morality and court masquerades in
Scotland and in France, and the interesting relation these
bear to the corresponding forms in England.

[81] *Opera Omnia,* 1725, II, 400 ff.

HEINE AND TENNYSON:
AN ESSAY IN COMPARATIVE CRITICISM.

By Charles Wharton Stork, Ph.D.

HEINE AND TENNYSON. AN ESSAY IN COMPARATIVE CRITICISM.

The Englishman or American who compares literary notes with a native of continental Europe is always surprised to find what English-writing authors are admired abroad. For instance, a German remarked to me that our three greatest geniuses were properly appreciated only in Germany, the three being Shakespeare, Byron and Oscar Wilde. Seldom indeed is it that the foreigner has read Spenser, Milton or Wordsworth, noblest representatives of our native Parnassus. It is evident, therefore, that many of the poets we most admire are somehow outside the interest of the cultured continent. A Shakespeare, a Dante or a Goethe can

"pass the flaming bounds of place and time,"

but in the class immediately following, the writer's nationality often excludes him from his proper place in the world literature. This is peculiarly true of English authors, whose "insularity" is so strongly marked as to be proverbial. Conversely, certain continental writers never obtain proper recognition in England.

We must all be aware of these two contrasting types in modern literature, the exclusively continental and the exclusively English. We deny, for instance, that Swinburne is in the narrower sense an English poet, and we feel in reading such an author as D'Annunzio that, despite his harmonies of language, he represents an artistic code which is distasteful to us because it violates our innate sense of fitness. Abstractions are futile. We therefore choose as examples of their respective schools, Heine and

(155)

Tennyson. Probably no modern lyrist is so widely accepted on the continent as Heine, whereas we of the narrower Anglo-Saxon traditions find our most intimate ideals expressed in the music of Tennyson.

The fact that first arrests our attention is that Heine had already written all the poems which have made him famous by the time he was twenty-six. Some dozen familiar songs and ballads fall within the next five years, but even here the productions are in the main but repetitions of the more spontaneous and exquisite melodies from the poet's youthful "Buch der Lieder." Where do we find anything more direct than the following from Heine's earliest period ?

> "Wenn ich bei meiner Liebsten bin
>   Dann geht das Herz mir auf;
> Dann bin ich reich in meinem Sinn,
>   Ich biet die Welt zu Kauf.
>
> Doch wenn ich wieder scheiden muss
>   Aus ihrem Schwanenarm,
> Dann schwindet all mein Überfluss,
>   Und ich bin bettelarm."

In the same series come "Wenn junge Herzen brechen," and soon after, certainly written by the time he was twenty, "Die Grenadiere." All the other incomparable songs follow in the "Lyrisches Intermezzo" and "Die Heimkehr" from 1822 to 1824.[1] To be sure we have later some spirited ballads, e. g., Schelm von Bergen, Schlachtfeld bei Hastings, König Richard, and Rudel und Melisande; but to my thinking Der Asra is the only one that brims over with the old pulsating fire. For the rest his only sincere note is one of regret for Germany and his early love. His satires and occasional verse may be interesting

---

[1] Heine was born December 13th, 1799.

to the special student of German literature; they have
nothing to detain the lover of belles lettres.

But what were the qualities which won the poet his
laurels at such an early age? The subject matter of his
masterpiece falls into two classes: first, youthful love,
happy or unhappy; and secondly, the ballad, always
strongly personal. His genius, in brief, is his personality,
for as he changes from passionate German sincerity to
the coldness of the Paris roué, the glamour fades and
vanishes.

> "Wermut sind die letzten Tropfen
> In der Liebe Goldpokale."

Heine was disappointed in what we may assume was
the one deep ideal love he experienced. The motive of
the heroine marrying a man of straw, and being finally
claimed by her affinity, the hero, under tragic circumstances occurs not only in numerous lyrics, but also
in Heine's two youthful tragedies. This devil's marriage
of the beloved was a thought he could not escape, and he
rings insistent changes on the theme. But then come
happier, quieter loves, full of rich imagination and tender
fancy. These are the poems which Heine himself, in
a preface written many years later, describes as "eine
Art Volkslieder der neueren Gesellschaft." And as such
we recognize them. They have the poet's native ecstasy
restrained, as we so often feel ourselves to be, by the delicate conventions of the drawing-room. Imagine Burns
discarding his homespun and adopting the dress, manners
and speech of the Edinburgh aristocracy, or conceive of
Percy's Reliques translated into the metre of Waller.
The decorous Heine loves in very truth, but he will not
fall down at the feet of his mistress while "der Garten
ist voller Leut'." The idea was a new one, this bringing of

sentiment into the very stronghold of sentimentality, and Heine, like all great innovators, left his successors to imitate what they could never surpass. Here is the quintessence of the whole in two quatrains:

"Die Jahre kommen und gehen,
    Geschlechter steigen ins Grab,
Doch nimmer vergeht die Liebe
    Die ich im Herzen hab'.

Nur einmal möcht ich dich sehen
    Und sinken vor dir aufs Knie
Und sterbend zu dir sprechen:
    'Madam, ich liebe Sie.' "

We can hardly realize how startling to Heine's contemporaries was the beautiful irony of the change from the "du" of the lover immemorial to the "sie" of polite address.

But later, especially after Heine's removal to Paris, the amours became even lighter and less satisfying. I quote the following not for its sordidness but to illustrate Heine's decline. The date is 1829, before his settling in Paris, and soon after his brightest blossom-period:

"In welche soll ich mich verlieben,
    Da beide liebenswürdig sind?
Ein schönes Weib ist noch die Mutter,
    Die Tochter ist ein schönes Kind.

Die weissen, unerfahrnen Glieder
    Sie sind so rührend anzusehn!
Doch reizend sind geniale Augen,
    Die unsre Zärtlichkeit verstehn.

Es gleicht mein Herz dem grauen Freunde,
    Der zwischen zwei Gebündel Heu
Nachsinnlich grübelt welch von beiden
    Das allerbeste Futter sei."

Heine had already burned himself out and, with characteristic frankness, was ready to admit it.

"Doch wenn ich den Sieg geniesse,
　Fehlt das beste mir dabei,
　Ist es die verschwundne, süsse,
　Blöde Jugend-Eselei?"

Another even more striking example of the way Heine came to regard his most sacred emotions is the poem "Frieden" from the Nordsee series. Here, after relating a marvelous vision of Christ moving across the waters, the writer suddenly turns and asks, "Which of you Berliner poetasters could conceive such a vision as that?" The effect is indescribably banal.

As Heine brought the direct emotion of the popular ballad into modern society, he infused reciprocally a modern, personal element into his ballads. Every observer has noted that the Lorelei begins with "ich," and Die Wallfahrt nach Kevlaar has a psychological intimacy beyond that of any other ballad ever written. Yet Heine's ballads, even as ballads, are thoroughly successful. The reason is that in them the feeling is not merely poignantly personal, the inspiration roots rather in that deeper poetic nature which touches the springs of all human passion, that of the peasant as well as that of the aesthete. Take, for example, the following:

DIE BOTSCHAFT.

Mein Knecht! steh auf und sattle schnell,
　Und wirf dich auf dein Ross,
Und jage rasch durch Wald und Feld
　Nach König Duncan's Schloss.

Dort schleiche in den Stall, und wart,
　Bis dich der Stallbub schaut.
Den forsch mir aus: "Sprich, welche ist
　Von Duncan's Töchtern Braut?"

Und spricht der Bub' "Die Braune ist's,"
So bring mir schnell die Mär.
Doch spricht der Bub "die Blonde ist's,"
So eilt Das nicht so sehr.

Dann geh' zu Meister Seiler hin
Und kauf mir einen Strick,
Und reite langsam, sprich kein Wort,
Und bring mir den zurück.

This has the true Percy ring with even greater intensity. And there is that most simple and inevitable of all, "Es war ein alter König." Pater says that what the artist gives the world is himself, and Heine gives this self nobly and fully in his earliest emotions. With him far more than with Byron who coined the phrase, "Poetry is passion." This self-revelation is his strength, but it is also his weakness; his strength when the emotions spring forth strong and pure, his weakness when they sink into sluggishness or stagnate with the scum of satiety.

Turning now to Tennyson, in the metrical experiments written before he came of age we find the incipient germ of a poet and one undoubted poetic achievement, Mariana. Two years later follow Œnone, The Lady of Shalott, A Dream of Fair Women and The Lotos Eaters, proving the writer a master beyond all question, but still leaving his rank in doubt. Only with the volume published at the age of thirty-three could it be said: "A great poet has been born into the world." And from that time on, if there was no marked advance, there was continued production of a high order. We have certainly in our English master a steady development from youth to manhood, and a long period of sustained activity. Tennyson is essentially a descriptive and reflective poet, appealing to our contemplative nature where Heine appeals to our emotions. For whenever Tennyson attempts to describe intense emotion he always fails to master it, and instead of carrying us forward with him, merely stands still and marks time. Note some of his failures in this respect, e. g., his handling of the Tristram story, or the conclusion to The Death of Œnone. Fortunately Tennyson usually knows how to moderate his passion till it is well within his control and moves the delicate engine of his verse in perfect rhythm. How he might rage in Pelleas and Ettarre, how he might storm in Guinevere; but he softens, idealizes, and the result is beautiful. We have only to look at the conception of Morris to see what an unreal figure is Tennyson's Guinevere, which has so much of sentimental charm and so little of human nature. She never could have been rude or womanly enough to have defended her woman's nature while she maintained,

"Nevertheless you, O sir Gawaine, lie."

The greatest harm one can do a poet is to praise him for qualities which he has not, and in Tennyson's case we had best admit that he is never properly dramatic, never depicts real, naked passion.

The two men are as different as can be imagined, and it must be confessed our instinctive preference will almost surely be for Heine. Frankly, I believe him to be the greater poet, but by no means in a higher class than his less emotional rival. However, the question of priority need not detain us here where the essential object is to define the types. Heine carries us by storm; the style is direct, the response immediate. So irresistible is the passion that we do not read Heine, we *are* Heine, are in love, sharing every rapture and torture of the gamut. No such love poetry has been written since Catullus.

Dante is more mystic, Petrarch more formal, no other so palpitatingly real. Quotation alone can do him justice:

"Mit deinen blauen Augen
    Siehst du mich lieblich an,
Da ward mir so träumend zu Sinne,
    Dass ich nicht sprechen kann.

An deine blauen Augen
    Gedenk ich allerwärts:—
Ein Meer von blauen Gedanken
    Ergiesst sich über mein Herz."

Here Heine reaches the absolute, but if we ask what else he has done in the field of poetry, the answer must be "Nothing that the world would not only too willingly let die." Love lyrics, love ballads, love dramas and this love of one sort only, the passionately sensuous.

Tennyson also is a love poet, but of how different a nature! He is never direct, always a trifle sentimentalized and, as we read him, always objective. The difference between the poets is not merely one of personality, important as that may be; the difference is even more largely one of education and environment. Heine's full-grown love poetry is the result of the continental regime which brings the young man immediately into the most intimate and passionate relations with women, leaving no room for sentimentalism. Tennyson, on the contrary, trained in accordance with the accepted English traditions, spent his youth among other young men, associated with girls as with comrades, and gazed upon woman in general with the eye that admires much but understands very little. So far, from the artist's standpoint, the odds are all in favor of the continent, but Heine's further progress is one of disillusionment; he drained the cup at the first draught, and as a result we find at thirty Tennyson mel-

lowed and Heine embittered. To be sure, youthful love
is the most exciting to read of, and we can well understand
that a man brought up under the continental regime
might fail to be charmed by such characteristically English
lines as those of Herrick:

> "I dare not ask a kiss."

But if this be the case, how much of true beauty and purity
the man of the continent misses! What pathos is more
tender than that of Elaine, of Œnone? What pastorals
more charming than The Miller's Daughter and Dora?
Locksley Hall and Maud delight us perennially with their

> "Passion pure in snowy bloom
> Through all the years of April blood."

And although these two great love poems are so peculiarly
English, they contain a world of beauty for all who may
be wise enough to take it.

Unfortunately the appreciation of one artist often prevents our doing justice to another, and in such cases it is
always the quieter genius that suffers. He who admires
a Velasquez will hardly take time afterwards to enjoy an
Andrea del Sarto. We should, therefore, if we wish to
be fair, give special attention to the calmer style. We
have observed the effect of their environment on the two
poets and have seen that the English mode of life, though
less stimulating at first, has in the long run its compen-
sations. To understand these the foreign critic may need
to cultivate a wider range of responsiveness in order to
feel the fascination of an author with whose point of
view he is not naturally in sympathy.

But admitting that Heine is the superior as a votary
of Erato, we must give Tennyson the credit of being more
impartial in his courtship of the Muses. How far above

Heine's bitter partisan satire are Tennyson's "Love thou
thy land" and those stirring patriotic ballads, The Revenge
and The Defense of Lucknow. No doubt violence was
required during Heine's lifetime to arouse the supine, but
Heine resembles the French Revolution in that he profanes
more than he purifies. German critics try very laudably
to prove that the exiled poet remained always true to the
Fatherland, but the reader feels that Heine, under French
influence if you will, would rather be witty than genuine,
would rather satisfy a private grudge than castigate a
public wrong.

I fear we must take the following for a belated bit of
Byronesque not borne out by his actual conduct, but the
passage deserves quotation not only as a record of his
better nature but also for itself as prose:

"Ich weiss wirklich nicht, ob ich es verdiene, dass man
mir einst mit einem Lorbeerkranz den Sarg verziere. Die
Poesie wie sehr ich sie auch liebte, war mir immer nur
heiliges Spielzeug, oder geweihtes Mittel für himmlische
Zwecke. Ich habe nie grossen Wert gelegt auf Dichter-
ruhm, und ob man meine Liede preiset oder tadelt, es
kümmert mich wenig. Aber ein Schwert sollt ihr mir
auf den Sarg legen; denn ich war ein braver Soldat im
Befreiungskriege der Menschheit." [2]

Such flashes, often a trifle lurid, appearing from time
to time in Heine's poetic satires and prose reflections, stand
out only too strongly against the shabby background of
the context. More characteristic of Heine's general tone
is the assertion that if he had to shake hands with the
people, he would be careful to wash his hand afterwards.

Again, Heine could never be called a philosophic
poet, although in Atta Troll and Deutschland, his

[2] Reise von München nach Genua. Cap. XXX.

satires, are brilliant passages of truth and blasphemy inseparably interfused. We admire the astounding imagination, but we cannot regard Heine's faith very seriously when he expresses it in such figures as that when we accept a personal god we receive the future life gratis like a piece of scrap-meat at the butcher's. Heine's genius maintains itself only for short, meteoric flights; he never could have held himself down long enough to evolve a philosophic creed, nor, supposing he had done so, was he earnest enough to have believed in it the next day. On the other hand, Tennyson, though not among the greatest English philosophic poets, thought earnestly and to a purpose. He rose from "honest doubt" to find a deeper meaning in nature and a deeper purpose in the seeming contradiction of the world of men. Though not equal to Browning, he has the advantage of thinking more lucidly and thus giving the results of his meditations to the average reader. Nor, despite his so-called didacticism, is Tennyson ever less than poetic. The "Flower in the crannied wall" is a fine example of an abstract truth made specific and comprehensible, and such poems as Faith, and God and the Universe bear witness to a well balanced and steadfast form of belief. Tennyson's political philosophy, most clearly portrayed in the second Locksley Hall, is the deeply reasoned conservatism of Burke which states that all advance must be based on the assured foundations of the past. Like Horace, Tennyson distrusts the "vulgus mobile," the thousand-headed monster, and exhorts the statesman to legislate with his eye fixed on a goal beyond the seething present.[3] Yet Tennyson, without waiting for the help of Mr. Bernard Shaw, perceived many of the evils lurking in modern society, as we see in an outspoken

---

[3] Cf. his poem, To the Duke of Argyll.

passage of Aylmer's Field. In his patriotic and philo-
sophical poetry Tennyson is again typically English, for
unswerving love of country and a firm belief in the God
above and the God within are an inalienable inheritance
of the Englishman, no less of the American, as opposed
to the spasmodic excitement and general indifference of
the continent. Supposing, what we should hardly admit,
that Tennyson were narrow in his creed, we must at
least admire his sincere and resolute expression of it.

One important observation must be made in Heine's
favor, namely, that the most important of his later writings
are in prose which is beyond the province of this essay
as are the plays of Tennyson, since neither represents the
writer at his best and neither gained a universal popularity. Heine's prose, however, is notable in many
ways, especially for its technical and artistic beauty.
Irresistibly fresh and charming is the style of the
Harzreise, while in such later works as the Florentinische
Nächte are imaginative passages not short of marvelous.
Still the writer shows himself to us here as in his poems;
in youth, enthusiastic and lovable; after thirty, world-
weary and cynical. The random raptures and daring play
of humor which we find delightful in the traveling student,
become unspeakably stale and mean, often mere sacrilege
and vulgarity, in the older man for whom no deeper mood
succeeded. The brilliance is forced and only the bitterness is from the heart. The beauty of the Florentinische
Nächte is morbidly exotic, and in the criticisms on Shakespeare's women a really enlightening passage of criticisms,
like that on Cleopatra, may be followed by trivialities or
would-be witticisms on Ophelia and Lady Macbeth. Perhaps the finest critique is that on Cordelia, whom he
describes as the modern Antigone who surpasses the

ancient, "a pure soul, but a trifle obstinate." Heine's
prose style is discursive, but he lacks the self-control needed
to write in the manner of Sterne or one of the great
French masters, the unevenness of his disposition and the
obtrusion of personal cavilling or rancor spoiling the effect
as a whole.   He is not earnest enough for a satirist, nor
good-natured enough for a humorist.

We all remember Arnold's lines:

> "The Spirit of the world,
>   Beholding the absurdity of men—
> Their vaunts, their feats—let a sardonic smile,
>   For one short moment, wander o'er his lips.
> *That smile was Heine!*"

The summary is just if we consider only the later Heine.
To the young enthusiast of the Harzreise, Arnold pays a
generous tribute in an earlier passage of the poem just
quoted, viz. Heine's Grave.

Turning from subject-matter to style in the narrower
sense, we shall at first sight incline again to prefer the
German.

> "Heine for songs, for kisses how?"

writes Browning, who felt, as we all do, that Heine was
the nearest approach to reality.   Heine fuses figures with
feeling, and runs them into a perfect mould of form.   The
imagery is not external, made to refer to the subject, but
eyes and stars are so described that we see both at the
same instant.   Heine's passion pervades all he sees.   The
setting sun sinks into his glowing breast; he bends over
his beloved in the star-sown sky, her voice is the nightingale, "Die Rose, die Lilie, die Taube, die Sonne" unite
in her; he seizes a Norway pine, dips it into the crater
of Etna, and writes on the black tablet of the night in
letters of fire, "Agnes, ich liebe dich!"   Even to the

most simple and conventional emotions, he can give such
unexpected yet profound expression as:

> "Wenn ich in deine Augen seh;
> So schwindet all mein Leid und Weh;
> Doch wenn ich küsse deinen Mund
> So werd' ich ganz und gar gesund.
>
> Wenn ich mich lehn' an deine Brust,
> Kommt's über mich wie Himmelslust;
> Doch wenn du sprichst: 'Ich liebe dich!'
> So muss ich weinen bitterlich."

Heine uses contrast and irony with the greatest effect, but
the style is never decorative. A man writing at white
heat has no time to pause for description or moral reflection. It is indeed only with a soaring imagination that
irony can be effective; if the poet flies too low his attempt
at humor may be taken for a mere accidental slip into the
ridiculous, and it is the boldness of Heine's contrasts that
makes both the passion and the anti-climax more effective.
The rapture of a lover and the agonies of the Weltschmerz
are in themselves an exaggeration which if carried too far
will seem strained or absurd. The artist, seeing this,
avoids the catastrophe by anticipating it, drops suddenly
from his exalted height, and thereby not only attains a
striking effect of irony, but also shows us to what a dizzy
height of emotion we have been previously carried. For
an example of this we may take the conclusion of
"Fragen," which the poet asks by the seashore:

> "O löst mir das Rätsel des Lebens,......
> Sagt mir, was bedeutet der Mensch?
> Woher ist er komen? Wo geht er hin?
> Wer wohnt dort oben auf goldenen Sternen?"
>
> Es murmeln die Wogen ihr ew'ges Gemurmel,
> Es wehet der Wind, es fliehen die Wolken,
> Es blinken die Sterne gleichgültig und kalt,
> Und ein Narr wartet auf Antwort."

In the above quotation we may also note the handling of the free rhythm; first the nervous, excited movement of the questions, then the monotonous indifference of the elements and the tremendous accent thrown on "Narr" in the final line. This brings us to Heine's versification, where he is once more a past master. His instinct, his ear is unerring; he loses no opportunity, and he makes no mistake. Considering the harshness of the German language, it is a wonder what music the great poets, especially Heine, can draw from it. For melodies of breathing tenderness almost any of the poems already quoted, and those even better known, which are in every memory, will suffice. Again, what unbridled restlessness chafes in the lines:

> "Mit schwarzen Segeln segelt mein Schiff
> Wohl über das wilde Meer,"

and what pathos echoes in the refrain where, this time with the deepest sincerity, he speaks of his country "in der Fremde."

> "Ich hatte einst ein schönes Vaterland.
> Der Eichenbaum
> Wuchs dort so hoch, die Veilchen nickten sanft.
> Es war ein Traum."

Indeed, Heine at his best seems not so much to have a beautiful style as to have the power of verbal incarnation for every mood and change.

We have seen that the essence of Heine's style is subjectivity and directness; of Tennyson exactly the opposite is true. As Mr. Bagehot has noted, the style of Tennyson is always objective, descriptive, decorative. He wreathes with flowers his classic goddesses, his medieval ladies and his English dairy-maids till we can hardly tell them apart. He is never too intensely centred on his subject to miss a chance for a graceful bit of detail, and at the end he is nearly sure to drift into a moral parallel. In "Break, break, break," for instance, he takes time to turn around and look at himself before going on. The interpolation is in this case surely a fault. Why does not the poet make us *feel* what he cannot utter, instead of saying he cannot utter it? One thinks of the typical traveler's letter or the typical popular novelist: "The scene was beyond description," "Words fail to express my emotions." Heine would simply have said

> "Mir träumt ich weiss nicht was,"

and we should have understood. Compare also the speech of Heine's grenadier, ready to spring full-armed from the grave at the sound of his Emperor's trumpet, with the more artificial figure used by the lover in Maud:

> "My dust would hear her and beat,
> Had I lain for a century dead;
> Would start and tremble under her feet,
> And blossom in purple and red."

Tennyson often loses himself in his figure and prefers the simile to the metaphor. Take the picture of Geraint:

> "Arms on which the standing muscle sloped
> As slopes a wild brook o'er a little stone,
> Running too vehemently to break upon it."

Here we shift our attention entirely from the thing described to the description. But no better illustration occurs than that cited by Mr. Bagehot, *i. e.,* the passage about the tropic island in Enoch Arden, extremely picturesque, but quite extraneous to the action of the story. We need not treat of Tennyson as an epic poet, because he is not properly an epic poet at all. He not so much tells as illustrates a story. His plots are either flimsy or

absurd, such as one would expect to find in novels written
for boarding-school girls. What could be more mawkish
than the bare narrative of Maud, of Locksley Hall, of
Aylmer's Field ?   Of the flimsy category are The Lady of
Shalott, Sea Dreams, The Village Wife, etc. As to the
Idylls of the King, the story is much better told in Malory.

What then are the merits of this description which
Tennyson has made an end in itself ? To this we must
answer that although Tennyson appeals to a very large
audience because of the lucidity with which he portrays
universal, if somewhat generalized, emotions, yet a true
appreciation of him as an artist does not come at once.
Heine's fiery nature burns in an indelible impression at
the first contact, but to feel the charm of Tennyson we
must allow it to steal over us gradually. Heine sweeps
us away and hurries us along with him; but Tennyson
is less a passion than a refuge after the burden and heat
of the day, a soft, half-evasive loveliness, not to over-
master, but to be yielded to. He gives us a picture of
settled English landscape, with more or less idyllic figures
moving about in the subdued light of summer afternoon,
for in Tennyson's land it is "always afternoon." Here
one has time to lean back and enjoy in their fulness all
the lesser beauties of nature:

> "A league of grass, wash'd by a slow broad stream,
>   That, stirr'd with languid pulses of the oar,
> Waves all its lazy lilies, and creeps on,
>   Barge-laden, to three arches of a bridge
> Crown'd with the minster towers."

But every line of The Lady of Shalott, The Lotos-
Eaters and twenty others is precious and loses half its value
in being wrenched from the context. Be it confessed,
however, one wearies of In Memoriam, some hundred

and thirty modulations of luke-warm grief slightly sweet-
ened by a modicum of philosophy. Exquisite lyrics there
are, but the subject offers too little variety for such interminable repetition. Infinitely greater are Lycidas and
Adonais.

Let us observe, next, the figures in this Arcadian
landscape. Heine displays only himself, an individual
product of the French Revolution, fervent and lovable,
violent and selfish, one complete but isolated personality;
whereas Tennyson gives us in general two types, the strong,
pure-hearted hero, and the gentle, somewhat Griselda-like
girl. These are, to be sure, the idealizations of the
English university man and the quiet-eyed English
maiden. The villain is always a man of straw—did any
one ever quite believe in Maud's brother or young Locksley's uncle?—and the peasant characters afford a background of homely humor as in the novels of George Eliot.
To point out the continental and English qualities in the
character-drawing of Heine and Tennyson respectively
would be superfluous. To be sure, we are all interested
in Heine, whereas the savant of the continent might find
the English hero tiresome and the heroine insipid. To
appreciate them one must drift into the poet's atmosphere,
as one might stand before Turner's "Crossing the Brook,"
until the day-dream becomes reality. Then we shall have
time to examine each flower and shrub, to enjoy the
branching elms, the oaks and smooth-boled beeches, and
to let the eye follow their perspective into soft, hazy dis-
tances of hill and cloud. And if the sound of church
bells vibrates solemnly from far away, we do not feel
it as an intrusion, but as an audible consecration of the
scene. So are we affected by Tennyson's moralizings,
which are so sweet and unforced that we not only accept

but enjoy them in the context despite all theories of art for art's sake.

We Anglo-Saxons have all felt the charm of Tennyson's descriptions, but we have not perhaps stopped to think how typically English this passion for description is. No other literature contains anything like the same amount; indeed Lessing maintains that poetry should never describe, since it thus encroaches upon the province of painting and sculpture. The answer to Lessing is that given by a German professor of English, who said that English poetry was in itself the refutation of such a thesis. English poetry is peculiarly fond of picturesque detail for its own sake, "loading every rift with ore," as Keats specifies it. St. Agnes' Eve is perhaps the shining example, but we can go back to Milton and Spenser or forward to Morris, Rossetti and Tennyson. And this will always be the justification of pictorial poetry, that it enables the writer to evolve from such airy nothings as the motive of The Lady of Shalott, a poem which wholly delights us. The taste may be an acquired one, but it is certainly as well worth acquiring as a fondness for the strained and distorted emotions of the present continental school.

Tennyson has also the rare gift of visualizing religious and political abstractions. He retells the newspaper account of some English victory so that it stirs our blood with the thought of the issues at stake, he states some governmental or moral axiom in so novel and perspicuous a way that he lends new meaning to the threadbare truth. The Ancient Sage, a commentary on the sceptic, is good reading and good poetry, the argument being summed up in the couplet from Locksley Hall Sixty Years After:

"Truth for truth, and good for good! The Good, the True, the
    Pure, the Just—
Take the charm 'for ever' from them, and they crumble into
  dust."

To be sure we must give Heine credit for saying that
pantheism is merely a compromise offered by the atheist,
but we have seen how little heart this maker of epigrams
had in the matter of religious faith. We think of Tennyson's poems as the common-prayer-book of English poetry,
but the volume contains many a sharp rebuke of narrow
conventionality and intolerance. Note his fine recognition
of the English spirit which made the American revolution.[4] Inconsistent as the traditional Englishman in one
point, he combines a love for the human race in general
with a holy hatred of the French. But his personal
philosophy has a high mobility. Akbar's Dream is in
truth a dream of something loftier than the world has yet
attained, a cosmopolitan religion, and nothing is farther
from Tennyson's mind than the fanaticism which consigns
its antagonists to fire and brimstone. His optimism,
though not so virile as Browning's, carries conviction as
to the progress and destiny of humanity, and his conservatism is well reasoned and well stated. His attack on
modern realism is especially telling.

> "Rip your brothers' vices open, strip your own foul passions bare;
>   Down with Reticence, down with Reverence,—forward,—naked,—
>   let them stare."

Heine might indeed have replied with his sardonic:

> "Der lieben Mittelmässigkeit droht hier, wie überall, keine Gefahr."

Tennyson is, as all critics have noticed, a remarkably
eclectic poet, and in this quality pre-eminently English,
which being interpreted means "retentive of tradition."
Glancing at the great poets preceding him, we find Burns

[4] Cf. England and America in 1782.

more universal and so less insular. Byron and Shelley, children of the Revolution, might have been born anywhere in Europe, Wordsworth is too metaphysical and Coleridge too far aloof from the visible world. Keats, of the early romanticists, is the most English, and forms the link in the line of royal succession from the Elizabethans to Tennyson, but Keats was born into a realm of fancy and died too young to acquire his full birthright in the outward world. In the contemporary period we have Browning rising to greater intellectual heights and Swinburne attaining more elaborate complexities of form, but Tennyson is triumphantly English in that he keeps the balance of excellence between matter and manner. He originates comparatively little, adapting his true poetic gift to the models of the past, whether of English literature or of what lies at the foundation of English literary tradition, the classics. He is never a mere imitator, but has the faculty of assimilating and re-employing the contributions of his predecessors. An ex-Haverford professor, Dr. Mustard, has given us an excellent book on classic echoes in Tennyson, showing that he not so much wrote as felt in the spirit of the originals. In the same way he used Wordsworth's philosophy of nature, the subtle music of Coleridge, the tenderness of Shelley, the lighter satiric touch of Byron. Above all, he assumes with dignity the gorgeous mantle of Keats' imagery. "Keats begat Tennyson, and Tennyson begat all the rest," says a critic. Yet, although Tennyson is inferior to each of the poets just mentioned in some one respect, he has given to literature a much greater body of good poetry than any one of them. He directs all the new-found beauties of the romanticists into the well-marked path of English literary tradition. Later he brings the dramatic monologue of Browning within the apprehension of the masses in such splendid poems as Rizpah, The Wreck, etc. A more independent trait is Tennyson's ability to write noble occasional poems such as that to Virgil, the Ode on the Duke of Wellington, and the Inscription on the Monument to Sir John Franklin:

> "Not here! the White North has thy bones; and thou,
> Heroic sailor-soul,
> Art passing on thine happier voyage now
> Toward no earthly pole."

Literary coteries discussing their favorites among the poets of the last century will never agree upon one name, but the great bulk of readers will recrown with grateful love the late laureate.

Although Tennyson is the poet of the average man, he is never an average poet. This is due, probably, not so much to his command of imagery as to the sustained flow and melody of his verse. His rhythm not ony fascinates us at the time, but lingers in our memory afterward, so that Tennyson is the most quotable of our modern poets. Lines seldom stand out like the mightiest utterances of Wordsworth and Browning, but on every page will be found some perfect fitting phrase, while the even balance of the context never jars us with commonplaceness or harshness. Tennyson's range of style, like the range of his emotions, is not great, but within his province he rivals the best. He has the faculty of the composer who develops a simple theme with perfect art in a hundred pleasing modulations. Mendelssohn is the best parallel— a musician never of striking originality, somewhat sentimental, whom the savants are compelled to admire for the mastery of his art, and the world at large for his graceful blending of feeling and form. So the unsophisticated, the simple hearted, love Tennyson, and the finest and most discerning critics love him. Those who dissent, compose that too large middle class of culture who have read or understood just enough to mislead themselves and others.

If Tennyson originated little in subject matter, he at least enlarged the technical resources of the literature by the introduction of a lyrical blank verse. His blank verse has a flexibility and melody exactly suited to the idealized tone of the substance.

> "Elaine the fair, Elaine the lovable,
> Elaine the lily maid of Astolat"

and

> "O mother Ida, many-fountain'd Ida,"

have a beauty of sound which, like the mist in our English afternoon landscape, lends softness and remoteness to the scene. A nobler note, typifying the sunset splendor which succeeds the milder light, sounds in the heroic cadences of Ulysses and the harmonies beginning with

> "So all day long the noise of battle roll'd."

The former rhythm reminds us of Turner's Crossing the Brook as contrasted with the larger effect of Ulysses deriding Polyphemus. The imitations of Tennyson are weak because they lack the stability and repose of classic inspiration, for only inherent strength and symmetry can sustain a wealth of ornament. But Tennyson's blank verse is so exquisite that he can use it for purely lyric purposes, to give atmosphere and touch the most delicate chords of emotion. No night-pieces of Heine breathes more rapturously than

> "Now lies the Earth all Danaë to the stars,
> And all thy heart lies open unto me."

Again, "Tears, Idle Tears" and "Come Down, O Maid" are so overflooded with music that we do not even notice the absence of rhyme. Doubtless a reason why Tennyson has been undervalued by foreign critics is that one must have not only a perfect ear but also a subtle appreciation of the values of sound in English in order to fully enjoy such an artist.

Yet admirable as Tennyson shows himself in the control of blank verse, he is more beloved for the simpler music of his songs and rhymed lyrics, the mere mention of which is enough to set one quoting or improving one's memory in any of the anthologies. There is a mystical use of sounds as symbols that gives these lyrics a deeper magic, even for the casual reader, than any other English songs possess. This melody was Tennyson's birthright, tinkling at once in Claribel, and persisting through his entire works, to chime its last tones in Crossing the Bar. How often do the elfin echoes of the Bugle Song,

> "thin and clear
> And thinner, clearer, farther going,"

enchant us! We are never deaf to the monotone of Mariana's lament, nor can we hear unmoved the crash of "Break, Break, Break," for these rhythmic sounds vibrate to the inmost depths of us. Tennyson's art was not at first unstudied—he speaks of the difficulties in handling esses in English—but soon he progressed far enough to trust his instinct. Swinburne's alliterative dithyrambs have always a certain trickiness, but Tennyson's felicities are as unsought as they are satisfying. Take, for example, A Farewell, which is more personal and delicate than the better known Brook.

A FAREWELL.

Flow down, cold rivulet, to the sea,
  Thy tribute wave deliver;
No more by thee my steps shall be,
  For ever and for ever.

Flow, softly flow, by lawn and lea,
  A rivulet then a river;
No where by thee my steps shall be,
  For ever and for ever.

But here will sigh thine alder tree,
  And here thine aspen shiver;
And here by thee will hum the bee,
  For ever and for ever.

A thousand suns will stream on thee,
  A thousand moons will quiver;
But not by thee my steps shall be,
  For ever and for ever.

The beauties of such a poem are not obvious, indeed they conform to Swinburne's definition of poetry in that they are indefinable.

In his technique Tennyson is not less English than in his subjects. He follows the traditions of elegant simplicity as we find it illustrated in the reposeful painting of Reynolds, Romney and Morland. With the poet, as with the painters, inspiration is inherent, but the form it assumes is redolent of the artist's environment. Tennyson's poetry belongs to England, but must we therefore conclude that it has no appeal for the connoisseur of the continent? At the recent exhibition of classic British paintings in Berlin, general surprise was evoked and unqualified praise was bestowed by sincere German critics, who recognized that a new and important field of beauty was here opened to them. Might not foreign literary

critics have the same sensation by allowing themselves to
fall under the similar charm of Tennyson?

Surveying the field of our subject from the vantage
point of the conclusion, we see that Heine developed almost
immediately under the forced growth of the continent an
intense but narrow personality which confined itself to
one phase of life, manifested itself in a remarkably brilliant subjective style, and exhausted itself in a few years.
In Tennyson we observe a slow but steady development,
a much broader field of interests, and a subdued, impersonal style.   Both are admirable artists; the one as an
individual romanticist, the other conforming the romantic
spirit to the bounds of classic convention.   This is a
natural result of their development, for Heine was greatest
in youth, Tennyson in maturity; and youth is usually
romantic and passionate, whereas manhood is stylistic and
restrained.   Heine was essentially a Bohemian, one whose
emotions were uncontrolled, whose opinions were antagonistic to a settled mode of life, whereas Tennyson was
composed, temperate, with that generous English tenderness which never gives way to the egoism or the irony
of the Parisian point of view.   Not many great English
artists have been Bohemian in the modern sense of the
word; that is, self-centred, discarding all of life that did
not minister to their passions.   They have felt themselves
a part of society rather than a sect at war with it, and
have consequently tried to reform it from within instead
of hurling promiscuous abuse at it from without.   Someone may be tempted here to enlarge upon Heine's misfortune, the ingratitude of his country, etc., but a clear view
of the case will show that Heine was well placed by fortune and that his destiny was in fact his character.   Nevertheless a ray of light is shed over his last hours.   In the

moonlight of his last dream the Passionsblume opens to
him mysteriously.   After the agony of

> Gut ist der Schlaf, der Tod ist besser—freilich
> Das beste wäre, nie geboren sein,"

comes a fine resignation, recalling Stevenson's "Under
a wide and starry sky" in

> WO?
>
> Wo wird einst des Wandermüden
>   Letzte Ruhestätte sein?
> Unter Palmen in dem Süden?
>   Unter Linden an dem Rhein?
>
> Werd' ich, wo in einer Wüste
>   Eingescharrt von fremder Hand?
> Oder ruh' ich an der Küste
>   Eines Meeres in dem Sand?
>
> Immerhin! Mich wird umgeben
>   Gotteshimmel, dort wie hier,
> Und als Totenlampen schweben
>   Nachts die Sterne über mir.

At first thought it would seem that a marked personality
was the highest form of poetic genius, since in such a
case we learn to know and love the poet, but after a
little consideration of the subject we must admit that the
greatest writers have often concealed themselves in their
art.   Tennyson's weakness is that his impersonality seldom goes beyond the English pale, so that to know him we
must first know his country.   But English virtues should
interest even when they do not coincide with the taste
of the cosmopolitan, and Tennyson has an undoubted claim
upon universality.   The man of the world may assert that
such poetry is fit only for women and school children, but

even so a large audience remains, and have we not all
our womanlike and childlike moods, which deserve to be
encouraged rather than suppressed? Ideal poetry must
preserve a balance between power and restraint, both of
which are essential. Of these qualities Heine excels in
the former, Tennyson in the latter, and a fair critic will
agree that the difference between them is not nearly so
much in degree as in kind. Each developed as impulse
drove, and if anyone goes further and insists that one
kind must be higher than the other, we must answer that
the greatest and most enduring poets have written imper-
sonally, rising from themselves to a purer and more ideal
form of expression. But this is going too far afield into
mere theory. In practice let us be broad minded, never
dictatorial in questions of taste. Here are two great poets,
both of whom we must admire, and each of whom we may
enjoy. Shall we destroy our pleasure by comparison
because their beauties are so different? Behold! one star
differeth from another in glory.

THE FRANKLIN'S TALE.

By Walter Morris Hart, Ph.D.

THE FRANKLIN'S TALE.

Considered as a Masterpiece of the Narrative Art, in Its Relation to the Breton Lay and to the General Framework of the Canterbury Tales.

I. THE FRANKLIN'S TALE.

The *Franklin's Tale* was manifestly written for the place which it now occupies. Not only did Chaucer connect it, by means of its prologue, with the preceding *Squire's Tale;* he gave also ample evidence that he was conscious of the dramatic situation; throughout the story he never forgot that the Franklin was talking, and talking to the Canterbury Pilgrims.* The tale has thus comparatively little of that impersonal quality which we think of as characteristic of medieval literature. In his choice of story, and in his way of telling it, the Franklin revealed certain phases of his own charming and relatively complex personality. It was not, indeed, so much the own son to Epicurus, the St. Julian for hospitality,[1] who was now

* See the passages (like "For o thing, sires, saufly dar I seye") where the Franklin, in the first person, addresses his audience, vv. 761, 829, 927, 1113, 1466, 1493ff., 1593f., 1621f. The Franklin's use of the word *wryte* is clearly a slip. See, however, Henry Barrett Hinckley, *Notes on Chaucer*, pp. 238f. Mr. Hinckley argues for an early date (1380) for the *Franklin's Tale*, on the basis of evidences of immaturity. But Professor Tatlock is clearly right in saying that "Chaucer's literary manner depended far less on the time of life when he was writing than on the character of his subject." *Development and Chronology of Chaucer's Works*, p. 18. This is a peculiarly valuable comment on the *Franklin's Tale.*

[1] Except in the description of December, vv. 1252ff.

speaking, as the vavasour, conscious of his "almost-baronial dignity,"[2] yet retaining his sturdy middle-class morality, condemning his son for wasting his substance at dice and for associating with low company.   This rare combination of delight in high living and high thinking must have carried with it unusual sanity, maturity of judgment, knowledge of the world, and a perhaps not unlearned interest in the problems of life.   Thus, although he may, as Professor Schofield maintains,[3] have intended his story as a compliment to the Squire, yet he could not refrain from siding against Aurelius, his attitude varying from the amusement excited in sober maturity by calf-love,[4] to a sterner condemnation of magic or black arts.[5]   Middle-class morality drew the picture of conjugal equality, in conscious contrast, apparently, to the ideals of courtly love and to the notions of Aurelius.   Upon this idealism, however, the man of the world made ambiguous comment concerning the ways of women.[6]   In much the same mood he declared his inability to use figures of speech, and gave an example of their absurdity.[7]   Such interest in questions of style implies some reading; the Franklin's familiarity with *Hieronymus contra Iovinianum,* revealed in Dorigen's exempla, should not surprise us, nor should his knowledge of astrology.   His whole character prepares us for his interest in the problem of evil.   *His* interest,— for Chaucer did not forget that the Franklin was speaking, and though their views and interests may have coincided,

[2] Cf. Skeat's note on v. 360 of the *General Prologue.*
[3] *M. L. A.,* XVI. 405.
[4] Vv. 1084, 1217f.
[5] Vv. 1119f., 1132f.
[6] Vv. 743, 803ff., 817f.
[7] Vv. 726f., 1016f.

as Shakespeare's and Hamlet's did sometimes, the "fallacy of quotation" is almost as delusive in the case of the great narrative poet as it is in the case of the great dramatic poet himself.[8]

It was, then, the Franklin, and not Chaucer, who said that he would relate one of the lays rhymed by the old gentle Britons in their first Briton tongue. The fact that the story was a very old one, that the events which it narrated must have happened long ago, may have invested it, for the Pilgims, with a peculiar charm. Yet no attempt was made to emphasize or to develop this glamor of the past, though the Franklin might well have learned from the Wife of Bath how to clothe his story in an atmosphere of beauty and mystery. How different was her beginning!

> In tholde dayes of the king Arthour,
> Of which that Britons speken greet honour,
> All was this land fulfild of fayerye.
> The elf-queen, wih hir Ioly companye,
> Daunced ful ofte in many a grene mede;
> This was the olde opinion, as I rede.
> I speke of manye hundred yeres ago;
> But now can no man see none elves mo (vv. 857ff.).

The Franklin made no such distinction between past and present; nor did he emphasize the connotation of the scene of his story, of "Armorik that called is Britayne." Doubtless his hearers were more or less familiar with Breton lays and knew that Brittany was the home of mystery and romance, the very threshold of fairyland, but that the Franklin so conceived it there is no evidence whatever. The sea and the dangerous coast with its hostile black rocks were necessary for his story, and to these the "places delitables"—conventional medieval gardens—formed

---

[8] Cf. Moulton, The Moral System of Shakespeare, p. 1.

effective contrast, and whatever charm of unreality may have been present was due merely to vagueness in conception, even to absence of clear visualization.[9] The time and the land seem empty; a May morning, a "Now" in December, a flowery garden, a bit of rocky coast, a busy street, stand out but dimly against a background of shadows.

This background is vaguely peopled—by the vanishing figures in the busy street, or those friends of Dorigen who walked with her by the sea, or danced in the gardens. Detached but slightly from these are individuals, who appear in receding perspective, Aurelius the social favorite, Arveragus the flower of chivalry, Dorigen the high-born, the magician, the squire and maid of Arveragus, and the servant of the magician.

The nearest of these figures are but dimly seen. Dorigen has the distinction of being "oon the fairest under sonne." Aurelius alone is honored by a formal description; he

> fressher was and Iolyer of array,
> As to my doom, than is the monthe of May.
> He singeth, daunceth, passinge any man
> That is, or was, sith that the world bigan.
> Ther-with he was, if men sholde him discryve,
> Oon of the beste faringe man on-lyve;
> Yong, strong, right vertuous, and riche ond wys,
> And wel biloved, and holden in gret prys (vv. 927ff.).

This conventional panegyric, absolutely without visualization, is to be contrasted with vividly descriptive lines from the portrait of the Squire in the *General Prologue:*

[9] It is noteworthy that the journey from Penmark to Orleans seems (vv. 1239ff.) to require but a single day, whereas Orleans lies 300 miles due east (not south, as Professor Schofield insists). Aurelius thus seems unconsciously to perform a task like that of Doon, who rode from Southampton to Edinburgh in a day to win a maiden.

With lokkes crulle, as they were leyd in presse.
Of twenty yeer of age he was, I gesse.
Of his stature he was of evene lengthe,
And wonderly deliver, and greet of strengthe.

    *   *   *   *   *   *   *   *

Embrouded was he, as it were a mede
Al ful of fresshe floures, whyte and rede.
Singinge he was, or floytinge, al the day;
He was as fresh as is the month of May.
Short was his goune, with sleves longe and wyde.
Wel coude he sitte on hors, and faire ryde (vv. 81ff.).

One should compare particularly "young" with "twenty years of age," "strong" with "wonderly deliver and great of strength," "one of the best faring men alive" with

Curteys he was, lowly, and servisable,
And carf biforn has fader at the table (vv. 98f.).

In each case the *General Prologue* is the more precise, specific, vivid. It is the same convention, but here far more effectively elaborated, so that one feels that, in this respect at least, the Chaucer of the *Franklin's Tale* is not quite the Chaucer of the *General Prologue*. Yet this is his nearest approach to that manner; except Aurelius, not one person in the *Franklin's Tale* is seen or described at all. Not one, in fact, is an individual; they are all idealized types, simply. Dorigen is the obedient and constant wife; Aurelius, the passionate lover; Arveragus, the worthy man of arms, flower of chivalry. Comparison with the Knight of the *General Prologue* is suggestive. The lines:

He loved chivalrye,
Trouthe and honour, fredom and courteisye.
Ful worthy was he in his lordes werre (vv. 45ff.),

are an admirable description of Arveragus. But what follows reveals, again, the typical vividness and concreteness of the *General Prologue*.

This conventional quality of the persons, however, should not blind us to the relatively subtle contrast between Arveragus and Aurelius—knight and squire; for one is the typical man of action, wise, sane, mature; the other, the typical sentimentalist, youthful, inactive, passionate. The distinction is made consistently throughout the story; the method is thoroughly characteristic.[10] Thus, at the outset, Arveragus, to make himself worthy to speak to Dorigen of his love, undertakes many a labor, many a great enterprise. In order that they might live the more happily, he was ready to swear never to take upon himself the mastery.[11] The Franklin is thinking of him in his general praise of those who are patient in love, who have learned to suffer whatever may be said or done amiss in wrath, or sickness, or sorrow, or because the stars above us govern our conditions, and who do not expect vengeance for every wrong. Much as he loved Dorigen, he loved honor more, and after only a year of happiness with her, set out for a two years' sojourn in England, there to seek worship in arms. On his return, in health and great honor, he, like Aurelius, danced, but he jousted also. He had neither suspicion nor fear that anyone had spoken to Dorigen of love. And when he had heard her story he did not accuse or reproach her. He sought rather to comfort her, and he saw at once a possible way, for one of his ideals of "trouthe," the only way, out.

> "It may be wel, paraventure, yet to-day.
> Ye shul your trouthe holden, by my fay!" (vv. 1473f.).

[10] Cf. the contrast of the more highly individualized Nicholas and Absolon (in the *Miller's Tale*), Troilus and Pandarus, even the more vaguely conceived Palamon and Arcite.

[11] His retaining the name of sovereignty for the sake of appearances does not seem quite in character; but this trait is, apparently, introduced here because it is necessary later.

When, with tears, he bade her tell no one "of this aventure," his grief was unmistakably caused, not by any fear
for the future, but by what had already happened, by the
same thought of appearances which led him at the beginning to reserve the name of sovereignty. It is because of
just this foreknowledge of what Aurelius will do that
Arveragus is not to be regarded as a "lewed"[12] man.
Dorigen, the Franklin tells his hearers, is to have better
fortune than they imagine.

Unlike Arveragus, Aurelius, the sentimentalist, does not
enter the story performing prodigies of valor, but dancing
"passinge any man." He is well-mannered, amiable, dis-
creet, and generally liked. Like Arveragus, he stood in
awe of Dorigen. He did not, however, seek to make himself worthy of her by great deeds, but luxuriated in passive
despair, expressing his grief, so far as he dared, in general
terms, in lays, songs, complaints, roundels, virelays. When
he spoke to Dorigen at last he began by telling her of his
desire to die, then begged for mercy. He declared at
once that Dorigen's condition was "an inpossible," and
desired nothing but sudden and horrible death. With
piteous heart he made his complaint to the gods, and when
they were deaf to his bootless cries, fell swooning and lay
for a long time in a trance. His brother carried him to
his bed, where he lay for two years in languor and furious
torment. Then at last his brother, not, as in Boccaccio's
story, the lover himself, bethought him of the magician.
When the rocks had been removed he saluted his lady with
humble countenance and heart full of dread. In his
forbearance to press his claim as a right which he had now
earned, he seemed to exhibit but another phase of his
sentimentalism, four parts selfishness and cowardice to

[12] V. 1494; "lewed" clearly means here ignorant, unskilful, bungling.

one of delicacy and consideration. And it was this same sentimentalism—lack of that will-power and decision which are developed by action, desire to stand well in the opinion of others—that led him to follow so promptly where another had shown the way, to vie with Arveragus in generosity, as Arveragus expected him to do, even though, clearly enough, he had not the same confidence in the outcome.

For Aurelius was quite capable of a noble deed; from the beginning there is no doubt of that. Viewed, not from the modern, but from the medieval point of view, there was nothing unusual in his falling in love with Dorigen; even Arveragus did not condemn him for that. What was unusual was the relation of Arveragus and Dorigen. He was her lover and her lord also, and the fidelity which she would, in medieval romance, have given her lover, she gave to her husband. Her scorn of Aurelius for loving another man's wife must have sounded strange in his ears. Yet, because of the unusual relation of Arveragus and Dorigen, the disturber of their happiness inevitably incurs the dislike and condemnation of readers. But this must not go too far. A villain would have destroyed the ideal mood of the story, would have given it a different ending. Aurelius, therefore, is made as attractive as possible; and even a sentimentalist may be— usually is—attractive, except for the over-strenuous man of action. If he loved Dorigen it was not his fault but his "aventure," his misfortune. It is noteworthy that he and Arveragus never came together. Such a scene would have been difficult to handle, and Aurelius would have suffered too much by the contrast. He has the qualities of his defects, however; his sentimentalism saves him. His youth, his popularity, his amiability, his sufferings, the very strength of his passion (for who could help loving Dorigen?), are all in his favor. It is his brother, not he, who thinks of the magician. And Aurelius makes no claim upon Dorigen, tells her simply that the rocks are removed, and leaves her without pressing his suit. That he should follow the noble example of Arveragus produces, then, no shock of unreality.

The impression of these three characters, consistent types, if not individuals, is conveyed to us by a variety of means, mainly, perhaps, by what they say and do in carrying forward the story; for of dialogue or action for purposes of characterization there is very little. Nor do their conventional good looks give us any clue. More significant are the effects which they produce upon one another or upon others; the "worthinesse" of Arveragus is capable of winning Dorigen to a very unusual fidelity; her undefined charm inspires love in very different men; Aurelius is "wel biloved and holden in gret prys," and subject to the good influence which springs from the powerful character of Arveragus. Epithets, giving the narrator's opinion of a character are, when used, conventional, like *virtuous, gentle, worthy, wise.* Beyond the contrast between Arveragus and Aurelius, and the necessary effort to make Aurelius attractive, it does not appear that Chaucer felt, in the *Franklin's Tale,* his usual interest in character.

The story seems to have been interesting to him mainly because of what it offered, or demanded, in the way of study of emotion. Not that he attempts any analysis so subtle as that in *Troilus and Criseyde;* not that there is any great scope or variety of emotions, for they are limited to joy and sorrow in their various degrees. What is striking is the completeness of the "lines of emotion;"

from beginning to end of the story we can trace the emotional rise and fall of Aurelius, fall and rise of Dorigen.[13]

[13] Complete illustration would require the quotation of a large portion of the tale. Dorigen's varying moods may be traced in outline as follows: "A yeer and more lasted this blisful lyf" (v. 806); in Arveragus's absence "wepeth she and syketh * * * moorneth, waketh, wayleth, fasteth, pleyneth" (vv. 817 and 819); her friends comfort her "til she Receyved hath, by hope and by resoun, The emprenting of hir consolacioun, Thurgh which hir grete sorwe gan aswage" (vv. 832ff.); "Hir freendes sawe hir sorwe gan to slake" (v. 841); she walked with them and saw the ships, "but than was that a parcel of hir wo" (v. 852); she saw the rocks, "For verray fere so wolde hir herte quake, That on hir feet she mighte hir noght sustene" (vv. 860ff.); her lament concerning the rocks and the problem of evil follows. Her friends try other places, where, however, she "made alwey hir compleint and hir mone" (v. 920); yet at last she must "with good hope lete hir sorwe slyde" (v. 924). When Aurelius declared his love, "she gan to loke" (v. 979) upon him,—evidently in surprise and scorn. "What deyntee sholde a man han in his lyf For to go love another mannes wyf" (vv. 1003f.); afterward, "And hoom they goon in Ioye and in solas, Save only wrecche Aurelius, allas!" (vv. 1019f.) (Has Chaucer forgotten Dorigen, or did he intend to include her in those who went home joyfully?) When Arveragus returns, "O blisful artow now, thou Dorigen!" (v. 1090). We hear no more of Dorigen until Aurelius tells her of the removal of the rocks; then "she astonied stood, In al hir face nas a drope of blood * * * And hoom she gooth a sorweful creature. For verray fere unnethe may she go, She wepeth, wailleth, * * * swowneth * * * With face pale and with ful sorweful chere." (vv. 1339ff.). Her Complaint follows. "Thus pleyned Dorigene a day or tweye" (v. 1547). "She gan wepen ever lenger the more" (v. 1462). She expresses no emotion when she hears Arveragus's command, but when she meets Aurelius and he asks where she is going,

> She answerde, half as she were mad,
> 'Un-to the gardin, as myn housbond bad,
> My trouthe for to holde, allas! allas!' (vv. 1511ff.).

Her relief is not described, except by "She thonketh him up-on hir knees al bare" (v. 1545). Finally,

> Arveragus and Dorigene his wyf
> In sovereyn blisse leden forth hir lyf (vv. 1551f.).

Equally striking is the contrast between rise and fall, joy and sorrow. Dramatic contrast heightens the effect of the despair of Aurelius after his rejection:

> And hoom they goon in Ioye and in solas,
> Save only wrecche Aurelius, allas! (vv. 1019f.).

There is the same sharp contrast between Aurelius's "Fy on a thousand pound" and his emotions when he finds himself beggared for nothing.

As in dealing with character, so also in dealing with mental states, Chaucer does not hesitate to use a direct or analytical method, to name emotions. Numerous epithets occur in the assignment of the speeches,—as when Aurelius is said to have begun his "pleynt" with "pitous herte,"—including almost every conceivable word for joy and sorrow.[14] At supreme moments, however, Chaucer is likely to let a "known cause" suggest the emotion. Thus little is said of Dorigen's relief when she is released from her promise, or of Aurelius's when he is released from his, and nothing whatever of the joy of Arveragus when Dorigen returns to him. Doubtless his feelings "can be better imagined than described." Rather curiously, as it seems to us,[15] Dorigen expresses no emotion when Arveragus commands her to keep her word. The rocks and ships, a notable instance of "known cause," are not allowed to stand alone and suggest; for purposes of

[14] Astonied, blisse, blisful, cares colde, comfort, compassioun, consolation, despeyred, dredful, fere, glad, herte soor, hope, good hope, humble, humblesse, Ioy, lisse, mad, penaunce, peynes smerte, pitous, pitously, routhe, solas, sorwe, sorweful, sorwefully, wo, woful.

[15] It is perhaps modern feeling about the matter which dictates the passionate outburst of Dorigen in Beaumont and Fletcher's *Triumph of Honor*. She speaks to the same effect, though more briefly, in Boccaccio's novella. In Chaucer's conception, perhaps, her vows demanded a silence like Griselda's.

"preparation"[16] their effect is explained and carefully emphasized.

Chaucer, as has been said, does not visualize the background or the persons of his story; all the more striking, therefore, is his constant conception of the expression of the emotions as audible and visible. Grief finds inarticulate expression,—sighs, groans, tears. Aurelius "knew not what he spoke;" Dorigen answered "half as she were mad." Contrasted with these are the conventional prayers, "complaints," exempla proving the necessity of death, brooding over the problem of evil. Action, "pantomime," accompanying these emotional utterances, serves to heighten their effects, as when Dorigen sat and stared at the sea, or (in surprise and scorn) "gan to loke upon Aurelius," or thanked him for releasing her "upon her knees al bare," or as when Aurelius turned away (in despair) with a single word, or, kneeling on bare knees, raised his hands to Heaven, or started up suddenly when his brother suggested to him a way of fulfilling Dorigen's impossible condition. In a singularly effective couplet, which almost dignifies Aurelius's passion, action stands alone:

> It may wel be he loked on hir face
> In swich a wyse, as man that asketh grace (v. 957f.).

More purely automatic reactions, the results, or, as Professor James would say, the causes of emotion, convey to the reader a sense of the sufferings or the joys of Aurelius and Dorigen.[17] In spite, however, of this

---

[16] Cf. pp. 204ff., below.

[17] The tale abounds in such studies in physiological psychology as "Anon for Ioye his herte gan to daunce" (v. 1136); "For verray fere so wolde hir herte quake, That on hir feet she mighte hir noght sustene" (vv. 860f.); "In al hir face nas a drope of blood" (v. 1340); or as "in swowne he fil adoun, And longe tyme he lay forth in a traunce" (vv. 1080f.).

insistence upon emotion and the more violent forms of its expression, the tale is not without a certain reticence, as in the case just cited, of Aurelius turning away in despair with a single word, or, still more noteworthy, the brief and restrained speech of Dorigen to Aurelius, when they met in the busy street:

"Un-to the gardin, as myn housbond bad,
   My trouthe for to holde, allas! allas!" (vv. 1512f.).

Chaucer's silence at supreme moments has already been noted.[18]

In keeping with this relatively elaborate psychology is the relatively elaborate study of motives. The central motive, however, the mainspring of the action, is not an emotion, but a concept, "the contagious influence of good." In this case the particular good is truth, honor, keeping one's word, remaining true to one's vows, without regard to the consequences to oneself or to others. "Trouthe is the hyeste thing that man may kepe" (v. 1479) declares Arveragus. It was a common medieval ideal. In one or another form it inspired most of the tales of the tenth book of the *Decameron;* it inspired romances like *Amis and Amile* or *Sir Gawayn and the Grene Knight.* It is at bottom the ideal of perfect faith, of "Though he slay me, yet will I trust in him," or of "Whosoever will save his life shall lose it; and whosoever will lose his life for my sake shall find it." It is an inspiriting belief; there is an encouraging optimism in the thought that virtue and self-sacrifice do in the end receive their reward. Stories illustrating it have a peculiarly stimulating quality; they are, too, essentially dramatic, in that tragedy seems inevitable, and the happy ending comes, with a shock of

---

[18] P. 195, above.

surprise, as an unexpected relief. Nor does the fact
that Arveragus foresaw the generosity of Aurelius destroy
this ideal quality in the *Franklin's Tale.* We delight to
find that his confidence was not misplaced, and our faith
in the essential goodness of mankind is confirmed.
Arveragus himself becomes, by virtue of his foresight,
less the fanatic, more the sane man of the world, who
conceives his ideal of truth in practical and rational
terms. He is still to be contrasted with Boccaccio's Gil-
berto, who acted simply through fear of the necromancer.

Common as was, in the Middle Ages, this high ideal
of honor, it is not to be supposed that it was realized every
day. To the charm of the idealism of the story must
be added the charm of its strangeness, not only in the
deed of Arveragus, but in his relations with Dorigen.
Sense of honor must take precedence of love; the greater
the love, therefore, the greater the triumph of honor.
The Franklin takes care to emphasize, to expound at
length, at the very beginning of the tale, the perfect
equality and harmony of Dorigen and Arveragus, this
paradox of married lovers. Only such an unusual wife
as Dorigen would, without question, obey her husband's
command, or would reject such a lover as Aurelius.[19]
Aurelius is from the very beginning doomed to defeat, a
defeat which he owes not only to the perfect union of
Dorigen and Arveragus, proof against any conceivable
attack, but also to the nature of his own passion, which can
stoop to attain its end by "constraint." The trap of his
making in which Dorigen finds herself (v. 1341), the

---

[19] Cf. Violet Paget's essay on Medieval Love in *Euphorion,* and
Bédier, *Les Lais de Marie de France, Revue des Deux Mondes,* CVII,
852.

chain of his forging (v. 1355), stand in sharp contrast with the "large reyne" proffered her by Arveragus.

The trap, after all, is not a real one; Dorigen's condition is not actually fulfilled, for the removal of the rocks is but a passing illusion, a seeming, an appearance,[20] not an objective reality, like Merlin's placing of the Giant's Dance at Stonehenge. The art which produced such illusions was practiced by heathen folk; it was "a supersticious cursednesse" (v. 1272),[21] and it is clearly not by chance that Aurelius is thus allied with the powers of evil, described as calling upon Apollo and Venus, and as thanking them when at last they seem to grant his prayer, while Dorigen is represented as swearing by the God of the Christians when she rejects Aurelius,[22] and apostrophizing him in regard to the problem of evil.[23] There is thus, in the *Franklin's Tale,* if not confusion, at least conflict, of creeds.

The central motive of the story is essentially an apologue theme, a theme for a moral tale. But Chaucer was, as has been said, interested even more in its concrete than in its abstract possibilities, that is to say, in the characters and emotions of the persons concerned, and by virtue of this interest the story becomes something more than mere apologue, still retaining, however, certain characteristics of apologue structure. This conflict of abstract and concrete interests, of two distinct literary types, accounts for most of the peculiarities of structure of the *Franklin's Tale.*

It is 896 lines, nearly 7,500 words, in length. It is a

[20] Cf. vv. 1140, 1158, 1264ff., 1295f.
[21] Cf. vv. 1132ff.
[22] Vv. 989, 1000.
[23] Vv. 865ff.

single episode, divided into five events, and preceded by
a relatively long introduction.[24] It is difficult to
draw hard and fast lines between the events; they
do not form distinct masses like the events in the
Reeve's Tale. Yet they are, relatively, not more
numerous, for the *Reeve's Tale* is less than half as long
(3,350 words) and has three events.[25] This relative
fewness of events makes possible a considerable elaboration, and all but the last two may be properly regarded
as scenes. In each of the first three, that is, there is
some emphasis of time and place relations, unity of
dramatis personæ, detailed incidents, and dialogue. From
the human point of view, because of its emotional possibilities, and from the point of view of dramatic structure,
the third scene (the disappearance of the rocks and its
results) is the most important; it is, therefore, the longest.
Next in interest and length is the first (Aurelius declares
his love). The last event (the magician releases Aurelius),
most important from the point of view of apologue, since
it forms the logical climax of the story, is emotionally
least interesting, and therefore briefest. Partly, perhaps,
in an attempt to avoid anti-climax, partly, perhaps, because
of a certain distaste for the inevitable symmetry of the

[24] Introduction (vv. 729-900) 19
   I. Aurelius Declares His Love (vv. 901-1086) 21
  II. Aurelius Brings the Magician from Orleans (vv. 1100-1238).16
 III. The Disappearance of the Rocks and its Consequences (vv.
      1256-1458) 23
 IV. Aurelius Releases Dorigen (vv. 1459-1556) 11
  V. The Magician Releases Aurelius (vv. 1557-1620) 07
Transitions and Connections 03

[25] The contrast with the *Man of Law's Tale* is striking. It is only
168 lines longer than the *Franklin's Tale*, but consists of a series of
more than a dozen events, grouped into several distinct episodes. It
is thus conceived as a long romance or an epic poem.

two events, Chaucer passes rapidly, too, over the fourth event (Aurelius releases Dorigen), which, had it not been for the impending fifth event, might have been effectively elaborated as climax and close of the story. Apologue treatment of the original theme demanded emphasis of three deeds of increasingly astonishing magnanimity, requiring increasing elaboration of the last three events. Fabliau or short-story treatment demanded emphasis of a series of emotional situations leading up to an emotional climax in the untying of the knot, requiring special elaboration of the fourth event of the story. Chaucer attempted to compromise these conflicting requirements, and the result is the apparent lack of firmness of grasp, and the anti-climax and symmetrical close, which we have in the *Franklin's Tale.*

Moreover, from the modern point of view, at any rate, Chaucer's method of elaborating his two great scenes leaves something to be desired. Even from the medieval point of view it was conventional.[26] For the third scene owes its length mainly (100 of the 211 lines) to Dorigen's enumeration of exempla; and of the first scene about one-third (60 of the 186 lines) is taken up with the "complaint" of Aurelius, and his prayer to Apollo and Venus. For the rest, however, these scenes are elaborated much as in modern narratives,—by emphasis of time, place, detailed incidents, dialogue, and description, or expres-

[26] Cf. Schofield, *M. L. A.,* XVI, 444f. Hinckley, *Notes on Chaucer,* p. 239, regards "the long and uninteresting list of virtuous women, which retards the story without exculpating the heroine," as an indication of Chaucer's immaturity and as evidence for the early date of the *Franklin's Tale.* Saintsbury, *Cambridge History of English Literature,* II, 217, is perhaps thinking of such passages as this when he says that "it is by no means certain that in his displays of learning Chaucer is not mocking or parodying others as well as relieving himself."

sion, of emotion. There is, as has been said, but little in the way of visualization; the background is but dimly seen, and the figures do not clearly detach themselves from it. The story is therefore not strong in pictorial situations, in moments when "the characters fall * * * into some attitude to each other or to nature, which stamps the story home like an illustration."[27] If the lines which tell how Dorigen gazed upon the rocks have any of this quality, it is due almost wholly to the reader's imagination:

> But whan she saugh the grisly rokkes blake,
> For verray fere so wolde hir herte quake,
> That on hir feet she mighte hir noght sustene.
> Than wolde she sitte adoun upon the grene,
> And pitously in-to the see biholde,
> And seyn right thus, with sorweful sykes colde (vv. 859ff.).

Visualization is left largely to the reader, yet the passage is immensely suggestive, and sets the imagination at work in the pictorial way, much as when Beowulf's faithful retainers stared at the sea, hoping against hope for their lord's return, or when stout Cortez and all his men stared at the Pacific, silent, upon a peak in Darien. Similarly pictorial by suggestion is the meeting of Dorigen and her lover, "amidde the toun, right in the quikkest strete" (v. 1502). With such passages as these, the best in their kind to the found in the *Franklin's Tale*, it is enlightening to contrast the description of Chauntecleer:

> He loketh as it were a grim leoun;
> And on his toos he rometh up and doun,
> Him deyned not to sette his foot to grounde.
> He chukketh, whan he hath a corn y-founde,
> And to him rennen thanne his wyves alle.
> Thus royal, as a prince is in his halle,
> Leve I this Chauntecleer in his pasture (B, vv. 4369ff.).

The difference in method needs no comment.

[27] R. L. Stevenson, *Memories and Portraits*, p. 256.

"Situation," however, has another meaning. It may be simply the point in a story "at which the actors are * * brought together significantly."[28] From the point of view thus suggested the *Franklin's Tale* may be regarded as mainly a succession of situations, of situations, perhaps, rather than events or scenes, for what Chaucer gives us is not so much action as a series of readjustments of the interrelations of the persons.

Not unexpected, then, is the large amount of generalized narrative, summing up the antecedent events of the marriage of Dorigen and Arveragus, the transitional events of the years of Arveragus's absence and of Aurelius's despair, or recounting the habitual actions of Dorigen. The exempla of Dorigen's long "complaint" are in the form of still more rapid summary. Like the exempla in the *Nun's Priest's Tale,* they constitute a descending series, in which the succeeding tales are dealt with in more and more summary fashion. Characteristic of this kind of narration are the "often's" (vv. 848, 853) and the generalizing "would's,"—"ther wolde she sitte and thinke" (v. 857), "so wolde hir herte quake" (v. 860),—which interfere somewhat with the pictorial suggestion of this situation. Curious enough is the effect of the passage quoted just above, in which it is said that when Dorigen *sat* by the brink and saw the grizzly black rocks, her heart would so tremble with fear "that on hir feet she mighte hir noght sustene" (v. 861), whereupon she would *sit down* on the green.[29] The lines that follow seem to imply that Dorigen was in the habit of repeating, word for word,

[28] C. S. Baldwin, *A College Manual of Rhetoric,* p. 150.

[29] Reconstructors of the "inner history" of anonymous poems would find in such a passage as this, with its inconsistencies and its "vicious repetition," ideal proof of "different hands" and "variant versions."

her interesting monologue in regard to the problem of
evil. This whole tendency, manifestly enough, makes
away from concreteness and vividness; in the last example
it even shows a complete failure to grasp as concrete at
all what is of necessity a concrete situation.

The large amount of merely introductory or transitional
matter, the failure to crystallize all the incidents of the
story in a few clear-cut scenes or situations, the very
marked tendency toward generalized narrative, seem to
imply a lack of sureness, a lack of firmness of handling,
almost a kind of fumbling with the matter in hand. And
yet the first part of the story is admirably managed. The
careful preparation for the peculiar form of Dorigen's
rash promise is indeed very noteworthy, and comparable,
in its way, with Shakespeare's treatment of the pound-of-
flesh motive in the *Merchant of Venice*. Just as Shakespeare leads up to the proposal of the bond by the discussion
of interest,[30] Chaucer avoids all shock of unreality in
Dorigen's condition by most careful and gradual preparation.[31] When, by force of time, and because of letters
which she received from Arveragus, Dorigen's great sorrow began to assuage somewhat, she consented to walk in
company with her friends. But her castle stood by the
sea, and as they walked along the shore, the many ships,
not one of them all bringing back her lord, served but to
renew her grief. Turning from the ships, her eye fell
upon their enemies the rocks, and her heart trembled so
with fear that her feet could not sustain her. These
hostile black rocks, she thought, were created for naught

---

[30] Cf. Moulton, *Shakespeare as a Dramatic Artist*, pp. 62ff.

[31] A closer and more modern parallel is to be found in *The Great
Divide*, where Mr. Moody is less successful than Chaucer, in solving,
however, a more difficult problem in preparation and motivation.

but to injure and destroy mankind. Her mind dwelt on
the problem of evil. Her friends now chose "places delitables" for their walks, and one day in a fair garden she
saw Aurelius dancing with the others. When they were
alone he declared his love. In her reply it is clear that she
is thinking first of Aurelius, then of herself, as a faithful wife, then, naturally, of her husband, with whom she
has now come to associate, through her hopes for his
return and through her fears for the danger of the voyage,
the black rocks of Brittany. Thinking of Arveragus, of
her love, her fear, the absurdity of Aurelius's petition
strikes her, and so "in pleye,"—by way of ironical
emphasis, not to spare her lover's feelings, but rather to
deride him, she says that she will grant him her love,—
yes, when he has removed all those dread rocks from the
shores of Brittany.[32] Her condition is "an impossible,"
as Aurelius declares; it is to be understood like the "when
sun and moon dance on the green" of the ballads, like the
"when a' the seas gang dry, my dear" of Burns, as a peri-
phrasis for *never*. Her final words are scornful:

> "What deyntee sholde a man han in his lyf
> For to go love another mannes wyf?" (vv. 1003f.).

Her threefold rejection of Aurelius is thus not emphatic,
courteous, scornful, but, in climactic order, emphatic,
derisive, scornful. As in the *Merchant of Venice,* this
jesting promise is taken seriously by an enemy, and
results as disastrous as they are unexpected seem imminent. Thus the whole matter of the rocks is significant
as leading to the threatened catastrophe, as a dramatic

---

[32] "The promise of Dorigen was really a vow to be constant as a
rock to her husband. In taking her literally, Aurelius knew that
he was taking her contrary to her meaning. This is explicitly
acknowledged in v. 1601." Hinckley, *Notes on Chaucer,* p. 239.

"moment of excitation," and in that part of the narrative
which deals with the fulfilment of Dorigen's condition and
with her escape from her predicament we have somewhat
the same sort of gradual approach to an objective point.[33]
The approach is now gradual, not so much for purposes
of emphasis and verisimilitude, as it is for purposes of
suspense created by delay. Otherwise suspense seems
little thought of; indeed the Franklin seeks rather to
reassure his hearers: Dorigen "may have better fortune
than yow semeth," he says. But one imagines that they
had guessed that already.[34]

The *Franklin's Tale* is, then, eminently dramatic, in
that it was conceived and written as an integral part of
the drama of the *Canterbury Tales,* springing from the
character of the narrator and his relation to his fellow-
pilgrims, from the dramatic situation of the Pilgrimage.
The Franklin described it as a Breton lay, yet did not
attempt to invest it with the glamor of the past, or to
relate it to the Celtic other-world. His settings, indeed,
are but vaguely conceived and vaguely described. The
persons of his tale, too, are but dimly seen and conven-

[33] There is an interesting instance of failure to provide for the
necessities of the working out of the story. After the removal of the
rocks, Arveragus, for purposes of suspense, must be away from home.
Otherwise Dorigen's despair, which she was unable to conceal, could
have no duration, would not be sufficiently impressive or "convincing." This, clearly enough, Chaucer has not foreseen, and inserts
only at the last moment, when the situation requires it, the line,
"For out of toune was goon Arveragus" (v. 1351). The careful
and timely motivation of his earlier absence ("I could not love
thee, dear, so much, loved I not honor more") is to be contrasted
with this. Stevenson's discussion of a similar omission in Scott is
interesting.

[34] It is possibly in the interests of suspense that Chaucer refrains
from laying greater stress upon Arveragus's foresight of the
behavior of Aurelius.

tionally characterized. Yet they are firmly grasped as types, and between two of them, the man of action and the sentimentalist, the distinction is clear and consistent, though never carried too far. Our impression of the characters is conveyed by means of what they do and say, and by the effects which they produce upon one another. The *Franklin's Tale,* however, is less noteworthy as a study of character than as a study of mental states; for completeness of the lines of emotion and for the dramatic,—audible or visible,—expression of all degrees of joy and sorrow it stands alone among the Canterbury tales. Yet its central motive is not an emotion, but a concept,—the contagious influence of good. This "good" is truth, honor; it involves self-sacrifice; and it constitutes, in its strangeness, its optimism, its dramatic quality, the essential charm of the story. It requires the emphasis of the unusual relation of a husband and wife. In conflict with their ideal and perfect love stands a baser passion, which, to attain its end, makes use of a passing illusion, the appearance of a miracle.

The contagious influence of good is an apologue theme, and the anti-climax and symmetrical close of the *Franklin's Tale* are doubtless due to an attempt to reconcile the technical demands of exemplum and pure narrative. The tendency to narrate in general terms, the absence of visualization and of pictorial situations may perhaps be traced to the same cause. Yet the tale abounds in suggestive situations, is itself perhaps to be regarded as a situation. And there is no lack of evidence of grasp of the whole, of "preparation" for purposes of verisimilitude, of steady approach, gradual, yet without suspense, to an objective point.

II. The Franklin's Tale and the Breton Lays.

Whether or not the Franklin's declaration in regard
to the source of his tale is to be taken seriously, it is at
least a challenge to compare his story of Dorigen and
Arveragus with undoubted Breton lays. Such a comparison reveals many resemblances, and these are not
merely of the obvious sort, such as the selection of Brittany
as the scene of action, but much that seems, at first glance,
peculiar to Chaucer, may be paralleled in the lays of
Marie de France, or in other stories of the same type.
The treatment of character is similar. Marie's hero,
Lanval, springing up and advancing courteously to meet
the attendants of the fairy queen, thus showing his breed-
ing, revealing his character by pantomime, may well
remind us of Aurelius, dancing "passinge any man."
Often, too, Marie's persons are like the Franklin's in
that they are not visualized, and in that, if they reveal
themselves by speech, it is by what they say merely, and
not by the manner of saying it. Both Marie and the
Franklin make use of the conventional epithets,—like
"valiant" and "courteous,"—for the conventional qualities. Equally conventional are the emotions; and in no
single lay is there greater variety than in the *Franklin's
Tale*. Professor Schofield calls attention to the resemblance of the despairing lovers, Aurelius and Lanval;
both experience the sharp contrasts of joy and sorrow.[35]
It is not possible, however, to trace complete "lines of
emotion," and Marie's vocabulary of the emotions is not
so large as the Franklin's. Yet she has not quite the
Franklin's reticence; she is not content with telling us
that Lanval's heritage was far hence, in a distant land,
all his money gone,—for King Arthur gave him nothing,

---

[35] Cf. *M. L. A.*, XVI, 428f., *Franklin's Tale*, vv. 1019ff., and *Lanval*,
vv. 255ff.

and he knew not where to seek for aid; she adds that he
was much perplexed and very sorrowful and heavy of
heart. Like Aurelius and Dorigen the heroes of the lays
reveal their strong feeling by "automatic reactions." The
frequent swoonings in the English *Emare* recall Aurelius. And a similar method is revealed in *Tyolet* in the
knight's wagging his head at those who mocked him, in the
false knight's saying never a word when he is caught in
a lie, but reddening and frowning as one ashamed. In
the same manner Guigemar's heart is set in a tumult by
love; he sighs in sore anguish, passes the night in sighing
and sore trouble, remembering her words and her manner,
her shining eyes and her sweet mouth, that had brought
this sorrow into his heart.[38]

In the matter of structure there are some general, though
not very significant, resemblances between the lays and
the *Franklin's Tale*. There is the same tendency to begin
with a formal introduction in general terms, the same
tendency to make use of narrative in general terms,[39] and
an absence of the vigorous handling and excellence of
proportion, so noteworthy in the fabliaux. Yet, where it
is necessary, Marie is quite capable of making careful
preparation for succeeding events, as where she emphasizes the silken mantle and the ring by which the heroine
of *La Frêne* is to be identified at a critical moment;[40] or
as where she carefully motives the transition from love
to hate in the queen's feeling toward Lanval.[41] Marie
is capable, too, of the gradual approach to an objective
point,[42] yet she makes no attempt to keep the reader in

[38] *Guigemar*, vv. 379ff.
[39] Cf. *Lanval* or *Bisclavret*.
[40] Cf. *La Frêne*, vv. 121ff., 301ff., 399ff., 484ff.
[41] *Lanval*, vv. 261ff.
[42] Cf. the "gradation" of the opening event in *Bisclavret*.

doubt, and, like the Franklin, tells what the end is to be before she reaches it.[43] It is interesting to compare her treatment of the werwolf with that of a modern author; Marie lets the reader into the secret at once. S. Carleton, in *The Lame Priest*,[44] gives the reader increasingly definite suggestions as to the solution of the mystery, yet never really solves it for him.

Finally there is in the lays a suggestion of that same idealism which is the essential charm of the *Franklin's Tale*. The persons are of noble birth, and their characters are vaguely idealized. The first wife of Eliduc, who gives up her rights to a second, and La Frêne, who consents in all humility to her lover's marriage with another, have a generosity as ideal (and as difficult for us to sympathize with) as that of Arveragus. Only for Frêne (from our point of view) does the story end well and encourage the timidly unselfish with an example of the safety of apparent self-sacrifice.

These are some of the technical similarities of the *Franklin's Tale* and the Breton lays; the differences are more striking.

Not one of the lays, in the first place, has the dramatic or personal quality of the *Franklin's Tale*. Few, if any, dispense so completely with the atmosphere, the glamor, of the past, which the subject-matter demands.[45] While

---

[43] Cf. *La Frêne*, v. 304, and *Les Dous Amanz*, vv. 185ff.

[44] *Atlantic Monthly*, LXXXVIII, 760ff.

[45] Cf. the opening lines of *Tyolet*, describing the England of Arthur's time, when there were fewer folk in the land, and knights, wandering through the country without even a squire for company, seeking adventures by day or by dusky night, often found neither house nor tower. "In Brittany of old time there reigned a king" sounds more like the *Franklin's Tale*, but in that Brittany Guingamor rode through the adventurous land, over a meadow where the turf was green and flowery, and saw the walls of a great palace, well built, yet without mortar.

some produce the same impression of isolation, others are
more elaborate in their geography than the *Franklin's
Tale,* and the lay of *Two Lovers* attaches itself to a locality
real and known. Marie usually surpasses the Franklin
in the visualization of the scene of action, in sense for
the beauty and color of the background. The Franklin
draws no picture so vivid as that scene in the lay where
Lanval lies alone in the green meadow, his horse grazing
beside him, and watches the approach of the two fair
maidens, clad in purple gray, bearing the towel of white
linen and the basin of gold. There is contrast of the same
sort in the treatment of the social setting; it is indeed
rather surprising that in this respect the lays should be
more realistic than Chaucer's tale, but such is the case.[46]
Not only by relating them to the world of men, but also
by visualizing them, are the persons of the lays made to
seem more real. While Chaucer is content with bare
mention of Dorigen's high rank, Marie is at pains to
describe the supernatural beings of her lays, in order to
convince us of their powers.[47] This visualization, moreover, is not confined to supernatural beings; the naively
charming, if somewhat conventional, passage in the *Earl
of Toulous* describes an empress "showing openly her face"
for the love of a knight.[48]

[46] Compare, for example, the historical setting of *Lanval:* King
Arthur was sojourning at Carduel because of the Picts and the
Scots, who had greatly destroyed the land, for they were in the
kingdom of Logres and often wrought mischief therein. The
heroine of *Doon* is not merely a lady of high rank, but has definite
powers as ruler.

[47] Cf. *Lanval,* vv. 553ff.

[48] The description recalls Chaucer's Prioress:

Aside from personal appearance, however, the reader learns far more of character from the *Franklin's Tale* than from the lays. In the latter the persons are scarcely even types; they are not, at any rate, differentiated; all are valiant, courteous, and beautiful. Even Dorigen seems real if we place her beside the heroine of *Doon,* who was also rich, noble, and averse to losing her freedom in marriage.[49] Contrasts are confined to characters merely good and bad; the lays have nothing so subtle as the difference between Arveragus and Aurelius. The persons in the lays are simply good and bad, and evil characters are not, like Aurelius, endowed with redeeming qualities.

The lays, as we have just seen, show something like

> Hur eyen were gray as any glas,
> Mowthe and nose schapen was
>   At all maner ryght;
> Fro the forhedd to the too,
> Bettur schapen myght non goo,
>   Nor none semelyer yn syght.

> Twyes sche turnyd hur abowte,
> Betwene the erlys that were stowte,
>   For the erle schulde hur see;
> When sche spake wyth mylde stevyn,
> Sche semyd an aungell of hevyn,
>   So feyre sche was of blee.

> Hur syde longe, hur myddyll small,
> Schouldurs, armes, therwythall,
>   Fayrer myght non bee;
> Hur hondys whyte as whallys bonne
> Wyth fyngurs longe and ryngys upon
>   Hur nayles bryght of blee (vv. 340ff.).

[49] Like Dorigen, she required of her suitors the performance of impossible tasks. But when they did ride from Southampton to Edinburgh in a day, she, instead of contemplating suicide, put them to death, after the manner of the märchen heroine.

Chaucer's interest in the emotions; with them, indeed, the passion of love is regularly the central motive, and they do not come nearer a pure concept than the general notion of love which underlies *Guigemar,*—that neglect of love leads to excessive suffering through love.[50] We find, indeed, the same insistence on the importance of a vow; Sir Degare has won a lady by his valor, but at the beginning of the very marriage ceremony, remembers his vow to marry no one whom certain gloves will not fit. We can find a fair example even of the contagious influence of good, when, in the *Earl of Toulous,* the Empress Beulyboon insists that Sir Trylabas must keep his word, bring the earl, her husband's enemy, to see her, and let him depart unharmed. Sir Trylabas felt that her reproof was well deserved, and did not at that time harm the earl. Later, however, though he owed much to the earl's generosity, he, with two other knights, treacherously attacked and sought to slay him. There is, too, a formulated moral at the end of *Equitan,* to the effect that he who digged the pit must lie in it, and the same notion is implied in the birth of the twins in *La Frêne.*[51] But all this is exceptional; normally the lay is not in the least interested in abstract or general ideas, and, normally, it is utterly unmoral. Thus in *Emare* the Pope is said to sanction the marriage of a father and daughter, or, in *Eliduc,* to permit the hero to take a second wife while the first one lives. In *Yonec* the hero kills his mother's husband; and in *La Frêne* the relations of hero and heroine are regarded as a matter of course. It was clearly not the

[50] *Seven Lays of Marie de France,* translated by Edith Rickert, p. 168.

[51] To a woman who had declared that twins and fidelity are incompatible.

way of the lay to seize upon an apologue theme and attempt to make of it a romantic story.

Most striking of all is, perhaps, the treatment of the supernatural. Beside the Franklin's scepticism stands simple belief; beside a mere sham, appearance, illusion, stand real fairy queens and kings, living in a real fairy-land, reached only through caves or over perilous rivers; stand also actual transformations from stag, or wolf, or bird to knight or lover. The draught, finally, which the young lover brought from Salerno was of a real, not an imaginary, potency; it would have made possible a super-human feat of strength. As it was, the land where the draught was sprinkled was the richer for it, and even to-day many a good herb is found there that had its root in the potion.[52]

The lay did not seize upon an apologue theme, and consequently was never marred, as is the *Franklin's Tale,* by an unduly symmetrical structure. To this the nearest approach is the coming of the maidens attendant upon the fairy queen, in *Lanval,* two by two, leading up to the climax of the appearance of the queen herself. In this, however, we have something akin to the simple art of the ballad or folk tale, but no attempt to shape by moral purpose or logic the wayward events of human life.

With its keener visualization of persons, with its relatively greater interest in things outward and tangible, the lay combines a greater delight in pictorial situations. This coming of the fairies in *Lanval,* the hero's first meeting with them, Guingamor's first glimpse of the fairy princess, Tyolet's first sight of a knight, who changes from stag to man-at-arms before his eyes,—all these, and many more, passages in the lays, stamp themselves upon

[52] *Les Dous Amanz,* vv. 225ff.

the mind like illustrations. Situation, both in the pictorial sense and in that of a significant assembling of the persons, is that fine passage in *Sir Degare,* where the hero, in a strange general silence, sups with a distressed damsel in her castle and is afterward put to sleep by her harping. The main interest in the lays, however, is in the plot and its strangeness; no lay could be described, as one may describe the *Franklin's Tale,* as a story of situation, where there is little action, but simply a series of readjustments of the characters' relations with one another.

The *Franklin's Tale* is, then, like the Breton lays, in that the scene is laid in Brittany; in its general treatment of character and mental states, its revelation of emotion by "automatic reactions;" in its summary of antecedent action and narration in general terms; in the absence of firm and vigorous handling of plot, and of due emphasis and proportion; in the relatively careful preparation for what is to come; in its steady approach, gradual, yet without suspense, to an objective point; and in its idealism.

The contrasts are more striking than the resemblances. The *Franklin's Tale* differs from the lays in its dramatic quality and all that this implies. It lacks their vivid backgrounds, their glamor of the past, their social setting, preudo-historical, yet realistic in effect. It lacks their visualization of character. Its persons are not mere doers of deeds, but relatively complex types; not contrasted as good and bad, but, more subtly, as man of action and sentimentalist; and none are merely bad, but the worst has redeeming qualities. While it betrays, perhaps, no greater interest in mental states, its lines of emotion are far more complete, and it is more dramatic in its hesitation to name emotions which are adequately implied in the situation. It differs from the lays in its concern with general or abstract ideas, with a moral concept, with an apologue theme. It differs from them in its use of a false rather than a true supernatural element, and in its curiously symmetrical structure. And it lacks their delight in pictorial situations and in action. Thus its art differs very materially from the art of the lays.

III. The Franklin's Tale and the Canterbury Pilgrimage.

The *Franklin's Tale* was, as has been said, written for the place which it now occupies, and is to be regarded as an organic part of the Drama of the Canterbury Pilgrimage. It must be studied not merely as an isolated work of art, not merely as an imitation of ˜the Breton lay, but also in its relation to the *General Prologue,* to the *Prologues*[53] of the various tales, and to the *Tales* themselves. The action of what I have ventured to call the Drama of the Pilgrimage begins, towards the end of the *General Prologue,*[54] after the descriptions of April, the Tabard Inn, and the characters of the Pilgrims, with the Host's suggestion for their entertainment on the road, and ends with his request to the Parson to tell the last tale. It has thus at least a beginning and an end, two of the requisites of plot. The middle is a series of loosely connected comic incidents, unified by the dominant personality

---

[53] These should be understood to include all the matter that intervenes between the tales,—Prologues, Introductions, Epilogues, various "Words of the Host," etc. The general term *Prologues* is used for convenience. The Drama of the Pilgrimage does not include the *Prioress's Prologue,* or the *Envoy* of the *Clerk's Tale,* or the *Man of Law's Prologue,* which are to be regarded rather as parts of the tales.

[54] At verse 715.

of the Host,[55] by the presence of the general plan through-out, and the mood or tone of the whole. Here and there are indicated the shifting scenes (by place-names and without visualization) and the passing time of the action. There are bits of narrative, too, but nine-tenths of the 2,347 lines[56] are dialogue. Of the speakers, those whom the Eighteenth Century would have described as "low"[57] have the most to say, dominate the whole, and produce the general impression. They are all comic, and, for the most part, confessedly, or very evidently, or apparently, drunk. Six of them,[58]—seven, if we include the Host,— and only four of the other group,[59] speak out of their own prologues. Inevitably we learn most of the low characters, and we get the impression that Chaucer was more interested in them than in the others.

There is little or no direct description of the persons; Chaucer's methods are here wholly dramatic and objective. Thus the Miller

> nolde avalen neither hood ne hat,
> Ne abyde no man for his curteisye,
> And in Pilates vois he gan to crye,
> And swoor by armes and by blood and bones (A, 3122ff.).

[55] He is silent only in the Prologue of the Summoner, and in that of the Second Nun, which has no connection with the general frame-work. Cf. Saintsbury, *Camb. Hist. Engl. Lit.*, II, 204.

[56] It is interesting to note that the longest of the metrical tales, the Knight's, has only 2,550 lines.

[57] That is, those low in rank, or those who show themselves, by what they say in their tales or their prologues, to be relatively low in the moral scale or in refinement. They are, in the order of the length of their parts, the Wife of Bath, Host, Pardoner, Canon's Yeoman, Summoner, Reeve, Maunciple, Merchant, Cook, Miller, Friar, Shipman, and Nun's Priest. Nearly nine-tenths of the dialogue (1,807 lines) is assigned to them, and but little more than one-tenth (279 lines) to the Man of Law, Franklin, Chaucer, Clerk, Parson, Monk, Knight, Canon, Squire, and Prioress.

[58] Friar, Cook, Wife of Bath, Reeve, Summoner, and Pardoner.

[59] Chaucer, Knight, Monk, and Parson.

The "pantomime," the voice, the oaths, all are typical; the reference to contemporary drama is significant.[60] Perhaps suggested by the drama is the convention of the *confession,* of persons' setting forth their own characters, exposing, for the benefit of the Pilgrims, good and evil, without shame. Thus the Reeve, in his northern dialect,—"But ik am old, me list not pley for age" (A, 3867). Thus the Maunciple confesses to the Host that the Cook might well reveal his dishonesty. It is only an extension of the same convention when the Pardoner discloses his methods, perhaps inspiring thereby the Wife of Bath's disclosure of hers. Clearly the Pardoner feels that she has outdone him: "Teche us yonge men of your praktike," he says (D, 187). The persons describe not only themselves but one another, and of this there is no better example than the gradual revelation of the true character of the Canon, by Chaucer, the Yeoman and the Host. The Host is elsewhere active in this way, serving as a kind of showman, calling the Pilgrims' attention to details of Chaucer's, the Monk's, and the Squire's manner and appearance and drawing his own conclusions in regard to character. He serves, too, as a kind of social barometer, his manner being adjusted, though not always with perfect precision, to the rank and importance of the person whom he addresses. It is interesting to contrast his "let the woman tell hir tale," addressed to the Wife of Bath, with

> "My lady Prioresse, by your leve,
> So that I wiste I sholde yow nat greve,
> I wolde demen that ye tellen sholde
> A tale next, if so were that ye wolde.
> Now wol ye vouche-sauf, my lady dere?" (B, 1636ff.).[61]

[60] Cf. Gayley, *The Plays of Our Forefathers,* pp. 111ff.

[61] In general we may contrast his respectful treatment of Knight, Squire, Prioress, Clerk, Merchant, Physician, Man of Law, with his familiar or rude manner in addressing Miller, Reeve, Parson, Nun's Priest, Monk, and Franklin.

Particularly interesting, as evidence not only of Chaucer's
tolerance, but also of his objectivity, his dramatic detach-
ment, is the Host's treatment of Franklin and of Parson.
In the *General Prologue* the former is described as a
person of great dignity, with nothing to his discredit more
serious than delight in high living; the latter is the most
highly idealized of all the Pilgrims.   Yet Chaucer permits
the Host, whom he describes as "wys and wel y-taught"
(A, 755), to say to one "Straw for your gentillesse, * *
telle on thy tale with-outen wordes mo" (F, 695ff.); and to
say to the other: "O Iankin,[62] be ye there?   I smelle a
loller in the wind" (B, 1172).   Later, indeed, the Host
makes partial amends, yet he still persists in the offensive
swearing, and urges the Parson to be "fructuous, and that
in litel space" (I, 73).   Additional evidence,—if additional evidence is necessary,—of Chaucer's delight in
describing "low" characters may be found in the portraits
of certain persons who, though not among the Pilgrims,
come to be pretty clearly individualized for us,—the
Franklin's account of his son, the Merchant's account of
his wife, the Wife of Bath's account of her five husbands,
and, finally, the masterpiece, the Host's discriminating
description of his wife.   She has not, he says, the for-
giving disposition of Dame Prudence in *Melibeus:*

> "By goddes bones! whan I bete my knaves,
> She bringth me forth the grete clobbed staves,
> And cryeth, 'slee the dogges everichoon,
> And brek hem, bothe bak and every boon'" (B, 3087ff.).

Yet he would not have us think that she was like the
heroine of the *Merchant's Tale;* though she is a labbing
shrew and has a heap of vices more, she is as true as
steel (E, 2426ff.).

[62] Skeat's note on this line calls attention to the derision involved
in the diminutive "Iankin."

Chaucer's interest in low characters was doubtless due in part to the fact that he found in them, as Goethe and Wordsworth did, centuries later, elementary feelings, simply combined and not under restraint, but expressed in plain and emphatic language. Certainly he permits them to express themselves more freely than their betters. The Host, who speaks so much, scarcely speaks at all except under the stress of strong feeling, of delight, or grief, or wrath; and it is from him and from such persons as the Cook, or the Shipman, or the Friar, that we get the frankest criticisms of the tales. For the Host it would be possible to trace from Prologue to Prologue a kind of "line of emotion." And it is of course the others of his type who are continually involved in quarrels and expressing most freely and most feelingly their low opinions of one another. Chaucer seems to have regarded restraint, on the other hand, as a differencing characteristic of the other class; Parson and Franklin make no reply to Host or Shipman; the Monk, it is said, took the Host's innuendo "al in pacience" (B, 3155).

Like description of character, the description of emotion is largely in the dramatic manner, of suggestion by words and actions, rather than direct naming or analysis. The Cook, for example, is seen in contrasting passions; while the Reeve spoke, "for Ioye, him thoughte, he clawed him on the bak" (A, 4326). But when the Maunciple told him he was drunk,

> the cook wex wroth and wraw,
> And on the maunciple he gan nodde faste
> For lakke of speche, and doun the hors him caste,
> Wher as he lay, til that men up him took (H, 46ff.).

Emotions, thus violently expressed, are often the results of the quarrels of the Pilgrims, conflicts sometimes of individuals, sometimes, rather, of the professions or trades which they represent. There is more of the personal element in the quarrels of Miller and Reeve, Host and Pardoner. The Host's good-natured criticism of Cook and Maunciple has reference, like the Shipman's attack on the Parson, mainly to the failings peculiar to their professions. The Yeoman, it may be supposed, represents Chaucer or society at large, in his exposure of the Canon's methods. The quarrel of Friar and Summoner is rather a matter of professional jealousy. Even in the case of the Miller and the Reeve, however, the latter's wrath is aroused by the part that a carpenter plays in the *Miller's Tale,* and he proceeds to get even by telling a tale of a miller. In all cases there is something of a conflict of trades or professions, or criticism of individuals as their representatives, so that the Prologues recall the manner of the old "debates" or flytings. No two of them, it will be seen, are quite alike; they vary not only in relative emphasis of individual and trade or profession, but also by virtue of the differences in the characters concerned and in their relations to one another. The series is further saved from monotony and given an air of reality and spontaneity by the apparent changes in the Host's plans for the tales, as when the drunken Miller insists that his tale, and not the Monk's, must follow the Knight's; or the Shipman, to save the Pilgrims from the Parson's sermon, insists upon telling his tale; or the Maunciple volunteers to take the place of the temporarily incapacitated Cook. There is much lively detail in the account of the latter's equestrian exploit. In this respect it is surpassed only by the lively dramatic incident of the *Canon's Yeoman's Prologue,* where sweating and foam-flecked horses gallop into the story, bearing the alchemist and his assistant. Details of dress are noted and interpreted, character is revealed by swift question and answer, and the Canon rides away again in shame, leaving his reputation to the tender mercies of the Yeoman. This little scene thus adds to an interest in character like that of the *General Prologue,* an interest in the action of a specific moment, with vigorous movement, suspense, climax, and lively dialogue. In the last respect, indeed, the scene is but typical of the whole Drama of the Pilgrimage, which is, as I have said, nine-tenths direct discourse. In the present instance the Canon twice takes part in the colloquy of Host and Yeoman; and elsewhere the quarrels, and reconciliaions through the mediation of a peace-maker, result in group conversation. For the rest, the utterance is all peculiarly indicative of character and emotion,—loquacity, oaths, coarseness, and dialect, contrast appropriately with brevity, refinement, restraint, and correctness of speech. On the whole, the variety and vigor, the life and spontaneity of the framework of the *Canterbury Tales* present an interesting contrast to the repose and to the monotonous, though by no means unpleasing, elegance of the *Decameron.*[63]

The Prologues are, then, mainly in dramatic form, and while Chaucer sometimes speaks with apparent sincerity, in his own person, he might have described them, as Browning did his *Dramatic Lyrics,* as "so many utterances of so many imaginary persons, not mine." Nevertheless they are, as Professor Mead has said,[64] "by far the most

[63] Chaucer's inconsistencies,—like the Host's forgetting, in the *Maunciple's Prologue,* that the Cook has already told a tale, or the reference, in the *Parson's Prologue,* to the *Maunciple's Tale* as just finished,—are doubtless due, as Skeat suggests, to the absence of a final revision. They are not, in any case, particularly significant. Even in finished work inconsistencies are common enough.

[64] *M. L. A.,* XVI, 388.

characteristic and original part of his writings. * * *
In them * * * we find, perhaps more than anywhere
else, the true Chaucer, working in his own way, and
controlling his sources instead of being partly controlled
by them." Thus, with all due regard to the "fallacy of
quotations," we can find in this part of Chaucer's work
very definite indications of his tendencies and interests,
of the questions that occupied his mind, if not always
of his answers to them. There is, certainly, very clear
indication of his self-consciousness; the Host's description,
in the *Prologue to Sir Thopas,* is not a sketch of a typical
poet, or a caricature; it has every mark of a portrait and
gives evidence of careful self-observation. In the *Man of
Law's Prologue* (B, 45ff.), moreover, as in the Apology
and the Retraction,[65] is ample proof that the poet thought
of himself as the author of his works, responsible for
their matter and their manner. He is a critic of other
poets, too, as in the Clerk's praise of Petrarch (E, 32ff.),
or the Man of Law's probable condemnation of Gower
(B, 77ff.). It is clear that each of the Pilgrims is
expected to tell a tale of a definite kind,[66] and where, as
with Monk or Wife of Bath, the tale does not seem, at
first glance, particularly characteristic of the teller, we
must regard it as necessary modification or amplification
of the portrait in the *General Prologue.* The criticism,

---

[65] A, 731ff., 3171ff., and I, 1048ff. The final leave-taking of
the author is not part of the Drama, but, whatever its sincerity,
must be considered in connection with the present phase of the
discussion.

[66] Thus the Squire is regarded as a specialist in love; ribaldry is
feared from the Pardoner; a dull sermon from the Parson; Chaucer's
appearance seems to promise some tale of mirth, "some deyntee
thing;" the Host feels that he must warn the Clerk against preach-
ing and the "high style."

too, is characteristic of the critics. Like the gallery in the modern theatre, it is the low characters who are the most outspoken, in praise or condemnation, yet the quieter appreciation of the gentles is not forgotten.[67] In general, Chaucer recognizes the important principle of basing criticism upon psychological effect. Thus the Host demands that the Clerk shall tell a tale which shall be intelligible, and shall neither cause his audience to weep nor put them to sleep. It is the soporific influence to which the Host objects in the Monk's tragedies, while the Knight interrupts them rather because of their too painful character. All the Pilgrims are deeply affected by the *Prioress's Tale*.

That Chaucer had relatively clear conceptions of certain literary types is revealed by the Prologues. "Tragedy" is defined for us by the Monk, whose instructive remarks are concluded by a line suggestive of the modern lecture-room: "Lo! this declaring oughte ynough suffise" (B, 3172). Host and Knight point out the defects of this type. The Parson, in his Prologue, distinguishes between fiction and the sermon,—chaff and wheat,—but promises to give his hearers all permissible pleasure. It is, however, the Pardoner who is the authority on the technique

[67] Thus the Host vociferously takes sides with virtue in his comment on the *Physician's Tale* (C, 287ff.), expresses violent disgust at *Sir Thopas* and the Monk's tragedies, strong approval of the *Nun's Priest's Tale* and the *Shipman's Tale*, and bestows perfunctory praise on the effort of the Man of Law. The Cook expresses intense delight in the *Reeve's Tale*. The *Knight's Tale* is unanimously declared a noble story, but especially praised by "the gentils everichoon." All are solemn when the Prioress has finished. The Franklin praises the wit and eloquence of the Squire; the Knight interrupts the Monk. Curiously enough, as it seems to us, the *Miller's Tale* is received with general laughter (A, 3855), and while there was some difference of opinion, only the Reeve was offended.

of the sermon; the confession of this conscious artist is, in large measure, a disquisition on methods of Persuasion, wholly with reference to psychological and other effects, including sample arguments, and reference to such minor details as the use of voice and gesture. Most noteworthy is his exposition of the theory of exempla:

"Than telle I hem ensamples many oon
Of olde stories, longe tyme agoon:
For lewed peple loven tales olde;
Swich thinges can they wel reporte and holde" (C, 435ff.).

Chaucer clearly distinguishes between such tales as "sounen in-to sinne" and those concerned with "gentillesse," morality and holiness. He describes his own *Melibeus* as a "moral tale vertuous" and he expressly refers to the Miller and the Reeve and "othere many mo" as telling tales of the former type.[68] He makes the realist's plea that he has no discretion, is under compulsion to tell all the tales, and adjures his readers not to "make ernest of game." While it does not appear that any of the Pilgrims were offended by the coarseness of the *Miller's Tale,* it is clear that the gentles stood in some fear of the Pardoner's ribaldry.[69] In obvious contrast to tales of this type stand those composed by the "gentle Britons."

Chaucer was conscious of a similar contrast in style. He apologizes not only for the subject-matter of Miller and Reeve and their like, but for their manner, their rough and coarse speech, as well. It is, as we have seen, one way of distinguishing them from those of higher rank and greater refinement, in the conversations of the Prologues. The Host, moreover, adjures the Clerk to tell

[68] A, 725ff., 3171ff., I, 1084ff.

[69] In this connection should be noted the Man of Law's condemnation of such stories as those of Canacee and Appolonius (B, 80).

his tale plainly and intelligibly, to keep his pedantic and
set expressions, his fine phrases, and his figures of speech,
until such time as he may write the high style appropriate
for kings.[70]   The Man of Law reveals Chaucer's interest
in matters of versification, declaring him unskilled in
meters and rhyming.   The Host finds the "drasty ryming"
of *Sir Thopas* to be "rym dogerel;" and the Parson holds
but a low opinion of rhyme and alliteration in general,
and associates the latter with the North and, apparently,
with "moralitee and vertuous matere."[71]   The Friar
displays an unexpected sense of relative emphasis and
proportion when he laughs at the Wife of Bath's "long
preamble of a tale."   More in character is the Clerk's
criticism of Petrarch's impertinent description of Pied-
mont and Saluzzo, introductory to the tale of Griselda.
It is clear that Chaucer had thought of such matters.   He
was alive, too, to the dangers of monotony, for it is partly
on this ground that Knight and Host condemn the Monk's
tragedies, and that the Host interrupts *Sir Thopas*.   The
variety of the *Canterbury Tales* is thus not to be regarded
as the result of their history, or of accident, or of instinct.

If the Prologues reveal Chaucer's concern with questions
of literary technique, they reveal no less his surpassing
interest in men and in human relations.   Nowhere is more
manifest his humorous tolerance, his sympathetic understanding of men of all degrees of rank, morality, and intel-
ligence.   He seems to know the peculiar vices incident to
every occupation.   His prevailing interest, however,
seems to be in the "war of the sexes," and especially in
the "wo that is in mariage."   Whether he is sincere in

---

[70] Cf. the *Franklin's Prologue*, F, 716ff.

[71] I, 37ff.   It is easy to read between the lines here a reference to
Piers Plowman.

his attitude, basing it, like the Wife of Bath, on experience
rather than on authorities, or whether, like Will Honey-
comb, he merely "shows his parts by raillery on marriage,"
he is clearly disposed to take the cynical view. The
longest of the Prologues, that of the Wife of Bath, is a
disquisition on methods of making husbands unhappy and
obtaining mastery over them. We women, she says, desire
what is forbidden us (D, 517ff.), and

> "We love no man that taketh kepe or charge
> Wher that we goon, we wol ben at our large (D, 321f.).

The Merchant, married but two months, echoes the closing
lines of Chaucer's *Envoy* to the *Clerk's Tale* to the effect
that "weping and wayling, care, and other sorwe" (E,
1213ff.) are the common lot of husbands. And the Host
adds to the descriptions of his wife, already noted, an
interesting glimpse of his relation to her, recalling that of
Simkin to his wife, in the *Reeve's Tale* (A, 3961f.); she
will persuade him to kill one of his neighbors some day,
he says,

> "For I am perilous with knyf in honde,
> Al be it that I dar nat hir withstonde,
> For she is big in armes, by my feith (B, 3109).

Characters such as the Miller, the Summoner, the Cook,
the Host, and, particularly, the Wife of Bath, display the
power of "lewed folk" to "report and hold" proverbial
sayings. Proverbs, therefore, are of frequent occurrence
in the Prologues, and most of them express, in crisp, sen-
tentious fashion, the speakers' cynical views of women.
These utterances are not all Chaucer's own, and it is not
to be assumed that they express his opinions. But it is
worthy of note that he mentions no happy marriage, and

no Pilgrim comes forward to extol the joys of matrimony
or the virtues of his wife. Silence about such matters
was doubtless characteristic of the gentles, then as now.
The Prologues, moreover, are comic, and happy marriages
and virtuous women have no great value as sources of
comic effect. Still, reference to them could have been
delicately managed, and would have heightened the effect
by contrast. In spite, then, of the Miller's declaration
that there are a thousand good women to one bad one, it
is difficult to believe that the Chaucer of the Prologues
was not inclined to share the traditional medieval view
of the sex. That he did share this view there is excellent
evidence in "The Counseil of Chaucer touching Mariage,
which was sent to Bukton."[72] Here Chaucer begs his
friend to read the Wife of Bath concerning this matter,
repeats her phrase, "the wo that is in mariage," and echoes
the Merchant's view of the married state. He advises
Bukton to take a wife, lest he do worse; but he will
surely have to endure much sorrow and be her slave.

A third interest of Chaucer's, that in astronomy,
appears, finally, in the Prologues. The method of calculating the time of day is given in the *Introduction to the
Man of Law's Prologue,* and again in the *Parson's Prologue.* In this connection it is convenient to mention the
references to astrology made by the Wife of Bath, who
sinned, she says, by virtue of her constellation (D, 614ff.),
and accounts for the mutual hatred of clerks and women on
the ground of the natural hostility of the children of
Mercury and the children of Venus (D, 697ff.). These
passages are doubtless purely dramatic, and with the irony
implied in them may be connected Chaucer's condemnation
of alchemy, in the *Canon's Yeoman's Prologue* and *Tale,*

---

[72] Skeat, *The Works of Chaucer,* I, 398.

and the Pardoner's exposure of his methods of gulling his victims.

Turning now from the framework to the tales which it encloses, we find that they are, finished and unfinished, twenty-four in number. Of these, twelve are serious and twelve are comic. Of the serious tales, two are in prose and five in stanzas. Of the remaining five, one, the *Knight's Tale,* is an older tale remodeled, and another, the *Squire's Tale,* is unfinished. This leaves three finished tales in the meter of the framework, written, in all probability, for the places which they now occupy, namely, the Physician's, the Wife's, and the Franklin's.

Of the comic tales,[73] one, the Cook's, is unfinished; one, *Sir Thopas,* is in stanzaic form, though only for purposes of parody.[74] The remaining ten are all finished and all in the meter of the framework. All twelve were evidently conceived and written as Canterbury tales. They are closely connected with the Drama of the Pilgrimage. Five of them,—Miller's, Reeve's, Friar's, Summoner's, Canon's Yeoman's,—spring from the quarrels of the narrators, and comic characters in them are counterparts of some of the Pilgrims.[75] The Miller insists upon telling

[73] Classed as comic are *Sir Thopas,* and the tales of Nun's Priest, Friar, Merchant, Cook, Shipman, Miller, Maunciple, Reeve, Summoner, Canon's Yeoman, and Pardoner. There may be some question as to whether the *Pardoner's Tale* should be placed in this group. Certainly it has serious elements. But the condition and character of the Pardoner, his Prologue, the conversation following the tale, and the fact that schwank and fabliau did not hesitate to find in death a source of comic effect, justify the present classification. The story is grim comedy, indeed, but still comedy.

[74] It is hardly conceivable that Chaucer ever intended to add anything to *Sir Thopas* or to the *Monk's Tale.*

[75] These are Miller, Reeve (Carpenter), Friar, Summoner, and Canon. There is no Palamon or Arcite, no Constance or Griselda among the Pilgrims.

his tale because he is drunk; the Shipman, upon telling
his, in order to save the company from a dull sermon; and
the Maunciple volunteers to take the place of the drunken
Cook.   Taken all together, the comic tales make a very
different impression from the serious ones, an impression
of greater uniformity,[76] and one practically identical,
speaking roughly and generally, with that produced by the
Drama of the Pilgrimage.   To sum up the characteristics
of that Drama is, therefore, to sum up the characteristics
of the comic tales as well.   The Drama, we have just
seen, is a series of comic incidents, realistic in relations
of time, place, and persons.   The latter are, for the most
part, "low" and comic.   These, at least, are more completely revealed than their betters, speak more frequently,
and dominate the whole.   Their characters are mainly
suggested by objective and dramatic methods, rarely
directly described.   Chaucer's attitude toward them is
detached and impersonal.   He is interested in their
thoughts and emotions, but here again there is little direct
description, the method is almost wholly dramatic.   These
emotions are mainly the results of the conflicts of the
characters, and in these conflicts are the elements of personal hatred and professional jealousy in varying degrees.
The drama consists largely of a series of these violent
differences of opinion, relieved from monotony by com-
pulsory changes of the Host's plans, and by vivid bits of
action.   It is carried on mainly by dialogue, vigorous and

---

[76] The serious tales represent a variety of literary types,—
romance, lay, fairy tale, saint's legend, tragedy, novella, and classical
tale.   The use of prose and stanzas has been noted.   The comic
tales, on the contrary, may all be fairly classed as fabliaux, except
the beast-epic of the Nun's Priest, which differs very little from the
fabliau manner, and *Sir Thopas*, which is, like the Old French
fabliau *Du Mantel Mautaillé*, a parody.

realistic, indicative of character and emotion, seldom taking the form of long monologues, and frequently taking that of group conversation.

While they are essentially dramatic and largely impersonal, the Prologues still reveal much concerning Chaucer's tendencies and interests. They reveal the fact that he was a conscious artist in literature, able to calculate the effects which he desired to produce, aware of the existence of certain literary types, interested in questions of technique, style, and meter. They reveal, too, his interest in human relations, particularly in marriage, and a certain cynical tendency in regard to women. And they reveal, finally, his interest in astronomy, and contain perhaps an ironical condemnation of astrology, and certainly a condemnation of the deceitful use of the pseudo-supernatural by alchemist and pardoner.

These characteristics are to be found in one or more,— most of them, indeed, in all,—of the comic tales. They are to be found also, whether faintly foreshadowed or clearly developed, in the Old French fabliaux, so that we may say with a fair degree of certainty[77] that in the technique of the Drama of the Pilgrimage and of the comic tales Chaucer was writing under fabliau influence. While the serious tales amount to 12,677 lines, and the whole framework and comic tales together only to 9,411 lines, it is clear that the latter group represents the Chaucer of the *Canterbury Tales,* for every part of it was composed especially for that purpose, in the style and

[77] The general influence of the fabliaux upon Chaucer's work is of great importance and should be studied. Evidence will be in the form, not of parallel passages and borrowings of stories, but of general similarity of technique. The present writer's article on the *Reeve's Tale* (*M. L. A.*, XXIII, 1ff.) is an attempt in this direction.

meter[78] and general tone peculiar to it. It indicates that the prevailing manner and point of view of Chaucer's work at this time were the manner and point of view of the fabliaux, and it leads us to expect that when he came to write stories of other types these would inevitably be contaminated; that classical story, Celtic fairy tale, or Breton lay, would have some fabliau characteristics. Of the finished serious tales, written, in heroic couplets, for the place which they now occupy, the classical story, the *Physician's Tale,* exhibits but few of these characteristics;[79] the Celtic fairy story, the *Wife of Bath's Tale,* exhibits more of them; and the Breton lay, the *Franklin's Tale,* exhibits most of all. It has the same consciousness of the audience, the power of calculating effects, inherited from schwank and fabliau; the same dramatic quality and technique; the same use of place-names with little visualization; the same passing references to time and season. In both the time is the present or an immediate past, without glamor or mystery. There is the same interest in character, love of contrasts (though this is more subtle in the *Franklin's Tale*), and preference for the dramatic method of suggesting character and emotion. The tendency to regard character with broad tolerance and from the comic point of view is present in the Franklin's attitude toward Aurelius. There is the same sustained interest in mental states; and something of the same con-

---

[78] With the trifling exceptions of *Sir Thopas,* which necessarily makes use of the meter of the genre which it parodies, and of its prologue, which continues for three stanzas the meter of the *Prioress's Tale.*

[79] The source of the *Physician's Tale* is the *Roman de la Rose,* and this, in a general division of medieval literature, is to be classed with the fabliaux. Bédier points out common characteristics. (*Les Fabliaux,* pp. 362, 371.)

trast between the free expression of emotion of the relatively "low" and the restraint of the relatively "high" in
character, in the contrast between Aurelius and Arveragus.
The question proposed at the close suggests the old
"debates," as the quarrels do in the Drama of the Pilgrimage; and there is something of the same conflict of
characters, not as individuals, but as representatives of
classes or professions, in the emulation of knight, squire,
and clerk. There is the same literary self-consciousness
and critical power, and interest in matters of style and
technique. There is the same interest in marital relations
and the same cynical tendency. The condemnation of
astrology, and the explanation of character and conduct by
planetary influence, connect the *Franklin's Tale* with the
Wife of Bath's Prologue. The use of a pseudo-supernatural trick to gull the credulous connects it with the
Pardoner's Prologue, the *Miller's Tale,* and the *Canon's
Yeoman's Tale,* as well as with the traditions of schwank
and fabliau. Like the comic tales, the *Franklin's Tale*
is closely connected with the framework. It springs, if
not from the quarrel, at least from the good-natured
rivalry, of Franklin and Squire. The Franklin is conscious throughout of the conditions under which he is
speaking. Two of his characters, knight and squire, are
more or less accurate portraits of Canterbury Pilgrims.
There are, of course, striking differences between the
Franklin's Tale and the Drama of the Pilgrimage,—its
moral purpose and serious nature, its preference for "high"
rather than "low," serious rather than comic, characters.
It is less vivid, less concrete and real. Its idealization of
character it may well owe to the Breton lay. Its lack of
vividness and concreteness may perhaps be regarded as
the result of the apologue theme. And this remains to be

accounted for.   Desire to illustrate and enforce a moral
concept is certainly not a significant part of the purpose
of the Canterbury Drama or of the comic tales.   Yet the
stories told by Nun's Priest, Pardoner, and Canon's Yeoman, together with Chaucer's interest in the general question of marital relations, are sufficient perhaps to account
for his moralization of a Breton lay.   Even the Old
French fabliaux are sometimes, by exception, moral in
intention,[80] witness the *Housse Partie, Bourse Pleine de
Sens,* and *Folle Largesse.*   Doubtless Chaucer was
familiar, if not with these, at least with fabliaux of this
type, and such familiarity may be added to the forces
which would lead a fabliau writer to compose a moral tale.
Furthermore, it is possible to account for part at least of
the curiously symmetrical structure of the *Franklin's Tale*
on the basis of an influence which relates it closely to
the most important of the Canterbury Prologues.   It is
exceedingly interesting to note that Dorigen borrows the
exempla of her complaint from the favorite book of the
Wife of Bath's fifth husband, from the treatise of Jerome
against Jovinian.[81]

So far as manner, point of view, general interests and
tendencies are concerned, Chaucer seems to owe nothing to
Boccaccio, either to the *Decameron* or to the *Filocolo.*
Whatever the provenience of the story, the technique of
the *Franklin's Tale* has every appearance of being simply
the result of a translation of *a* Breton lay, or an imitation
of *the* Breton lay, by a great poet who happened to be
writing at the time mainly in the manner of the fabliaux
To say this is by no means to deny the originality of the
great poet; whatever he may have learned from his
predecessors, selection, recombinations, improvements of
every sort were his own; the main source of Chaucer's
technique was Chaucer himself.

[80] Cf. Bédier, *Les Fabliaux,* p. 34.
[81] Cf. F, 1367ff. and D, 711ff.

IPOMEDON,
AN ILLUSTRATION OF ROMANCE ORIGIN.

By Charles Henry Carter, Ph.D.

IPOMEDON, AN ILLUSTRATION OF ROMANCE ORIGIN.

About the year 1187,[1] Hugh of Rutland, living at a little place named Credenhill, near Hereford, on the Welsh border, launched a three-decker metrical romance, written in good French and entitled *Ipomedon*.[2] Hugh was probably a friend of Walter Map, for they lived near each other and Hugh mentions Map familiarly, if not jocosely:

> "Sul ne sai pas de mentir l'art,—
> Walter Map reset ben sa part."

Other famous contemporaries, somewhat older than Hugh, were Marie de France and Chrestien de Troyes. Even when compared with the work of the notable Chrestien, Hugh's performance is not insignificant. *Ipomedon* is

---

[1] Ward, in his *"Catalogue of Romances in British Museum,"* Vol. 1, p. 728ff., shows by internal evidence that both *Ipomedon* and *Prothesilaus*, the other extant romance by Hugh, must have been written between 1174 and 1190-1. Neither Ward nor any other investigator, however, has cited the evidence of the following passage (Ip. 1. 8937ff.):

> Si fist uns reis gualeis jardis,
> Jo quit, k'il l'apelerent Ris;
> Il fut mut larges d'Engleterre,
> A ses hirdmans parti la terre,
> E Herefort e Glovecestre,
> Salopesbure e Wircestre;
> Mes il en lava ben ses mains.
> Il e li son ourent li meins,
> Kar il fust vencuz e laidiz,
> Vilment chacez e descumfiz.

This refers without doubt to Rhees ap Gryffyth, fomentor of insurrections in Wales from 1158 till his death in the next century. A careful examination of his career (Cf. R. W. Eyton: *"Court, Household and Itinerary of King Henry II,* p. 39ff.; also, Lyttleton's *History of Henry* II, Vol. 3, p. 80 ff.) shows that the only one of his forays into the English counties which fits this reference by

composed with a good degree of leisurely literary skill; it has humor, a lively style, a lack of tedious incident unconnected with the main plot, and a good climax. Excellences of style were lost in the English versions of *Ipomedon*[3] produced by later redactors.

Aside from the literary value of *Ipomedon,* a study of the poem makes clear certain points of interest in regard to romance origins. We can discover this twelfth century poet manufacturing his story from sources at hand and from his own invention. We can show that one-half the story is based on a widespread type of folk-tale, a type which has also influenced various other romances. We can show what are probably definite borrowings from the work of the poet's immediate predecessors. We can therefore secure a fair idea of the way in which this particular romancer set about amusing French-speaking Englishmen, two centuries before Chaucer amused their English-speaking children.

Hugh took place in 1186. Ultimate authority is found in the *Peterborough Chronicle* (*De Vita et Gestis Henrici II et Ricardi I.* Pub. by Hearne, 1735. Vol. II, p. 457). Under date of 1186 is found the following passage: "Interim, rumor ille nefandus venit in Angliam ad aures Regis, qui misit Ranulfum de Glanvil, Justiciarium suum, ad Resum filium Griffin, et ad ceteros Wallorum Regulos, ad Pacem faciendam inter eos et Herefordenses et Cestrenses (qui paulo ante in quondam [sic] Conflictu, multos Walensibus interfecerant)—" Apparently, therefore, Hugh's fellow townsmen in 1186 had joined with men from Chester in driving back this Welsh king. Probably Rhees had been boasting of the way in which he would divide England among his followers: this would agree well with his character. If it be granted as probable that Hugh was referring to this event, both *Ipomedon* and *Prothesilaus* must have been composed between the years 1186 and 1190-1. *Ipomedon,* the earlier of the two romances, is therefore dated, with probable accuracy, 1187-8.

[2] *Hue de Rotelande's Ipomedon, ein französischer Abenteuerroman des 12ten Jahrhunderts.* Kölbing und Koschwitz. Breslau. 1889.

[3] *Ipomedon, in drei englischen bearbeitung.* Kölbing. Breslau. 1889.

The plot of *Ipomedon* falls easily into two main themes: the three days' tournament, and the rescue of a besieged lady by a knight who plays the fool. With the latter is woven the theme of finding a lost relative by means of a ring, after the relatives have fought each other.

I. RESEMBLANCE TO FOLK-LORE.

The first of these, the three days' tournament, is a theme which appears in certain other romances and also in a large number of folk-tales gathered from all over Europe. Ward cited in this connection a tale named "*Le Petit Berger,*" No. 43 of Vol. II of E. Cosquin's edition of "*Contes Populaires de Lorraine.*"[4] A study of the folk-tale group to which this belongs reveals points of interest in regard to *Ipomedon.* The writer has examined many of these folk-tales as found in collections[5]

[4] Also cited by Karl Breul in connection with *Sir Gowther.* Cf. *Sir Gowther, eine englische romanze aus dem XV Jahrhundert.* Oppeln, 1886.

[5] Cosquin: *Contes Populaires de Lorraine,* II, Nos. 43, 55. Luzel: *Traditions Orales des Bretons-Armoricains,* p. 34. Zingerle: *Tirols Volksdichtungen,* etc., II, pp. 96, 326, 91, 198. Wolf: *Deutsche Hausmärchen,* pp. 269, 356, 369. Wolf: *Deutsche Hausmärchen u. Sagen,* No. 2. Grimm: *Kinder u. Hausmärchen,* No. 136. Meier: *Deutsche Volksmärchen aus Schwaben,* No. 1. Schambach u. Müller: *Niedersächsische Sagen,* p. 278. Karl Müllenhof: *Märchen u. Lieder der Herzogthümer Schleswig, Holstein u. Lauenberg,* p. 432. Gaal: *Mährchen der Magyaren,* p. 25. Milenowsky: *Volksmärchen aus Böhmen,* p. 147. Karadzic: *Volksmärchen der Serben,* p. 12. Schiefner: *Awarische Texte,* No. 4. Hahn: *Griechische u. Albanesische Märchen,* No. 26. Wenzig: *Westslawischen Märchenschatz,* p. 1. Dietrich: *Russische Volksmärchen,* No. 4. Gonzenbach: *Sicilianische Märchen,* No. 26. Ebert's *Jahrbuch,* etc., VIII, p. 253. Comparetti: *Canti e Racconti del popolo italiano,* VI, p. 93. Campbell: *Popular Tales of the West Highlands,* I, p. 72. Curtin: *Myths and Folk-lore of Ireland,* p. 157. Larminie: *West Irish Folktales and Romances,* p. 196. Others are cited by Hartland: *Legend of Perseus,* III, p. 7.

made by students of folk-lore about the middle of the nineteenth century.

These tales may be summarized as follows: (1) The hero is either someone of low rank, or else a prince in the disguise of the menial. He is a shepherd boy in tales from Lorraine, Germany, Italy, Swabia, Tyrol, Brittany, and Western Russia; a goat-herd in Tyrol; a fowl-herd in Schleswig-Holstein and the Odenwald; a cattle-herd in still another tale from the Tyrol, also in Scotland and Ireland; a swine-herd in Hungary; a gardener in Spain; a prince without menial position in Servia and Transylvania; a prince disguised as a gardener in Germany; a prince in disguise in Sicily; the son of a knight in disguise of a gardener in Russia, etc., etc.   (2) By some means, usually magic, he gains control of a horse, or more frequently of three horses. He may slay giants or other malevolent beings and thus gain access to their secret stables,—as in the case of fifteen tales examined by the writer; he may, however, simply find the mysterious castle where the horses are (Odenwald); or procure them from a subterranean vault (Russia); or from a magic nut (Sicily); or from a magic tree (Saxony); etc., etc. (3) These horses are of various colors, and with them frequently go suits of armor of three different colors. The horses may be: white, black, and brown (Tyrol, Germany); white, red, and black (Servia, Western Russia); black, red, and white (Odenwald, Tyrol); copper, silver, and gold (Schleswig-Holstein); etc.   In several cases the color of the horses is not given, and in more, no color is given to the armor.   In one instance, dogs are mentioned, corresponding to the three horses as in Ipomedon (Schleswig-Holstein).   (4) Having now got possession of the horses, and keeping his exploits secret, the hero

performs a thrice repeated feat by which he wins the hand
of a princess. The feat may be winning at a three days'
tournament (four tales, with two others where the feat
resembles a tourney); it may be winning in a three days'
battle against the foes of the kingdom (four tales); it
may be fights with dragons (eight tales); it may be a
race; a contest in riding at the ring; a contest in riding
at golden apples; in catching golden apples as thrown by
the princess; in jumping a horse over a tower; etc., etc.
(5) Before this, the hero may have won the friendship,
or even the love, of the princess; in some cases he has
married her, but has attained no honor. In one case (Lorraine) she urges him to take part in the contest, and in
another (Sicily) invites him to be present as a spectator.
(6) At the end of each day's exploits, the hero invariably
escapes unknown, and is often modestly reluctant about
showing himself and receiving his reward. In one case
(Sicily) he, like Ipomedon, expressly declares that he has
no interest in the outcome of the battle. In two tales the
hero is regaled in the evening with an account of his
own exploit. (7) In several tales the hero is wounded on
the last day, either in the fight (Swabia, Tyrol, Russia),
or more often in the endeavor of the onlookers to keep him
from making a third escape unknown (six tales). In
one case (Sicily) when asked about the wound, he answers,
like Ipomedon, "Ich habe mich gestossen." (8) Now follows his identification, often by a piece of weapon left
in the wound, and then the inevitable marriage with the
princess.

For the sake of convenient comparison, let us put side
by side the points of resemblance between Ipomedon, the
elaborate romance, and this variegated group of folk-tales.

We postulate the right to select incidents as we choose from the tales.

Ipomedon.	Folk-tales.
Ip. hears of the beauty of La Fiere, goes in disguise to her court, and takes service with her.	Prince becomes enamoured of princess through seeing her portrait and goes to seek her. He disguises himself.
They fall in love.	They become at least very friendly.
After a reprimand, Ip. leaves court. Her barons compel La Fiere to choose a husband, and she decides on the three days' tournament as a means for making choice.	Hero slays giants, or in some other way gets possession of three horses. King announces three days' tournament for hand of his daughter. The three days' feat is more frequently something other than a tourney.
Ip. brings his three horses, white, red, and black, and his three suits of armor of the same colors.	Hero uses horses colored white, red, and black, and clothes or armor of the same color.
He wins on each day and departs secretly, keeping his identity unknown.	He wins on each day and departs secretly. keeping his identity unknown.
After each day's fight, he sends word to La Fiere that he cannot be present on the next day, thus leaving her in continual suspense.	Princess each day implores hero to take part; he says he will, but apparently does not, thus keeping her in continual suspense.
On his return each day, Ip. is laughed to scorn by the court ladies.	Hero is laughed at as he returns on his decrepit nag. (Germany).
In the evening Ip. hears Thoas narrate the incidents of the day.	In the evening hero hears eyewitness tell of his deeds.
Ip. is assisted in his deception by his master, Tholomeu, who hunts with dogs matching the horses in color.	Hero is helped by dogs distinguished like the horses by certain adornments.

On the last day Ip. is wounded in the fray.	On last day hero is wounded in conflict, or as he escapes.
He tries to keep his wound secret, and when he cannot, explains it away.	He tries to conceal wound, and explain it away, but is identified by it later.
Ip. ultimately marries La Fiere.	Hero marries princess.

These resemblances to the first half of the plot of *Ipomedon* are so close and so pervasive that it seems impossible to regard them as accidental. The theme is too complicated to have arisen, quite independently, once in the mind of Hugh, or some literary predecessor of his, and again among the folk all over Europe. To be sure, no great stress can be laid on certain isolated resemblances; for instance, the mention of the three dogs corresponding to the horses, found in the variant from Schleswig-Holstein, very doubtfully shows occult relation to the dogs in Ipomedon; this is an idea which might easily have been added independently in England, or in Schleswig-Holstein, or anywhere. But the cumulative resemblance of Ipomedon to the widespread type is strong. The folktales usually contain magic, and the romance is rationalized; but the framework is practically identical, so that, on the whole, one must believe the romance and the folktales historically dependent.

The great gap of seven centuries between the writing of the romance and the writing down of the folk-tales, together with the general obscurity resting on folk-tale origins, might lead a critic to hesitate to accept the folk-tale as in any way the source of the romance. Foerster and his school of critics, espousing "Methode streng literarhistorische," think that reasoning from folk-lore is unsafe. But to derive the folk-tales from the literary forms of the story would require us to suppose that the unlettered folk seized upon the essentials of the story and decked them out in fairy-tale paraphernalia—magic castles, talking horses, etc.—in other words, reversed the usual tendency in early literatures to go from the simple and the supernatural to the intricate and the rational. This supposition is not tenable.

On the other hand, the romance has the appearance of being a complex and rationalized development of a primitive theme,—and folk-tales are undoubtedly old enough to be the ultimate sources of twelfth century romance. After the investigations of Wilhelm Grimm, Emmanuel Cosquin, Andrew Lang, and others, this last statement will hardly be questioned. Moreover, a wide distribution of any folk-tale, as in this case, is a good indication of its antiquity. It seems reasonable, therefore, to suppose that the first part of *Ipomedon* is dependent in some way upon the folk-tale, which has itself lasted unwritten among the peasantry of Europe till modern times.

Here, however, should be made a reservation. It is impossible to believe that Hugh (or his literary predecessor, if he had one) could have derived from a folk-tale the tournament. The reason is that in 1187 the tournament was still a rather recent institution.[6] The folk-tale represents the old ideas of the people, and therefore the tournament in *Ipomedon* is probably a literary substitution for some primitive form of the feat, such as the fight with the dragon, found in eight of the folk-tales. Much later, after the tournament became a common-place in

---

[6] Freeman: *History of the Norman Conquest*, V, p. 488, says, "The tournament appears among us as a novelty of the twelfth century." A. P. Budik: *Ursprung des Turniers:* quotes Wm. of Newburgh, Bk. V, ch. 4 of *Historia Anglicana*, when he says that in 1194 people in England began to use warlike practices commonly called tourneys.

Europe, it naturally stole into a few variants of the oral folk-tale, independently of the romances. It is not a common feature of folk-lore.

The exact history showing *how* the romance is dependent on the folk-tale is probably not to be determined. One or several literary adaptations may have intervened between the simple, magic story, told perhaps by somebody's nurse, and Hugh's long poem. In his introduction Hugh professes a Latin source for his story, but this profession, as we may see more clearly later, is very doubtfully true.

II. THE THREE DAYS' FEAT IN OTHER ROMANCES.

Meanwhile, if we have established the ultimate dependence on folk-lore of this part of Ipomedon, let us turn to glance at various other literary versions of the three days' feat. Will they help in tracing the literary history of this theme?

These other versions[7] are found (1) in *Sir Gowther* and in *Robert the Devil;* (2) in *Lanzelet,* and in three othe. rather unimportant passages where Lancelot is the hero; (3) in *Cliges;* (4) in *Partonopeus;* (5) in *Roswall and Lillian;* and (6) in *Richard Coeur de Lion.* Let us consider them in order.

(1) *Sir Gowther* and the various versions of the widely distributed *Robert the Devil* story are very similar to each other in those points where they resemble *Ipomedon,* and

[7] Ward first called attention to the resemblance between *Ipomedon* and one incident in the *Prose Lancelot.* The credit for first citing *Lanzelet,* a passage in the *Dutch Lancelot,* and Chrestien's *Cliges* in connection with *Ipomedon* is due to Miss Jessie L. Weston in her book "*The Three Days' Tournament*," London, 1902. Kölbing mentions *Gowther* and *Partonopeus.* Lengert (Eng. Stud. XVI, 321ff., and XVII, 341f.), and Child (*Eng. and Scot. Ballads* No. 271) mention *Ipomedon* in connection with *Richard* and with *Roswall.*

it is therefore convenient to consider them together. These resemblances may be briefly summarized as follows: The hero, in disguise of a menial, is at the court where the hand of a princess is at stake. We are not told that he loves her, but we feel sure that she loves him. On three successive days he is provided (here miraculously) with three horses. In *Gowther*[8] the horses are colored like Ipomedon's. The hero escapes unknown on each occasion,—unknown except to the dumb daughter. (La Fiere in *Ipomedon* knew each evening who the hero was.) The hero appears like a fool at the suppers in the evening. He is wounded on the last day. To be sure, the thrice repeated contest is a battle, not a tournament.

Breul[9] has industriously examined the *Gowther-Robert* story, but does not mention *Ipomedon* or any other literary version. Instead, he seeks the basis of the story in folk-lore, and, as a basis for that part which concerns *Ipomedon*, finds the same group of folk-tales which we have been considering. He cites three examples and then constructs an ideal märchen with which to make his comparison. His conclusion is that the *Gowther-Robert* legend is the clerical working over of a widespread folk-tale of the youthful knight voluntarily lowering his social standing and finally rewarded by the hand of the princess,—the story of the male Cinderella. This working over belongs to the twelfth century, perhaps earlier, and becomes essentially the tale of a sinner and his repentance.[10]

---

[8] *Sir Gowther* may be more than a mere retelling of the *Robert* story, as Breul would have it. In view of such tales as the Breton *Lay of Tydorel*, and *Sir Degore*, Dr. Schofield thinks it may represent the combination of such a story with that of *Robert*.

[9] *Sir Gowther, eine englische romanze aus dem XV Jahrhundert.*

[10] Reviewers of Breul's book find no serious error in his derivation of the story from folk-lore. Cf. *Romania*, XV, 160. *Englische Studien*, XII, 78-83.

Sir Gowther dates from the fifteenth century, and the earliest known version of *Robert* is found in the Latin of Etienne de Bourbon, about 1250. (Printed by Breul, p. 208.) Etienne says he heard the story from two brothers who said they had read it. Is it possible that the *Robert* story was directly influenced by *Ipomedon* (1187) ? No. The three days' tournament as we saw, is probably a literary injection as it appears in the romance; and both *Robert* and *Gowther* keep the old (?) three days' battle. The three colors do not appear in *Robert,* and in *Gowther* they are not in the same order. None of the complications exhibited in *Ipomedon,*—the hunting, the dogs, the two women open to the hero's love, and so forth, appear in the other stories, which in nearly all points keep closer to the simplicity of the folk-tales, and retain some of the magic elements.

It is equally impossible to suppose that *Ipomedon* is based directly on the *Robert* tradition, which Breul thinks may have existed in the twelfth century. For there is nothing of the clerical element in *Ipomedon,*— none of the devils, popes, miracles found in *Gowther-Robert.* It seems probable, therefore, that the *Robert* and the *Ipomedon* are independently based on the same general group of folk-tale. The *"clerical elaborator"* of Breul's theory would find it easy to account for the appearance of the horses and armor as the answer to prayer; it was not necessary to follow the folk-tale in its slaying of dragons, finding of subterranean castles, or what not. To bring in the Saracen king that he might be soundly drubbed by the Christians was natural to him. Also, to have the princess dumb offered a good chance for a miracle. Hugh, or his predecessor, on the other hand, though keeping

fairly close to the folk-tale framework, has developed
the theme romantically.

(2) We turn now to the three days' tournament theme as
found in various stories where Lancelot is the hero. The
story most to our purpose is the *Lanzelet* of Ulrich von
Zatzikhoven. Here the tournament episode is simply one
of a series of detached incidents in this biographical
romance. *Lanzelet* is said by its author to be the translation of a romance in French taken from England by
Hugh de Morville. This was in 1194. The story runs
as follows: One day Lanzelet learns of a tournament at
which all good knights should be present. Gawain, with
whom Lanzelet has been having a friendly bout at arms,
urges his young opponent to accompany him to the tournament; but the young hero says he may not do so. After
entreaty, Gawain sees that he cannot prevail, and therefore
departs alone. Later Lanzelet decides to go with Ade,
his amie, and her brother Diebalt. Bedecked in green, he
takes his place. He overthrows the boaster Keiin (Kay)
and others. That he may not be recognized on the following day, he bids Diebalt prepare for him a white shield,
banner, and coat of mail. He wins again and departs
unfollowed to his inn. On the third day he comes in red
and joins battle with Gawain. King Lot, fearing for
his favorite knight, rides at the unknown knight. With
that, Lanzelet turns his attention to King Lot, who, though
soon aided by his retainers, is presently captured. At the
end of the day Arthur and Gawain ride down to the
lodging of the hero, who will not give his name, say the
proper things, and invite him to come to Arthur's court.
This, however, Lanzelet refuses to do, and rides off for
another adventure.

This account is nearer to *Ipomedon* and to the folk-tale

type than any of the other accounts where this adventure is ascribed to Lancelot.[11] That the theme, however, though in modified forms, turns up three times again with reference to him, indicates the strength of this tradition.

In spite of obvious differences between *Ipomedon* and *Lanzelet*—dissimilar colors, no princess concerned, the sketchiness of *Lanzelet* and the elaboration of *Ipomedon*—there are yet certain strong points of resemblance. Miss Weston pointed out the likeness between the overthrow of Keiin in *Lanzelet* to that of Caeminius in *Ipomedon*. She might have mentioned even stronger similarities: (1) The hero is urged by the chief knight, his friend, to take part in the tourney, but refuses, only to go later in disguise. (2) The king in person rides to the assistance of this chief knight when in the tourney the latter is too sorely assailed by the unknown hero, and is in turn vigorously assaulted. (3) Ade in *Lanzelet* is similar to

[11] The Dutch Lancelot, cited by Miss Weston, (*Roman van Lancelot*, ed. W. J. A. Jonckbloet) gives a long-winded and dull account not strikingly similar to the other versions. Ward cites a passage in the *Prose Lancelot* (*Les Romans de La Table Ronde*, ed. P. Paris, Vol. 3), dating from the middle of the thirteenth century. Young Lancelot fights in white, red, and black. The fight, however, is not a tournament, and a year intervenes between the second and third appearances.

Another account, unnoticed hitherto, can also be found in the *Prose Lancelot* (See Sommer's notes on Bk. XVIII of his edition of Malory's *Morte Darthur*. On this part of Malory, Tennyson bases the incidents of *Lancelot and Elaine*.) Lancelot goes in disguise to the tournament to test his strength. His armor is red. He fights unknown, and casts down all. His kinsmen, thinking a stranger is gaining fame due to Lancelot alone, run at him in a body, and Sir Bors wounds him in the thigh. He wins, however, and departs unknown, to be nursed by Elaine and the hermit. He had planned to appear in a second tourney in white, but his wound, bursting forth afresh, detains him. A third tourney is decreed, but again an accident prevents him from going.

a rather mysterious niece of Ipomedon, whom he leaves with Meleager's queen until he departs after the tournament; and (4) Diebalt, who aids Lanzelet in the tournament by carrying spears and taking charge of captured horses, is much like Jason, who in *Ipomedon* performs similar services for the hero.

These resemblances occur in no other version of the story, either literary or popular. They render plausible the theory that Hugh may have known the French original of *Lanzelet* extant in England some time before 1194, or some closely allied version. That he did not build up the whole first half of his story from this incident is shown, however, by the close resemblances to the folk-tales, retained by him and lacking in *Lanzelet*.[12]

(3) Now for the theme as it appears in the *Cliges* of Chrestien de Troyes. Cliges, leaving his court in Constantinople, learns that Arthur has appointed a fifteen days' tournament. (Only four days are told of.) He at once devises the scheme of fighting there in differently colored suits of armor. He already has four horses, white, sorrel, fawn-colored, and black. He sends three squires off to London to buy three suits of armor, black, red, and green. His original suit was white,—a gift from the emperor,— so that he is now provided with four suits. On the tourney day, Sagremors is the first knight to take the field; at him spurs Cliges, in black armor, on Morel, his black steed.

---

[12] Miss Weston, following Ward, contends that Walter Map wrote a romance on Lancelot, and hints that the French original of *Lanzelet* was this romance. As evidence she cites the couplet quoted at the beginning of this article: "I am not the only one who knows the art of lying,—Walter Map knows his part too." This can hardly be cited as proof, in view of its extremely general character and its likeness to other personal hits by Hugh at his contemporaries. Cf. *Ipomedon* l. 5345ff.; and l. 5511ff. The Map authorship of such a romance appears doubtful.

Sagremors is overcome, and at the end of the day Cliges is pronounced the winner. When he goes back to his lodgings, he hides his black armor and hangs up the green in a conspicuous place. Thus he escapes being known. Next day in green armor on the fawn-colored horse he overthrows Lancelot. In the evening he hangs up the red armor. In red on the third day he rides the sorrel horse to the tourney and defeats Perceval le Galois. Again he escapes and hangs up the white armor. By this time the wise heads recognize that the victor on each day must be one and the same man. Gawain proposes, therefore, to meet him the next day and learn his name. Cliges appears in white. At the first joust both he and Gawain are unhorsed. Then they fight an even battle with their swords until Arthur parts them. Cliges, by the way, is Gawain's sister's son. This ends the tourney. Cliges goes in state to the court and makes himself known. He soon returns to Constantinople.

Foerster, the enthusiastic editor of Chrestien, believes that in *Cliges* (1160) the three days' tournament theme was first introduced into literature, and that from it *Lanzelet* borrowed directly. When Miss Weston attacked this theory,[13] Wolfang Golther[14] replied in defense of Foerster, and went so far as to maintain that *Cliges* is also the source for this incident in *Ipomedon*. The present writer agrees with Miss Weston in thinking that the natural impression one would derive from *Cliges* is that of a four days' tournament, and that any version based entirely on *Cliges* would be likely to follow it in this respect. The four days'

---

[13] She endeavors to prove that *Cliges* is dependent for this episode on the lost French original of *Lanzelet*, but from lack of conclusive evidence, falls short of proof.

[14] *Zeitschrift für französische Sprache und Literatur.* 1903.

fight in *Cliges* looks rather like an elaboration, in the style of Chrestien, of the simpler three days' theme. If the test from folk-lore is of value, *Ipomedon,* which adheres much more closely than *Cliges* to the folk-tale type, is not likely to be derived wholly, if at all, from *Cliges,* where the incident is so sketchy and so changed. Hugh must have known some other version. Of course it is possible to imagine Hugh finding an abbreviated account of the tournament, in *Cliges,* for example, or in the lost French original of *Lanzelet,* and expanding it from his own knowledge of the folk-tale. More probably he had before him some literary version of the incident nearer the usual folk-lore type.[15]

(4) Still another version of the three days' tournament with which *Ipomedon* may be compared is found in the

[15] However, it is not unlikely that Hugh knew Chrestien's work. The fight of Ipomedon with Capaneus, his half-brother, is somewhat like that of Cliges with Gawain, his uncle: they fight to a standstill and then discover their relationship. Moreover there is some resemblance between the love of Alexander and Soredamors in *Cliges* and that of Ipomedon and La Fiere. The parallel is one of style rather than of incident. There are in each long monologues, which are psychological analyses of new-born love. The same device is used of having the speaker make some statement and then catch himself up on the last words, which he repeats as a question. Gröber (Grundriss der Rom. Phil., p. 585) recognizes this stylistic influence.

Kölbing sees dependence of incident on Chrestien in the following points: (1) Ipomedon placed as sweetheart of Meleager's queen imitates Lancelot placed as sweetheart of Guinivere in *"Le Chevalier de la Charette;"* (2) the fight between Ipomedon and Capaneus is like a fight in *"Le Chevalier au Lyon;"* (3) the coming of Ismaine for a champion is like the coming of Lunete in *"Chev. au Lyon."* Upon careful investigation, the writer sees no evident dependence in these details: the first point is based on resemblance extremely general; the second is almost no parallel at all; and the third passage in *Ipomedon* is so evidently drawn from a different source, *Le Bel Inconnu* story, that the slight resemblance to Chrestien's work counts for nothing.

Partonopeus story.[16] Kölbing cites the parallel. This story
does indeed give a good version, but two very distinctive
features, the disguising colors and the secret escape, are
lacking. In some particulars *Partonopeus* resembles
Ipomedon, and in some it rather strikingly resembles por-
tions of the *Lancelot* story. Without pausing to give a
summary of this tale, let us enumerate these resemblances. How is this romance like *Ipomedon?* The
heroine by her capricious pride has driven away her lover.
Her courtiers, to procure her a husband, decree a three
days' tournament, the victor at which she is to marry.
She mourns her lot, but considers that she is being justly
punished for her pride. The hero comes, but does not
make himself known to the lady. On the first day he is
in white. The ladies watch his success from a tower. At
the end of the three days he is announced the victor.
Detailed descriptions of fights are given. After the
tournament the hero fights a special duel with a rival
suitor. The heroines, when trying to speak the name of
the lover, stick in the middle of it,—in one instance a
mighty sigh cleaves it in twain, and in the other she
stammers. (Kölbing calls attention to this last point.)
How is the romance like the *Lancelot* story? The hero,
on being driven away, runs demented into the woods,
where he is later found and cared for. He had already
won extreme favors from the lady. She girds his sword
upon him. He is taken prisoner by a cruel knight. The
wife of the knight frees him on parole that he may attend
the tourney. She furnishes him with horse and armor.
He wins and returns to prison, but is able to go again to
court. He slays the cruel knight who had imprisoned him.

---

[16] *Partonopeus de Blois,* by Denis Pyramis, ed. G. A. Crapelet,
Paris, 1834. *Partonope of Blois,* ed. Buckley, London, 1862. *Par-
talopa Saga,* ed. O. Klockhoff, Upsala, 1877.

When these points are thus singled out, the resemblances seem stronger than they really are, for a large number of incidents and details which lend peculiar cast to each story are absolutely lacking in the others.

Opinions differ somewhat as to the date and origin of the *Partonopeus* story. It seems probable, however, that the French version, ascribed to Denis Pyramus, dates from the latter part of the twelfth century. Whether its composition precedes or follows that of *Ipomedon* has not been determined. Since *Ipomedon,* however, as we have pointed out many times, seems to stand near the standard form of the folk-tale, much nearer than *Partonopeus,* it seems doubtful that Hugh borrowed his tournament from such a source. The broken name of the lover looks like a literary borrowing on somebody's part, but it is as apt to be on the part of Denis as of Hugh. It is suggestive, however, to find the tournament theme turning up in a romance which recalls again the *Lancelot* story. It makes one wonder if both Hugh and Denis may not have known some lost *Lancelot* story with similar features.

Two more romances, both late, contain the tournament theme. (5) One of these, *Roswall and Lillian,*"[17] resem-

---

[17] O. Lengert (*Englische Studien*, XVI, 321f., and XVII, 341f.), in a careful edition of this romance, cites many apposite folk-tales, and incidentally compares *RL* with *Ipomedon.* He does not radically disagree with Ward, who thought that *RL* borrowed from *Ipomedon.* Part of the story, minus the tournament theme, is found again in various ballad forms, notably *The Lord of Lorne and the False Steward.* (Child's *Eng. and Scottish Ballads,* No. 271). Child thought the ballad derived from RL; but it is rather noteworthy that the ballad omits altogether just that part of *RL* which offers close parallelism to *Ipomedon.* This circumstance seems to indicate that the author of *RL* adapted the tournament and the hunting from *Ipomedon,* possibly one of the English versions, to the simple ballad story, which still persisted till modern times.

bles *Ipomedon* so obviously in the hunting combined with
the tournament, that one may regard its direct dependence
on *Ipomedon* as certain. The other, (6) *Richard Coeur de
Lion,*[18] contains the three disguises, black, red, and white;
the secret departure of the hero after each appearance;
the detailed account given the hero of his actions by those
who do not know that he is the knight under discussion.
However, the contest is all on one day, the purpose of the
tournament is not to win a lady, the hero is worsted twice,
the colors are not used in the same order as in *Ipomedon.*
This romance, nevertheless, shows the persistence of the
old idea. It is conceivable that Richard may have actually
done some such thing, incited by the old romances,[19] but
it is more probable that the writer of the romance was
the one who adapted the idea. Direct literary dependence
on *Ipomedon* of course cannot be shown.

The foregoing consideration of the tournament theme
shows at least how widespread and persistent it is. We
can point to no literary version of it as the undoubted
source of *Ipomedon.* Folk-lore would seem to be the
ultimate source. Probably much in *Ipomedon* is due
to Hugh's own imaginative ingenuity. The literary original from which he adapted the idea may yet be discovered.

III. Relation to *Le Bel Inconnu.*

We turn now to other aspects of the plot, and
find a literary original from which Hugh probably
adapted a motif. His exact debt to it has never

[18] Weber: Metrical Romances; *Richard Coeur de Lion*, 1.257f.

[19] Kittredge (*Harvard Studies and Notes*, Vol. V, p. 94) cites an
interesting case of fact in the life of Richard Warwick, about the
year 1416.

before been definitely pointed out.[20]   This is *Le Bel Inconnu* by Renaud de Beaujeu.   Certainly, if Hugh did not know this romance itself, he must have known a closely allied form of it.   Not only is the action similar, but also at times the phraseology.   Let us put side by side sufficient summary and quotation to make this fact evident:

Ip. goes to Meleager's court in the guise of a fool, to escape recognition. King and knights are at table. Ip. enters, does not dismount, but forces his old nag along with blow and spur. He addresses king, boasts of former prowess, and causes great merriment. He makes covenant with king that he be granted the option of accepting or refusing the first quest in defense of maid or gentle lady which may offer. Queen and steward enter the conversation. King grants covenant. Ip. dismounts, thanks him politely, sits down at table.

Stranger appears at Arthur's court. King and knights are at table. Stranger rides up, salutes king and knights. Arthur invites him to dismount; he replies that he must first be assured of being granted the first gift which he may ask for. The king promises. Stranger then dismounts, is given a mantle, and sits down at table. When asked his name, he says his mother called him "biel fil." Arthur decides to call him "Li Biaus Desconneus."

Then comes into room a maiden on a white mule. Trappings of horse are described at length: ivory saddle, cover of purple "samit," gold, tinkling bells, etc. Ismeine is described elaborately: velvet mantle, "li cors pareit lunc e bel," "le chars blanche," "e cum esteit beas sis visages," "Un cercle d'or el chef aveit, La crine bloie avant pendeit."

Before the tables are moved, comes to court a maiden on a "palefroi." Description of her: "Gente de cors et de vis biele." She was clothed with "samit." "Face ot blance," "cors avenant," "Bel cief avoit, si estoit blonde," "En son cief ot un cercle d'or." Description of horse and trappings: covered with silk, gold and precious stones. With her comes a dwarf, of whom is given a short description.

[20] Kölbing and Miss Weston spoke in passing of parallelism, but no one has compared them closely with reference to other versions of the story.

Ismeine speaks:
"Meleager, reis pouestis,

*　*　*　*　*　*

Entendes, sire, ma querele:
Saluz vus mande la pucele,
La fere, ke nostre nece est.

*　*　*　*　*　*

El mund n'at tant triste pucele.

*　*　*　*　*　*

Sa grand joie turne a reburs,
Se par vus n'at aukun sucurs.
Ma dame se deit desredner
Par le cors d'un bon chevaler."

*　*　*　*　*　*

Li reis entendi sa resun,
Esgarde envirum sa meisun
E n'ot nul d'eus un sol mot dire."
Ismeine reproaches king and
knights. Ip. jumps up and
"Sire, fet il, vus savez ben
Ke reis ne deit mentir pur ren."
He claims the quest. After some
bickering, the king replies,
"Volenters, fol, ore i alez!"
Ismeine objects: "N'irat pas
issi; Od moi ne voil pas, ke il
aut." She leaves and returns to
a dwarf whom she has left outside of the city. Dwarf counsels
her to admit the foolish knight
to her company. She refuses.

Ip. arms:
"un bon hoberc ad tost vestu,
Elasca un heaume gemme.

*　*　*　*　*　*

Menez li fut un bon cheval,
Muntez i est cest bons vassal.
Un escu prent e lance el poing."
He sets out after Ismeine.

Helie speaks:
"Artur," fait ele, "entent a moi.

*　*　*　*　*　*

La fille au roi Gringars te mande
Salus, si te pris et demande
Secors.

*　*　*　*　*　*

Moult a painne, moult a dolor,
Moult ert entree en grant tristor.
Envoie-li tel chevalier
Qui bien li puisse avoir mestier,
Trestot li millor que tu as."

*　*　*　*　*　*

Li rois esgarde et atendoit
Qui le don li demanderoit;
Mais n'i trove demandeor,
Car n'i ot nul qui n'ot paor."
Li biaus Desconnus jumps up
and claims the quest. "Raison
feras, ce m'est a vis;
Rois es, si ne dois pas mentir.
Ne covent a nului faillir."
Ce dit li rois, "Dont i ales."
Helie objects: "Non sera.
Ja, par mon cief, a moi n'ira!"
She cries out against the Round
Table, and leaves the court with
the dwarf.

Bel Inconnu arms:
"Ses cauces lace, l'auberc vest,
Et en son cief son elme trest.
Puis est monte en son destrier;
Son escu li porte et sa lance."
BI takes leave of king, and sets
out after Helie with his squire
Robert. "E le retorne, si le
vit." Helie swears that she will

"Ele ot l'esfrei, s'est returnee
Et veit celui venir l'estree."
Dwarf refuses to send Ip. back,
so that Ismeine herself turns
upon him and tells him peremp-
torily to go back. Ip. answers
in his role of fool.

not willingly suffer his company,
and counsels him to go back.
BI says he will not return, and
dwarf intercedes for him.

About here the direct parallelism ceases, for the succeeding adventures in each story differ widely. In
Ipomedon we have the three fights with the relatives of
Leonin, and in *Le Bel Inconnu* we have the fight at the
ford, the fight with the three avengers, the adventure
with the giants, the sparrow-hawk adventure, all the adventures at L'Ile D'Or, the disenchantment of the serpent
woman, etc. It is interesting to observe, however, that
Hugh has evidently retained a proper name from the
story he was following, namely, that of Malgis, whom he
represents as first to fight for possession of Ismeine. This
is doubtless Malgeris, the knight who fights against BI
at the Ile D'Or. In the Middle English *Libeus Desconus*
he is a giant named Maugys. It is rather remarkable that
Hugh should have derived nearly all his proper names
from classical sources, and yet should have retained this
one as an additional foot-print to mark where he had been
for material.

Schofield[21] has had occasion to compare carefully
four versions of this maiden and dwarf episode: *Libeaus
Desconus, Le Bel Inconnu, Wigalois,* and *Carduino,* in
Middle English, Old French, Middle High German, and
Italian, respectively. An inspection of the parallel sum-
maries which he gives, coupled with the comparison just
given above, shows that, as compared with the others,

[21] *Studies on the Libeaus Desconus,* Harvard Studies and Notes,
Vol. IV.

Ipomedon and *Le Bel Inconnu* are very closely related. Let us point out details common to these two and lacking in the others. (1) Hero rides up while the king is at table. (2) He remains obstinately seated on horse-back till his request is granted. (3) The dwarf takes no part in the conference with the king. (4) Elaborate description is given in similar phraseology of the messenger lady. (5) She begins her speech by delivering salutation from her mistress. (6) Messenger explains at length the adventure to be undertaken. This is true of *Carduino* also, but not of the others. (7) The king looks around and waits for someone to offer himself. (8) The hero prevails on the king by saying that, since he is a king, he should not lie. (9) The messenger is loud in her complaint of the treatment given her. (10) Elaborate description of the arming of hero. This is also true of *Libeaus Desconus.* (11) Tholomeu in *Ip.* somewhat resembles the squire Robert in *BI.* No such character in other versions. (12) Similarity of phraseology when the messenger looks back and sees hero approaching. In only two minor points does *Ipomedon* resemble the other versions as opposed to *BI.* (1) The messenger rides on a white mule. In *BI* the horse is simply "un palefroi," but in *Libeaus Desconus* and in *Wigalois,* the color white is given. (2) Ipomedon wishes to have the option of undertaking or of refusing the first fight in defense of lady who asks aid. In *BI* the hero asks simply that he be granted the first request (unspecified) that he shall make. In *Lib. Desc.,* like Ip., he asks definitely for permission to undertake the first fight which offers. Wigalois also makes a definite request, but not until after the messenger has come and stated her case. Very little significance, however, can be seen in these details of difference. In regard to the

second point of deviation from *BI,* we should remember
that Ipomedon comes to court with a very special purpose,
namely, to meet that messenger who, he feels sure, will
come thither. He must therefore make the special request
to provide for the contingency of someone's coming on a
similar errand before Ismeine. We therefore see that
Hugh was forced to depart from the story before him, in
order to adapt the incident to his own plot, and therefore
his agreement here with the other versions might well be
a coincidence.

In view of this strong resemblance, and of a few other
passages[22] where the phraseology is similar, it seems probable that Hugh had before him Renaud's poem, or else a
French source for Renaud's poem. Hippeau places the
date of *Le Bel Inconnu* as approximately 1190. If Hugh
made use of it, it almost certainly was written before 1187.

With this whole episode should be remembered the
Gareth and Lynet story in Book VI of Malory's *Morte
Darthur.* Weber has said:[23] "The treatment which Ipomedon receives from the damsel * * * bears great similarity
to that experienced by Libeus Desconus * * * and by
Beaumains in Caxton's *Morte d'Arthur.* The latter adventure is undoubtedly borrowed from one of the two former;
but whether the author of the *Libeus* or he who penned
Ipomedon is entitled to the claim of priority of invention
it is now impossible to decide." (Weber probably knew
only an English version of *Ipomedon.*) Sommer, in his
investigation of Malory's sources, has found no source for
Book VI; the presumption, however, is that the source
was French prose, possibly a lost section of some *Prose*

---

[22] Cf. Ip. lines 377f., 395f., 407f., 2225f., 2245f., and 7956f., with
BI, lines 3255f., 2198f., 2214f., 2408f., 3255f., and 4658f.

[23] Metrical Romances, Vol. III, p. 363.

Lancelot. Certainly Malory did not base his story wholly or directly either on the *LD-BI* story, or on *Ipomedon,* or on any other known version. It agrees now with *LD-BI,* now with *Ipomedon;* and again it differs widely from them and from any other version of the story.

IV. RELATION .TO *Tristan.*

Through the maiden and dwarf episode, one feature is essentially characteristic of *Ipomedon:* The hero's assumed role of fool, adopted in order to accomplish his designs the better. This idea is clearly a skilful way to avoid logical difficulties in Hugh's ·plot. Ipomedon had been at Meleager's court before, and could not therefore ride up, like the Fair Unknown, to demand the quest openly. He must go in disguise. Kölbing at this point cites the story of *Tristan;* and investigation shows that Hugh may very probably have remembered Tristan's "folie."[24] Surely this Tristan episode, which space forbids us to summarize and compare carefully with Ip., is much like the corresponding episode in *Ipomedon.* The hero has already been at court, and, wishing to return, adopts the disguise of fool; he cuts his hair, scrapes his skin, and puts on old clothes; he comes in while the king, queen and nobles are feasting; he sets the whole company in a roar of laughter with his fooling. The essence of his fooling is this: he tells the absolute truth about certain former

[24] Two versions are preserved in Old French verse, pub. by Michel: *Tristan,* Londres, 1835. Vol. II, p. 89, and Vol. I, p. 215. The second is much shortened. The episode is not found in the English *"Sir Tristrem,"* nor in Gottfried von Strassburg's *"Tristan."* It appears in a greatly changed form in Old Norse prose, printed by Kölbing: *"Die Nordische und die Englische Version der Tristan Sage."* Heilbronn, 1878.

occurrences, of which at least one other in the company besides himself knows; but because of his disguise his remarks are not taken in earnest, or are not understood, so that in his mouth they seem broadly witty. Of course, many other instances of assumed foolishness or madness may be cited, but that particular type which manifests itself in making fun at the expense of the hearers by allusions to past events which they do not recognize as true, appears, as far as the writer knows, only in *Tristan* and *Ipomedon*. Versions of the *Tristan* story existed before Hugh's time; Chrestien, for example, often refers to Tristan, and probably wrote a version himself. Though the episode does not occur in all versions of the *Tristan* story, there is no reason for thinking that it is not sufficiently old for Hugh to have known it.

V. Fight Between Brothers.

One of the principal minor themes of *Ipomedon* is the hero's discovery that Capaneus is his half-brother. This discovery is prepared for by the poet with some artistic skill. He does not give away this point of his story at the beginning, as many mediaeval poets might do. No hint is dropped of the relationship between the two knights, until they have fought to a standstill and Capaneus has caught sight of the ring. Then, however, we can see how their lives have been converging.

The fight between relatives, when neither knows the other, is a dearly beloved situation among mediaeval writers. Very frequently the combat is between father and son. This subject has been carefully investigated by Potter,[25] whose book contains an appendix giving a

---

[25] M. A. Potter: *Sonrab and Rustum*, London, 1902. See appendix, p. 207.

list, gathered from folk-lore and romance, of twenty-seven combats between brothers. In not one of these, however, does the identification by a ring occur. *Ipomedon* seems to be unique in this respect. Identification by a ring, however, is not unusual in stories of combat between father and son. Good examples of this are found in the lays of *Doon*[26] and *Milun.*[27] It cannot be said that Hugh adapts the idea very happily to suit his situation, for he apparently does not see the logical difficulties in the way. It is quite natural for a father to leave a ring with the mother to be placed on the boy's finger when he should grow up, but does the ring idea suit brothers? Capaneus and Ipomedon are apparently about the same age, and how should Capaneus know the ring given Ipomedon by the mother of them both? If the queen had known where Capaneus was, she would not have resorted to the ring as a means of bringing the brothers together. It would then appear that she had lost all knowledge of her former son, in early years, and we are not told how a long-lost son should know that his mother had another son by a second marriage, and that he might recognize him by means of a ring. Probably Hugh derived his idea from some such story as *Doon* or *Milun,* but did not show his usual skill in adaptation.

VI. Claim of Latin Original.

Thus far in investigating the sources of *Ipomedon* we have not considered the words of the poet himself in his

[26] *Romania,* VIII, p. 59.

[27] *Die Lais de Marie de France.* Ed. K. Warnke. Halle, 1885, p. 152f.

prologue. After commenting on the duty of transmitting
one's knowledge for the benefit of others, he continues in
substance as follows: "I marvel greatly at those wise
clerks who understand several languages, that they have
passed by this history, so that they have not kept it in
memory. I don't say that he did not tell it well, who has
written it down in Latin; but there are more laymen
than learned men, and if the Latin be not translated,
scarcely will they understand. Therefore I wish to tell
the story in French as briefly as I know how, and· then
both clerk and layman will understand."

This claim of a Latin original is very doubtfully true.
After once getting the prologue off his hands, Hugh does
not in any subsequent passage of his long poem allude to
an original of any kind. Moreover, it seems to have been
a rather common trick for a romancer to protest
that his original was written in Latin, in order to gain
the readier hearing for his own fabrications. The authority of Latin was great. Ward, in his Catalogue, considers several cases in point. There is much doubt that
there ever existed a certain "grand liure del graal" in
Latin, kept in the abbey of Salisbury, out of which are
said to be translated Map's *"liure del graal"* (cf. Ward,
p. 348); the *Tristan,* by Luces de Gast (Ward, 357, 363);
and the *Meliadus* by Helie de Borron. The ascription to
a Latin source in *Perceforest* is a clear case of lying
(Ward, 378). The prologue to a prose *Saint Graal*
says the book was first written by Christ, and then came
"mes sires robers de borron qui ceste estoire translate de
latin en franchois" (Ward, 340).

We have still better reason, however, than this *a priori*
reason, for doubting a Latin source for *Ipomedon.* Let
us compare with Hugh's prologue two others, that of the

Roman de Thebes, and that of the *Roman de Troie.* I
first quote certain lines from the *Ipomedon.*

> Moult me mervail de ces clers sages,
> Ky entendent plusurs langages,
> K'il ont lesse ceste estorie,
> Ke mis ne l'ont en memorie; etc.—
> Si li Latin n'est translatez
> Gaires n'i erent entendanz;
> Por ceo voil jeo dire en romanz
> A plus brevment qe jeo saurai,
> Si entendrunt and clerc and lai, etc.—
> Mes pur hastiver la matire,
> Nos estovra par bries motz dire:
> Fors la verrour n'y acrestrai,
> Dirai brefment ceo que j'en sai, etc.—
> Ne voil tut mon sen celer mes:
> Or m'escotez si aiez pes!

Certain lines from the prologue to the *Roman de Thebes*
are as follows:

> Qui sages est nel deit celer
> Ainz por co deit son sen monstrer
> Que, quant serra del siecle alez,
> En seit pues toz jorz remembrez, etc.—
> Por co ne vueil mon sen taisir
> Ma sapience retenir;
> Ainz me delet a aconter
> Chose digne de remembrer,
> Or s'en voisent de tot mestier,
> Se ne sont clerc o chevalier
> Car aussi pueent escouter
> Come li asnes al harper.

From the prologue to the *Roman de Troie* come the following lines:

> Salemons nos enseigne et dit
> Et si lit len en son escrit
> Que nul ne deit son sen celer,
> Ainz le deit len si demostrer
> Que len i ait prou et enor.

(They who find valuable old books and keep silent about
them verily do foolishly).

Et por co me voil travaillier
Et une estoire comencier,
Que de latin ou gie la truis
Se j'ai lo sen, et se jo puis
La voldrai si en romanz metre, etc.—
Dire vus dei ci a bries motz
De quel fait iert li livres toz.

It looks as if Hugh were adapting ideas for his
prologue from these. Moreover, his debt to the *Roman de
Thebes* does not end here. It seems very probable that
Hugh derived from it many of his proper names. The
following names appear in each romance: Adrastus,
Amphion, Amphiaras (in *Ip.*, Amfiorax), Antenor,
Capaneus, Creon, Daire (in *Ip.*, Daires), Diana, Drias,
Egeon, Eurimedon, Ipomedon, Ismaine, Meleager, Minos,
Nestor, Tholmes (in *Ip.*, Tholomeu).[28] Kölbing, following Ward, thought that Hugh might have known enough
Latin to read in the *"Fabulae"* of Hyginus about the seven
kings slain before Thebes. Kölbing states that in Hyginus
Capaneus and Hippomedon are mentioned as uterine
brothers—the relationship which they bear in Hugh's
romance; but this is an error. The words in Hyginus are
these: "Capaneus Hipponoi filius ex Astynome Talai filia
sorore Adrasti Argivus," and later, "Hippomedon Mnesi-
machi filius ex Mythidice Talai filia sorore Adrasti
Argivus." It thus appears that Capaneus and Ipomedon
were merely first cousins, their mothers being sisters; so

[28] Kölbing and Ward were apparently unacquainted with this fact.
L. Constans, however, recognized it in his preface to the *Roman de
Thebes: "Le Roman de Thebes*, a resu un prologue et une suite. * * *
Je veux parler des romans d' *Ipomedon* and de *Prothesilaus*, dont
l'auteur est Huon de Rotelande, de Credenhill, en Cornuailles. * * *
Ipomedon * * * emprunte presque tous ses personnages au *Roman de
Thebes*, auquel il se réfère dans un passage curieux." Of course it
is not fair to call *Ip.* merely a prologue to the *Roman de Thebes;*
neither is Credenhill in Cornwall.

what at first seemed like a fairly strong argument that
Hugh knew Hyginus, since in the *Roman de Thebes* these
two heroes are not mentioned as relatives, becomes weaker.
In the *R. de Th.*, however, they are introduced together.
Cf. 1. 2003 and 2007. Ward says that Hugh may have
been distorting a little knowledge from Hyginus when he
says of Amfiorax (*i. e.,* Amphiaraus) that he was a "devin"
attached to Adrastus the duke of Athens. But this fact
was easily derivable from the *R. de Th.*, cf. 1. 2025ff.
The reference in Hyginus is very vaguely appôsite. Cf.
Fab. LXXIII. Still further, it seems likely that in
several places Hugh kept the *R. de Th.* in mind as a model,
especially in descriptions of persons.[29]

At the end of *Ip.* we find this significant passage, 1.
10539:

> De ceste estorie, k'ai ci faite,
> Est cele de Thebes estraite:
> A Thebes fut Ipomedon,
> Aillurs querrez, si vus est bon,
> Cument ilokes li avint.

"From this history that I have made, is that of Thebes
continued; Ipomedon was at Thebes,—seek elsewhere, if
you wish, to see how he fared there." Hugh may be trying
to find a proper place for his story in the eyes of those
who already knew the *R. de Th.* Where have you heard
about these people? In the History of Thebes, to be sure.
My story belongs in time just before the events chronicled
there.

In view of this evidence, it looks as if we had caught

---

[20] Compare R. de Th. 733ff. with Ip. 401ff.; Th. 1. 3802 and 8427ff.
with Ip. 2201ff.—very similar passages. Also Th. 1. 4355 with the
tournament descriptions in Ip. Also Th. 1. 3391-3407; 4412ff.;
4427ff. One of Hugh's favorite tricks of style is anaphora, and this
device is frequently employed also in Th. Cf. 1. 2810, 4899, 4555.

Hugh practising his "art of lying" when he professed a
Latin original for his romance. Especially in those por-
tions where he appears to be adapting from contemporary
French literature is a Latin original almost impossible.
The *Roman de Thebes* goes back ultimately to Statius,
and we can conceive Hugh claiming for his story the same
authority in Latin which this romance, already popular
perhaps, claimed and possessed. Several other works
besides the *Roman de Thebes* and the *Roman de Troie* were
adapted, if not translated from Latin about this time and
before. We may cite the *Alexander* story, resting on the
Latin version by Julius Valerius of the Pseudo-Callis-
thenes; the *Eneas,* perhaps by Benoit, a travesty on the
Aeneid in the spirit of the middle ages; Chrestien's
adaptation of Ovid, now lost; and *Jules Cesar* (13th cent.)
from the *Pharsalia* of Lucan.[30]   It was natural, therefore,
for a poet who wished to give currency to a romance of
home manufacture to tell a white lie about a Latin source.

VII.   Place Among Romances.

Now Gaston Paris[31] classes both *Ipomedon* and *Pro-*
thesilaus as coming into French from Byzantine sources
by oral tradition without passing through Latin. This
would happen during the time of the crusades, when connections between Frenchmen and Greeks became direct.
Under the same caption he places the following romances:
Eracle, by Gautier d'Arras, 1160; *Floire et Blanchefleur*
(12th cent.) ; *Florimont* (1188) ; *Athis et Porphirias;*
Comte de Poitiers (12th cent.) ; *Roman de la Violette*
(1225) ; *Floire et Jeanne; Guillaume de Dole; Constant*

---

[30] For these and other examples see Gaston Paris: *La Litt. Fran-*
çaise au Moyen Age, second ed., 1890. Chapter II.

[31] *La Litt. Française au Moyen Age.* Chapter III.

l'empereur; Manekine (13th cent.) ; *Partenopeus de Blois*
(12th cent.) ; *Cliges; Cleomades; Floriant et Florette;
Guillaume de Palerme; L'Escoufle; Clarus;* and *Berinus.*
Of the group as a whole, he says in substance: "All these
have in general the same style and the same tone, as they
have the same form,—octosyllabic verses rhyming in
couplets. The principal subject is love, which, hindered
during the story, ends by triumphing. There are mingled
with this innumerable adventures on sea and land, enchantments, predictions, and metamorphoses. Destined for
elegant society, these romances have usually sought part
of their success in the portrayal of its customs, in the
exact and brilliant description of its exterior life."

It is noteworthy that for nearly every one of these
romances, except for *Ipomedon* and *Prothesilaus,* Gaston
Paris adds a clause or two, sometimes more, to show the
Greek or Byzantine element which he discovers. It might
appear that he wished to classify *Ipomedon* somewhere,
and, influenced by the Greek names, possibly, and the
scene laid in Sicily and Italy, thought it convenient to
call it Byzantine. We have seen, however, that the names
do not imply a direct Greek source, and that the scene does
not necessarily imply such. The character of the story,
moreover, is not happily described as "innumerable adventures on sea and land, enchantments, predictions, and
metamorphoses." Still less is it described by Ten Brink,[32]
who, in speaking of the romantic themes brought through
the crusaders from Byzantine and Late Greek sources,
says: "As to subject-matter, we find a pair of lovers who
are pursued or parted, who endure all sorts of adventures,
and are happily rescued from ever-recurring perils. The
execution shows an absence of all analysis of motive and

[32] *History of English Literature,* I, p. 170. Translated by Kennedy,
1889.

of all portrayal of character. There is a predominance of chance, an effeminate sentimentality in the treatment of the erotic element, together with detailed descriptions of beautiful gardens, fountains, etc. The favorite romantic apparatus consists of storms, shipwreck, land or sea robbers, caves in which men hide, and the like." He does not include *Ipomedon* under this head, however,—does not mention it at all, indeed.

Ipomedon can hardly be placed, as Paris places it, in such company, however honorable that company may be. *Ipomedon* seems essentially like a manufactured romance, in which Hugh has made free use of the ideas of his predecessors. In a stock prologue he invested his story with the authority of a Latin source. With much skill he elaborated, keeping his attention well fixed on the main plot of the story which he had outlined, and resisting the besetting mediaeval sin of rambling digression. His romance cannot be called Arthurian, though if he had borrowed his names from Chrestien's romances instead of from the *Roman de Thebes,* and had localized the story in England instead of Sicily, the difference from Arthurian romance would not be great. It is not among the biographical romances, so-called, where the romancer traces the fortunes of his hero from the days of his father to the days of his grandchildren, and strings adventures on the life thread of each. It belongs to none of the great cyclic romances. It can hardly be called Byzantine. It might be called a sporadic romance, based partially on folk-lore, and manufactured with conscious literary art by an Englishman, who, like the other dominant Englishmen of his day, happened to write French, and who had never heard of the modern sin of plagiarism.

THE MOORS IN SPANISH POPULAR POETRY BEFORE 1600.

By William Wistar Comfort, Ph.D.

THE MOORS IN SPANISH POPULAR POETRY BEFORE 1600.

Sismondi, together with Fauriel, Schack, Wolf, Durán, Dozy, Menéndez y Pelayo and the whole century of historians who have dealt with the influence of the Mahometan peoples upon European civilization, do full justice to the mediaeval foes of Christian Europe. Not only are the Arab triumphs in science, philosophy and literature rehearsed in general by nineteenth century historians, but individual enthusiasts stand out here and there who would have us believe that Christian Europe owes a great part of what is best in its arts and sciences to the learning and accomplishments of those divers races which we may group under their mediaeval appellation of Saracens.

Leaving aside the unquestioned interchange of influence upon the natural sciences, philosophy and architecture which resulted from the shock of Christian and Moslem in southern Europe during a period of seven or eight centuries, it is interesting to consider the aspect under which the Saracens appeared to the purveyors of popular literature in southern Europe. It is not a question here of borrowed *motifs* in the French *fabliaux* and *contes,* or of the alleged adopted forms of verse in the early Provençal and Spanish lyric poetry. The inflow of oriental fable upon European literature is as unquestioned nowadays by scholars as the development of lyric verse forms in southern Europe independent of all Arab influence is stoutly maintained. Rather are we concerned to learn just what was the impression made upon the mind of the European from the twelfth to the sixteenth century by the legendary or actual presence of the Saracens. To borrow the convenient phrase of Gaston Paris, what was the "poetic history" of the Saracens in European literature ? How much of a position did they occupy, and in what fashion did the Christian poets use them as *dramatis personae?*

To answer this question in complete detail is too great an undertaking for our present purpose. The Spanish *romances,* the Old French *chansons de geste* and *romans d'aventure,* the Italian court epics of Pulci, Boiardo, Ariosto and Tasso,—all present the Saracens. They are stock personages in the heroic poetry of the Romance domain until the sixteenth century. The literary field which they have invaded is of vast size,—co-extensive, indeed, with the European territory once threatened by their arms. For the purpose of making our observations more tangible, we may confine our attention in this essay to the treatment of one of the Saracen peoples, in this case the Moors, in the Spanish popular poetry before 1600. By referring in the course of our examination to the Saracens as they appear in France and Italy, we shall at the same time get some comparative view of their treatment at the hands of the three Christian nations with which the Infidels came chiefly into contact. Though not as exhaustive as we hope to make this study at a later date, the general history of the Saracens in Christian poetry may here be traced more distinctly than has been done heretofore by those literary critics who have been concerned with the Saracens only incidentally.

It must be stated at the outset that nowhere in the literature which we are about to survey are the followers of Mahomet represented as we must believe them actually to have been. Nowhere, except in Spain, were circumstances favorable to any sympathetic and detailed examination of a people from whom the western Christians felt themselves to be separated by that widest of dividing clefts —religion.   Even in Spain, during the eight centuries of partial occupation by the Moors, the essential separation between the two races seems to have been always felt, and by many laws to have been accentuated.   Schack's observation commends itself as being very near the truth: "One cannot escape the tremendous cleft which separated the Christians and Mahometans in matters of belief, and made excessively difficult any contact of the two civilizations."[1]   If, in spite of numerous qualifications, the truth of this remark may be asserted in the case of Spain, with much greater confidence can it be asserted in the case of France and Italy, where the contact between the oriental and occidental peoples was never more than of a fortuitous and temporary nature.   The actual incursions of Saracens into the territory of France and Italy occurred, for the most part, so long before the composition of the earliest poetry we have in the vulgar tongues, that any description of the Infidels based upon observation was out of the question.   Before the time of our earliest French epic poems, the Saracens had become assured of a prominent and permanent inheritance in the *trouvère's* pack of legendary lore, but an inheritance saddled withal by literary convention and popular prejudice.   Strange to relate, the revival of interest in the Saracen awakened by the Crusades and by the later piratical onslaughts of the Berbery corsairs availed little to bring the true Saracen any nearer to the popular mind.   Not until Cervantes took up the subject with his practical experience and his love of realism, as part of a political crusade, do we

[1] *Poesie und Kunst der Araber* (1865), v. II, pp. 91, 92.

get any true picture of the life and manners of the hostile races.[2]   Nowhere in the mediaeval literature of France, so far as we are aware, is a Saracen to be found portrayed with the truth and the colors we should expect from an eye-witness. Yet, in French narrative poetry of the eleventh to the fourteenth century the Saracen is everywhere. He is well-nigh as inevitable in a Franch *chanson de geste* and in many of the *romans d'aventure* as are the Moros and Moriscos of Spain in the heroic poems and popular *romances* of the Peninsula.

In the earliest monuments of Spanish heroic poetry, such as the *Poema del Cid* (1150 circ.) and the *Poema de Fernan Gonçalez* (1250 circ.) one is struck by the fact that the Moors are taken for granted. The Christian poets feel under no necessity to explain their presence, nor do the Moors possess the slightest romantic interest for the Christian public. Since the time of Don Pelayo's stalwart resistance until the reconquest of Alfonso, as narrated in the *Crónica General,* it was one long up-hill fight to regain the northern and central kingdoms from the Infidel invader. Thus, we should expect to find the Moors consistently regarded as enemies of the true God, to be uncompromisingly converted or slaughtered. So, indeed, we do find them in the earliest French *chansons de geste.* But in Spain we have to reckon with the innumerable jealousies between local Christian monarchs and the frequent quarrels between these monarchs and their powerful vassals. In other words, the unified resistance of Christian Spain opposed to the solid attack of the Moors is in popular poetry as far from being established as it is in history. It is unnecessary to cite the numerous instances

---

[2] Cf. Emile Chasles, *Michel de Cervantes: Sa vie, son temps* (2d ed., 1866), Chapter V.

of political alliances for private gain narrated as existing between individual Moorish and Christian chiefs. In Spain we find no parallel to the French and Italian conception of Christendom uncompromisingly arrayed under Charlemagne against the definitely planned aggression of the Infidels. Policy and expediency weighed more than religious affiliation in the early relations of the two races in Spain.

As Dozy has well shown,[3] the people were interested in the Cid primarily as a great independent vassal, who could dispense with the favor of an ungrateful king. The *Poema del Cid* does not sing the praises of a defender of Christendom, but of an independent free-booter, who as time went on became more refined and religious to meet the requirements of a higher civilization. There is this essential difference between the first great national expressions in the *Roland* and the *Poema del Cid*. To the Cid the killing of Moors is only an occasional incident in the securing of booty (470f., 498f., 1236, etc.). When it suits his purpose, the Cid is lenient with the Moors. When he leaves Casteion

"Los moros y las moras bendiziendol estan" (541).

When he leaves Alcoçer, the Moors exclaim

"Vaste, myo Çid; nuestras oraçiones uayante delante" (853).

One of the most sympathetic of the secondary characters in the poem is the Moorish king, Avengaluon of Molina, a useful ally of the Cid throughout, and called by him, with good reason, "myo amigo de paz."

It is not unusual to find Moors and Christians fighting on the same side: as when Count Remont of Barcelona

---

[3] *Recherches sur l'histoire et la littérature de l'Espagne pendant le moyen âge* (2d ed., 1860) v. II, pp. 222, 223.

led a mixed host against the Cid (*Cid,* 988), when Bernard
del Carpio joined with Marsil(io), king of Saragossa, to
defeat the Twelve Peers of Charlemagne (*Fernan Gonçalez,* 141), and when Fernán González reproves Don
Sancho of Navarre for having in the past allied himself
with Moors to fight Christians (*F. G.,* 288). There is
just a suggestion of that bitter religious competition
familiar in the French epic poems: when the Cid, after his
conquest of Valencia, established Jerónimo (that Spanish
Turpin) as bishop of Valencia, the poet says:

"Dios, que alegre era todo christianismo,
Que en tierras de Valençia señor avie obispo!" (*Cid,* 1305-6).

In the other camp, we read (1620) of how Yucef, king
of Morocco, grieved to hear of the victory in Valencia of
those who worship "Jhesu Christo." But we suspect these
to be concessions to the deepened religious convictions of
the twelfth century, and that the Cid was right when he
thanked the Creator for his victories and spoils regardless
of the religion of his victims:

"Antes fu minguado, agora rico so,
Que he auer y tierra y oro y onor,
E son myos yernos yfantes de Carrion;
Moros y christianos de mi han grant pauor; (*Cid,* 2494f.)

The point upon which we would insist, then, is the
matter-of-fact, business-like tone which is employed here
in speaking of the Moors. They are enemies, of another
religion, to be sure. But no personal hatred is expressed
for them, no religious crusade is preached against them,
and, if it be expedient, alliance with them is winked at.
There is no trace here of that bitterness employed by
Ibn-Bassâm, the Arab writer of 1109, whom Dozy quotes,[4]

[4] *Op. cit.,* v. II, p. 7f.

and who accompanies every mention of Alfonso with the
hearty exclamation: "May God curse him!"

In the *Poema de Fernan Gonçalez* (1250 circ.) we feel
a distinct advance in the sentiment of Castilian nationality
and, consequently, in the hostility toward the Moors.
Though we are still following the career of an individual
hero, we realize at once that his chief claim to popularity
rests in his valor against the Moors, "la gente descreyda"
(173, 174). Indeed, F. G. dedicates himself solemnly
in God's name to the reconquest (184f.). The Moorish
king, Almozor (*i. e.,* Almanzor of the tenth century, and
hence not really a contemporary of F. G.),[5] rallies a great
host to fight F. G.,—a host of 5,000 legions. The *Crónica
General*[6] is more conservative with its allowance of seven
legions of 6,666 men each on the Moorish side. But the
exaggeration of the enemy's numbers is a constant trait,
especially in the French heroic poems, and is used to
enhance the credit of the Christians' victories. It may
be added that the mediaeval audience accepted the proportion of ten Saracens to one Christian as about the
proper odds to provide an interesting fight. In the
Spanish poems, where the Christians are counted by hun-
dreds, the Moors are rated by thousands; and in the
French poems, where the French are counted by thousands, the Saracens move like a vast horde:

> "Des tentes issent aussi espesement
> Come li pluie, quant le cachent li vent."
> (*Anseïs von Karthago,* 6658-59)

When fighting against such odds, it was no disgrace to
succumb; to win was sublime.

The religious element is prominent throughout the

---

[5] Cf. the note of Professor C. C. Marden in his edition of the poem.
[6] Ed. of Menéndez Pidal, p. 392.

Poema de Fernan Gonçalez, and brings this poem well within the sphere of our observations made in another place[7] regarding the Saracens in the *chansons de geste.* The hero is supported by the promises of God made through chosen vessels, and upon these promises he rests confident:

> "Alli fue demostrrado el poder del Mexyas,
> El conde fue David e Almozor(re) Golias" (*F. G.*, 267).

After this great victory it is true that the booty is still detailed with satisfaction as a valuable asset;[8] but the Count uses his share in endowing the Church, as he had previously promised to do (278, 246f.).

This poem contains one other interesting reference to the popular estimation of the Moors as enchanters and experts in black art. Explaining the nature of a fiery serpent in the heavens, whose appearance had terrified his men, Fernán González says:

> "Los moros, byen sabedes,(que) se guian por estrellas,
> Non se guian por Dios que se guian por ellas,
> Otrro Criador nuevo han fecho ellos dellas,
> Diz(en) que por ellas veen muchas de maraui(e)llas.
>
> A y (avn) otrros que saben muchos encantamentos,
> Fazen muy malos gestos con sus esperamentos,
> De rreuoluer las nuves e (de) rreuoluer los vyentos,
> Muestra les el diablo estos entendymientos.
>
> Ayvntan los diablos con sus conjuramentos,
> Aliegan se con ellos e fazen sus conventos,
> Dizen de los pas(s)ados todos sus fallimientos,
> Todos fazen conçejo, los falsos carvonientos.
>
> Algun moro astroso que sabe encantar,
> Fyzo aquel diablo en syerpe fygurar,
> Por amor que podies(s)e a vos (otrros) (mal) espantar,

---

[7] Vid. *Publications of the Modern Language Association of America,* v. XXI.

[8] Plunder by the Christians is but rarely mentioned in the French and Italian poems. Cf., however, *Les Enfances Ogier,* 6899; *Gerusalemme Liberata,* XIX, 52; *Mambriano,* XVII, 67f.; XXXV.

Con este tal enganno cuydaron (se) nos tornar.
Commo sodes sesudos byen podedes saber
Que ellos non han poder de mal a nos fazer,
Qua quito les don Cristo el su fuerte poder,
Veades que son locos los que lo quieren creer."

F. G., 473-477.

Here the Moors are represented as astrologers in league with the devil, who has taught them his arts, but of which the true Christian need have no fear. This reputation of the mediaeval Saracens as astrologers, soothsayers, or wizards may be regarded as a frequent, though not greatly emphasized, trait in popular poetry.[9] That it is the pale reflection of the actual superiority of the Arabs in the domain of the natural sciences seems probable. To this superiority and to the attitude of the Church toward Arab learning the historians of Arab civilization have done full justice. But as Schack,[10] D'Ancona,[11] Renan[12] and others have remarked, the ignorance of the Saracens' religion displayed by the mediaeval Christians is monumental. It is difficult for us to conceive how such gross misrepresentation of the Infidels' tenets could have been accepted, even by the most ignorant of the Christian masses. Leaving aside the ecclesiastical attitude toward Mahometanism, we have found nothing in the popular poetry of Spain which would indicate any interest in or knowledge of the religion of the Moors. If the popular poets possessed any such knowledge, they made no use of it,—not even as much as did the French poets.[13] By

[9] The Saracen magician is a standard character in the *Ger. Lib.* and in the Italian court epic poems.

[10] *Op. cit.*, v. II, p. 92f.

[11] *Giornale storico della Lett. ital.*, XIII, pp. 192-281.

[12] *Etudes d'histoire religieuse.*

[13] Cf. *Couronnement de Louis*, 847f.; *Floovant*, 373; *Gaufrey*, 3582; *Aiol*, 10090; *Conquête de Jérusalem*, 5546.

way of compensation, in the Spanish poems there is no
ridiculous talk about the Saracens' gods and idols, such
as Apolin, Cahu, Tervagan, Diana, Mahom and the rest.
Beside Allah, Mahomet alone is mentioned, and is regarded
not as one of the grotesque fraternity just mentioned, but
as the counterpart of the Christians' Messiah,—a prophet
of God. Usually devoted to Mahomet and his cause, the
Saracen is often represented by the Christian poets as
disgusted with his Mahomet and disappointed with his
protection. For instance, after Almozor had lost the battle to Fernán González, he exclaims: "Alas, Mahomet, in
an evil hour did I trust in thee. All thy power is not
worth three beans."[14] With this compare the outbreak
of pagan fury against their idols described in the *Roland*
(2580-91) and in *Fierabras* (p. 156). This puerile doubt
in the efficacy of their gods must have been introduced
for a humorous purpose, to contrast with the abiding faith
of the mediaeval Christian in his God of battles.

To conclude, the religious element in the strife between
Christian and Saracen comes out in the French far more
than in the Spanish narrative poems. From the *Roland*
on till the close of the epic period, the French poet puts
religion in the foreground; for conversions and argument
on religious beliefs between hostile warriors there is always
room in the most animated narrative.[15] Before the
promise of conversion the avenging arm of the French
falls. The things of the Spirit are given the first chance.
In Spain there is little to indicate any altruistic religious
interest on the part of the Christians. We may doubt if
there were actually any such interest during the early

[14] *F. G.*, 268.
[15] Cf. *Roland*, 3661-74; *Mainet* in *Romania*, IV, p. 330; *Cour. de
Louis*, 847f.; *Aliscans*, 1223-27; *Enf. Ogier*, 4453-56; *Chev. Ogier*,
11316-21.

centuries of the Moorish occupation, when the Christians were in the minority. After the taking of Granada in 1492, history tells us of the strenuous endeavors of the State egged on by the Church to coerce the Moorish population to an empty conversion.[16] But even in the *romances* of the sixteenth century, as we shall see, the religious note is lacking. We suspect that the living religious enthusiasm bred by the Crusades, in which the French played so much larger a part than did the Spaniards, may explain this difference in attitude. In the twelfth and thirteenth centuries, when the highly civilized French nation considered itself in a position to dictate to the Saracen foe in the East, the Spaniards were still fighting for their existence on the *frontera*. If one may risk the remark, we should say that the Spaniards from actual experience know far more of what they are speaking when they introduce the Moors in their early poetry, but that they saw nothing in the subject worthy of description or amplification. The French, with far less actual knowledge, made of the Saracen an Infidel *chevalier,* and personified in him the idealized opposition to themselves in the "lutte de l'Europe chrétienne sous l'hégémonie de la France."[17] The Italian poets took over this conception *in toto,* while introducing into the treatment many traits of levity and romance. The Spanish poems reflect an actual state of affairs, with the Christians fighting for their fire-sides, with expediency and compromise as counters in the game; the French and Italian poems reflect an ideal strife between Christendom and Paganism, in which compromise with principle has no place, and where the extermination of heresy is the ultimate goal.

[16] Cf. H. C. Lea, *The Moriscos.*
[17] Gaston Paris, *Histoire poétique de Charlemagne,* p. 16.

The practical realism of the Spanish treatment of the Moors in the historical poems, and the poetic idealism of the French treatment of the Saracens, is explained by the historical relations of these peoples. This fact should be borne in mind by anyone who reads these pages. The French were freed from any imminent danger of invasion by the Saracens at an early date. In our period they did not know as a nation what the African peril was. We should see the romantic side of their relations with the Infidels finding expression at a comparatively early date. The Spaniards until within two centuries still knew the danger of the Berbery corsairs at their very ports. Not until they had gained a heavy upper hand in the fifteenth and the sixteenth centuries do we note the lenient and romantic literary treatment of the Moors and Moriscos invading the *romances*. The struggle for existence is then passed, and the Christian poets can afford to use for artistic purposes the faded orientalism of the western Caliphate.

As bearing upon the twelfth and thirteenth century knowledge concerning the Saracens, a word is in order as to their geographical distribution and their physical characteristics according to the popular poets. The Spanish poems, as we should expect, have the Moors distributed with due regard to the facts. The topography of the wars of reconquest is observed in the heroic poetry with sufficient exactness to make comparison with historical records interesting and profitable. The *Poema del Cid* and the *Poema de Fernan Gonçalez* are as full of topography as the *Crónica General* is full of dates. Whether the enemy be called *Moros, Moriscos, Alárabes, Turcos, Sarricenos* or *Berberiscos,* the Spanish poets of all ages know pretty well what they are talking about, and present their enemies within proper geographical limits. What extravagant notions the French popular poets entertained of the origin and whereabouts of the Saracens it is hardly necessary to tell. Anyone who has read any mediaeval French narrative literature will have given up the fruitless task of identifying the names of Pagan peoples and countries. In this confusion the *Roland* leads off with a score of names before which the most zealous speculation retreats in confusion. Who are *les Ormalois, les Leus, les Eugles, les Soltras?*[18] Where are *Valpenuse, Occiant la déserte, Balide-la-Forte, Floredée?* As to many of the other places and peoples mentioned and which have been identified (?), it may be safely said that the modern scholars know far more about them than did the mediaeval poet. As time went on, confusion became worse confounded. The one desire of the poet, as Professor Geddes has said, is "to name the peoples who have terrorized Christian Europe during the last centuries."[19] Thus we find masquerading as Saracens the Saxons,[20] the Normans,[21] the Danes,[22] and the Albigenses.[23]

As to the individual, there is no attempt in early Spanish verse to describe him either seriously or grotesquely. The great crowd of Africans who arrive at Almozor's summons after his first defeat offers a fine chance for such description (*F. G.*, 383, 384). Their equipment is described in this place, as so frequently in the later *romances;* but not a Pagan in the vast host stands out so that we can see

---

[18] *Les Enfances Ogier* (1275 circ.) offers a somewhat more recognizable assortment of Saracen peoples: Turs, Persant, Arrabis, Esclers, cil de Barbarie, Achopars, Esclavons, Aufricans, Arragons.

[19] Geddes, *La Chanson de Roland* (1906), p. 223.

[20] In the *Chanson des Saisnes.*

[21] In *Aquin* and *Le Roi Louis.*

[22] In *Chronique de Phil. Mouskes.*

[23] In *Garin de Montglane.*

him. And why should the poet describe the dark-skinned peoples ? All his audience had seen them. There was no exotic charm for the Spaniard in an African complexion. He wanted events, not portraits. But in France, where neither the poet nor the audience had ever seen a Saracen, a loose rein was given to the *trouvère's* fancy. Consequently, we have such delightfully naive portraits as those of the *Roland* (1217; 1917-19; 1932-34), *Les Narbonnais* (3803-8), *Gaufrey* (p. 90), and *Couronnement de Louis* (504-510). In these latter a purely conventional portrait of bigness, blackness and fierceness has been evolved as a grotesque embellishment of the poem. Without falling into this comical exaggeration, the French poets were incapable of depicting the Saracen warrior in any different guise from that of the Christian knight. He fought in the same way, his standards of conduct were the same. The poet knew no type of warrior except that which he saw about him; so he contented himself with crying of a sympathetic Saracen hero:

> "Deus! quels vassals, s' oüst chrestientet!"
> *Roland*, 3164.

After having remarked the very slight artistic use made of the Moors in the two great heroic poems of mediaeval Spain, we turn next to the *romances,* or popular ballads, composed, as we have them, from the fifteenth to the seventeenth century. Few questions are more intricate than the origin of many of these *romances*. They have been variously classified: chronologically according to their supposed antiquity, chronologically according to the antiquity of the subjects of which they treat, and thirdly according to the nature of the *genre,*—such as historical, romantic, chevaleresque, burlesque, etc. In any system

of arrangement many escape from all categories and
remain without any certain indication of their pedigree.
We may, however, summarize what has been written as
to the development of the *romances*. There are three
great periods of bloom. The first dates from the earliest
expression of the Spanish people in the vulgar tongue,
when ballads were sung by the people and for the people.
This period closed before 1200, and from it we have no
remains except as they are incorporated in later and more
artistic poetry and in the prose chronicles. The second
period is that of the popular poets,—the *juglares* by profession, who sang for the people in more ambitious strain
the same songs of national heroes. To these were added,
without much regard for chronology or congruity, subjects
borrowed from the "matière de France," the "matière
de Bretagne," and the "matière de Rome la grant." This
period includes the fifteenth century and represents a
rich midway stage between the really popular expression
of the first period and the thoroughly artificial and conventional ballad poetry of the sixteenth and seventeenth
centuries. In this last period, where we meet the work
of Sepúlveda, Laso de la Vega, Timoneda, and even
Góngora, cultivated society has taken up the old popular
material and clothed it now in a new travestied dress, now
in a dress of pseudo-antiquity which it is not always
easy to distinguish from the genuine article. The great
anonymous ballad collections of 1510, 1550 and 1593 contain the meat of this period, to which must be added the
artistic imitations and the *rifacimenti* of such poets as
have just been mentioned.

From Durán's enormous collection of almost two thousand *romances* in his *Romancero General* of 1849, it
requires an internal criticism of exceptional competence

to cull with any certainty those poems which are essentially popular, and to distinguish them from those that are tainted by subjectivity and art. Ticknor says of the *romances:* "Few can be found alluding to known events or to personages that occur before the period immediately preceding the fall of Granada; and even in these few the proofs of a more recent and Christian character are abundant."[24] Wolf, too, maintains that the surest antiquity may be claimed for those relating to wars with the Moors during the second half of the fifteenth century; and, though these contain features which go back to early times, they hardly antedate in their present form the sixteenth century.[25] We have hesitated over what method to pursue in bringing the Moors into the foreground from this vast body of material where they occur at every step. Durán's division, painstaking and conscientious though it be, helps us little for our present purpose. We have decided at last to adopt what is perhaps the most evident plan: that is, to study the Moors first in the poems where they are only incidental, and then to take up the great body of poems in which they are the chief *dramatis personae* After the adoption of this division, it was found that the *romances* divide themselves chronologically upon somewhat the same lines. That is, that the ballads in which the Moors are incidentally treated are relatively early and have some pretentions to historic reliability, while those which present the Moors as an end in themselves are late, artificial and romantic. These last will appropriately conclude our study with some interesting evidence bearing upon the ultimate invasion of Spanish

[24] *History of Spanish Literature,* v. I, p. 156.

[25] Cf. *Studien zur Geschichte der spanischen und portuguesischen Literatur,* pp. 459, 460.

lyric poetry by the exaggerations of that *Orientalismus* which was the Moors' revenge for their banishment from Spain.

The oldest *romances,* at least in their inspiration if not in their final version, are those of the reconquest, such as those dealing with the Cid, Fernán González, Bernardo del Carpio and the Seven Infantes de Lara,—all standard subjects of popular verse for centuries. In them we find all the essential facts narrated, as borrowed from earlier ballads and from the lengthy *crónicas* which stand in such close relation to the *romances.* In most of these ballads the attention is fixed upon the Spanish hero, and the Moors are only incidentally introduced. Hence, we find in them little to add to the primitive evidence already presented. The under-current of religious hostility is still upset by the exigencies of politics and expediency. Christians and Moors mingle fraternally in battle against some common enemy. Courteous and chivalric attentions are shown to distinguished representatives of the opposite faith. Examples of conversions become more frequent, and the rift of religious separation becomes at times well defined as an actual factor in the life of the nation and of the individual. A few instances of this evolution may be noted. They may be the literary reflection of that increasing confidence and didactic tone affected by the Spaniards about 1500 toward their weakening opponents. When Mudarra, the bastard brother of the Infantes de Lara and the son of Count Gonzalo Gustios grows up and is told of the family tragedy by his Moorish mother:

> "Mudarra se baptizó.
> Cristiano tornado había."
>   (No. 693, attrib. to Sepúlveda).

In the Cid's last testament, which is a late poem, he makes a bequest to

> "Gil Diaz tornadizo,
> Que de moro á Dios volvióse."   (No. 896.)

We are saved an excursion afield by the Cid in a sixteenth century ballad, when he politely refuses to visit the Sultan of Persia because the latter is a Pagan. He says to the messenger:

> " 'Si tu Rey fuera cristiano
> Fuera yo á verle á su tierra.' "   (No. 891.)

It is a narrow escape, but happily the condition imposed was sufficient to deter him from the expedition. These are but typical of many instances where the religious distinction is touched upon in individual cases.

Intercourse between the sexes when separated by religion seems to have been forbidden as a theory, just as it is throughout the French epic poems. Two notable passages dealing with historical personages may be quoted, though they are of late composition. Alfonso the Fifth of León gives his sister in marriage to King Audalla of Toledo against her will, in return for aid against other Moorish kings. But she forbids her new spouse to approach her: "I tell you you shall not approach me, because I am a Christian and you a Moor, of another religion very different from mine. I care not for your company, and the sight of you gives me no pleasure. If you lay hands on me and from you I suffer dishonor, the angel of Jesus Christ will strike your body with his trenchant sword" (No. 721). In the ballad the king disregards her wishes, is smitten with the plague, and returns her to her country, where she becomes a nun. Strange as this story may sound in its late pious setting, Dozy has found the historic basis for it in the tenth century.[26] Gabriel Lobo Laso de la Vega has treated another episode in which figure Alfonso the Sixth and the beautiful Zaida, daughter of the king of Seville. Zaida, who has fallen in love with Alfonso by hearsay, is determined to marry him. In reply to her ardent addresses the Christian king replied "that he could not marry her, because his religion forbade him to do what she requested; but that if she would give up her own faith for a better one, he would accept her." This the Moorish maid consented to do, for one who loves knows no law. She became a Christian with great ceremony, and became queen of Castille, whom afterward they called the great Christian Mary (No. 913). This conversion of Saracen women had become a constant trait of romance after the doctrine of all-conquering love was firmly established in European literature. In admitting it, the poets were far enough from the facts, and we should be tempted to say that it is a sure mark of late composition, did we not recall Charlemagne's solicitude in the *Roland* for the conversion of Bramimunde, the captive wife of Marsile. (*Roland*, 3673-74). The later French poems show very artistic use of these international unions, postponed only until the happy conversion and baptism of the Saracen maid can be effected (cf. Guillaume and Orable in the *Prise d'Orange*, Aiol and Mirabel in *Aiol*, Elie and Rosamonde in *Elie de Saint-Gille*, Berart and Flordépine in *Gaufrey*, Gui and Floripas in *Fierabras*, and Gerart and Malatrie in *Beuves de Commarcis*).

The religious reconquest of the Moorish territory is more than once referred to, as it was cursorily in the *Poema del Cid* (see above). When under the reign of Alfonso the Sixth the city of Toledo was taken, the Chris-

Op. cit., v. I., p. 205.

tians proceed to convert the Moorish *mezquita* into a church again. This they do by "cleansing it of false rites, rededicating it to God, and celebrating Mass" under the new archbishop (No. 911). (Cf. No. 931).

But alongside of such traits as these which possess a certain color of historic reliability stand others of a purely romantic nature. Even the so-called historic ballads, dealing with the national heroes, early fell under the romantic influence. The Moors commence to appear in an ever more romantic light. For example, when the Cid was at Valencia, King Búcar comes and makes love to Urraca, the Cid's daughter. The Cid bids his daughter detain Búcar in suitable converse until he can come and administer the chastisement which such temerity deserves (No. 858). When, after the Cid's death, the Christians sally forth from Valencia to fight Búcar, in front of the Moorish host they fall in with a female warrior at the head of a hundred companions like her:

> "Una mora muy gallarda,
> Gran maestra en el tirar
> Con saetas del aljaba
> De los arcos de Turquía;
> Estrella era nombrada
> Por la destreza que había
> En el herir de la jara."[27]   (No. 901.)

Elsewhere we find the romantic element softening the conventionally hostile relations between the two people. The Master of Calatrava, for example, assists a Moor of Granada to elope with his lady-love who was betrothed to another (Nos. 1096-99). Again, that Don Manuel Ponce de León, who was the doughty champion of many a single

---

[27] The female Saracen warrior became a regular romantic feature of the Italian poems.

duel upon the frontier, released his defeated Moorish opponent in order that the latter might join his sweetheart
(No. 1134).   In both cases the sympathy for a lover
outweighs the prescribed attitude which called for the
speedy beheading of the Moor.   These instances are but
straws which show the turn of treatment bestowed upon
the Moors in the so-called historical ballads.   It is only
with general tendencies that we are concerned, and to
multiply quotations is needless.   As Durán has noted,
there is no essential difference between his late historical
ballads and the *romances moriscos novelescos* to which we
shall presently come.   The latter certainly affected the
former.   Indeed, the same known poets wrote both kinds,
and the historical ballads are only historical in so far as
they mention historic characters upon one side or the other.
In spirit they are identical with the avowedly romantic
Moorish ballads in which the Moorish characters and
colors furnish the whole interest.   Before leaving the
historical ballads it should be added that in their last period
of bloom at the end of the sixteenth century they still
present the Spanish sovereigns Charles the Fifth and
Philip the Second in their historic struggle with the Turks
in eastern Europe and with the corsairs upon the sea.
These last ballads are simple history in poetic form, and
add nothing to what has been said regarding the literary
presentation of the Moors.   They lead directly to the classic
period of the Spanish drama in the seventeenth century,
where we still find the Moors playing their ancient rôle,
now treated historically, now romantically.

We come now to the ballads in which the centre of
interest shifts from the Christians to the Moors.   Durán
includes 243 of this class in his first volume, and calls
them *romances moriscos novelescos*.   Though some of these

date from the fifteenth century, the great majority date
from the sixteenth century.   Most of them are anonymous,
but the work of Sepúlveda, Padilla, Laso de la Vega,
Encina, Lucas Rodríguez, and even of Góngora is well represented in this class.   They show forth that literary
tolerance and sympathy for the conquered people which is
far from being equally manifested in the historic treatment of the scattered Moriscos by Church and State.

Here war is only in the background, useful as a chance
for the Moorish braves to exhibit their prowess and honors,
as in a tournament, to be laid at the feet of their ladies.
Indeed, war has now passed into the tournament stage.
The array of one people against another, so familiar in
the French epic and in the Italian poems, has no counterpart here.   We still hear at intervals of battles and sieges
of frontier towns, but the religious interest is out of it.
The scene is described from the stand-point of the individual warrior, and the assets of victory are reckoned in
terms of love.   We find a mixture of European chivalry
with a graft of oriental coloring and Moorish names
which at least sound historical.   That lamentable strife
in Granada between the two great factions of the Aben-
cerrajes and the Cegríes finds its echo all through this
group of ballads.   Many are the fierce jealousies and
hatreds, the plots and deeds of violence which so tore
the Moors apart that they became a prey for the Christian
enemy, ever more consolidated.   The men are shown
fighting or love-making; the women appear a prey to the
passion of love or jealousy.   The women reprove the men
for cowardice as warriors, or for boasters as lovers; the
men berate the women for their fickleness.   The love passion is depicted as all-absorbing.   No division of favors
is tolerated.   No suggestion of oriental polygamy is to

be found.[28]   One must be off with the old before one is on
with the new.   The lovers communicate over the bal-
conies, or, when separated, by letters.   That extreme sus-
ceptibility and suspicion which mark the love passion
among the hot-blooded races is everywhere uppermost.
Yet there is nowhere a suggestion of the carnal, which is
more than can be said of the Italian romances.   The
relation between the sexes before marriage is altogether
above reproach.   What these rites of marriage are, we are
not told.   The disposal of the woman is in the hands of
her father or of the king.   To interfere with the wishes
of the king entails banishment from the court and exposure
of the lovers to all the pains and torments of enforced
separation.

Inasmuch as these romantic ballads deal chiefly with
the period of the frontier wars, the taking of Granada
and the occasional early insurrections of the Moriscos,
the taking of captives is frequently mentioned.   The
beauty of the ballads dealing with the Christian Moriana
and the Moor Galván are, perhaps, the most artistic
and among the oldest of the *genre*.   The setting of the
game of drafts between the rich Moor and his unwilling
captive is in the best ballad style:

> "Moriana en un castillo
> Juega con el moro Galvane;
> Juegan los dos á las tablas
> Por mayor placer tomare.
> Cada vez qu'el moro pierde
> Bien perdía una cibdade;

[28] We can recall no reference in popular literature to polygamy
among the Saracens, except that in the *Chanson d'Antioche* V, 42,
where the crusade against the Christians is preached:

> " 'Bien peut avoir dis femes cil qui or cinc en a,
> Ou quinze ou vint ou trente, ou tout com lui plaira.' "

Cuando Moriana pierde
La mano le da á besare.
Del placer qu'el moro toma
Adormescido se cae.
Por aquellos altos montes
Caballero vió asomare:
Llorando viene y gimiendo,
Las uñas corriendo sangre
De amores de Moriana
Hija del rey Moriane.
Captiváronla los moros
La mañana de Sant Juane,
Cogiendo rosas y flores
En la huerta de su padre."   (No. 7.)

Exterior description, indeed, is the special charm of the
Moorish *romances,* rather than any light they throw upon
the personal character of the Moors. The coloring, so
long as it is not overdone, is very pleasing, and helps us
to people in imagination the groves and gardens of
Granada, the courts and baths of the Alhambra and Gen-
eralife, the banks of the Genil and the green stretches of
the great *vega.* Is it asserting too much, to say that the
Moorish joy in Nature's beauty happily inspired the
Spanish poets, sons of a harsher clime, and gave them
an inheritance of feeling for the out-door world which
succeeding generations of Spanish lyrists have never lost?

There is, then, no essential difference between the
Moorish ballads and the contemporary ballads dealing with
other personages, save the oriental coloring conventionally
employed in the former. Tournaments, duels, love-making with the inevitable quarrels and reconciliations,—all
these developed that *pundonor* among the Moors of the
ballads as among the Spaniards. At a time when the
Moriscos were leading a sorry existence in exile from
their old homes, the Spanish poets were representing them
as riding about on proud chargers, adorned with orna-

mented armor, courting their sweethearts, and vowing their undying devotion in a setting of oriental wealth and magnificence. The whole thing is artificial, conventional, and contrary to the real estate of the Moors, as the Christian poets must have very well known.

The question arises, then, why did the Spaniards make out the Moors to be leading a chivalrous existence in the sixteenth century just like themselves? As Durán has pointed out, it became a conventional trick of such poets as we have mentioned to sing their loves in oriental imagery. The Fátimas, the Zaidas, the Vindarajas, the Boabdils, the Zaides, the Audallas, Gazuls and Tarfes of this poetry stand for the less romantic names of the actual Christian lovers. The situation is in no wise different, nor is any effort made to differentiate the exterior of the personages. The vogue for Moorish scenery and local color had come in with the beginning of the sixteenth century, as the Moorish peril had ceased to be a constant threat within the country. This is not the place to mention individual ballads of great beauty. But it may be stated in a general way that this numerous class of romantic Moorish ballads yields us no matter for this study beyond the totally false historical aspect under which the Moors are portrayed. If the Spanish poets tried to do so, they failed to give us the domestic and intimate life of the Moors among themselves. Take away the Moorish names and the conventional colors of oriental chivalry, and we have left the Spaniards of the *comedias de capa y espada*. The constantly recurring words in the Moorish *romances* are the identical ear-marks of the later Spanish *comedias: celos, penas, pundonor, cuidados, contentos, retratos,* etc.

One is surprised that the mysterious life of the harem had no charm for the Christian poets. As has been said.

there is no attempt to describe it. The Moorish women
deport themselves exactly as their Christian sisters. They
employ their time in making favors for their lovers, in
discussing their merits, in writing love-notes, in quarreling
and making up. They are even fair of hair and white of
skin,—a fact which shows how completely the conventional Spanish type of beauty was imposed upon the Moors.
A Moor sings of his lady:

> "Ay bella Soltana mía!
> Ay mi rostro delicado!
> Ay bellos cabellos de oro,
> Que me tienen enlazado!" (No. 165.)

The three most beautiful maidens in Granada are thus
described:

> "Tiene Fátima en los ojos
> Paraísos de las almas,
> Y en sus rubios cabellos
> El rico metal de Arabia,
> En cuyos lazos añuda
> Las almas más libertadas.
> Tiene Jarifa la frente
> De un liso marfil sacada,
> Con sus mejillas hermosas,
> Y sus labios de escarlata:
> Son las manos de cristal,
> Nieve el pecho y la garganta,
> Adonde el fuego de amor
> Invisiblemente abrasa;
> Y aunque en su comparación
> Es algo morena Zara,
> En discreción y donaire
> A las demás aventaja,
> Que la flor de la hermosura
> En breve tiempo se pasa,
> Y es don que jamás se pierde
> La discreción y la gracia."[29] (No. 76.)

[29] For the fair type of Saracen beauty cf. *Enfances Ogier*, 1470 f.;
4245; *Beuves de Commarcis*, 715; *Gerusalemme Liberata*, IV, 24 f.;
VI, 92; VII, 7; XVII, 26.

Thus, superficial description triumphed over any satisfactory detail of observation, and we fall into the deplor-
able taste of the latest Moorish ballads, where the fair
women are compared with Venus, Juno and Diana (cf.
No. 77). In this train pass by the god of Love, the
Muses of Parnassus (No. 77), and the whole motley crew
of Renaissance mythology. This incongruous migration
of the gods and goddesses to Moorish Spain is especially
noticeable after the favor of the *Orlando Furioso* caused
it to be imitated in Spain. Durán prints thirty-three of
these ballads taken, in almost all cases, from the *Orlando
Furioso*. Here we meet Sacripante, Rugero, Angelica,
Mandricardo, Roldán, Bradamante and the rest, all faith-
fully transplanted from the Italian poem, and with the
romance and mystery of Ariosto and Doré still clinging
to their garments.

And thus in the strange irony of literary history, we
have completed the circle. How far we have got from the
Moors of Granada and Valencia! We have followed them
from Spain to France, from France to Italy, and from
Italy to Spain again. Such has been the course of the
literary current which we have been following. There is
no more curious spectacle in literary history than that
afforded by the Spanish poets of 1600 going for their
Moors to the Italian poem of Ariosto. The reason, of
course, is that Ariosto was admitted then, as he is admitted
now, to have given in his poem the final word of the
artist on the mediaeval strife between the two Religions.
When the Spaniards talked about the Moors in poetry
in 1600 they wanted art and color,—not truth.

Yet it is not to be supposed that all were so blind as
not to realize how far astray the poets had wandered
from the Moors as they actually were in sixteenth century
Spain. This brings us to our last division,—that of the

romances moriscos satíricos.   These ballads give grateful
reading, indeed, to one who has made his weary way
through the preceding mass of false coloring and characterization.   One is quite in the mood for a dash of satire.
The contemporary poets are berated by these patriotic
iconoclasts for deserting the old traditional heroes:

> "Los Sanchos, y los de Lara,
> Qué es de ellos? y qué es del Cid?
> Tanto olvido á gloria tanta!"   (No. 244.)

Another says more forcibly than elegantly:

> "Váyase con Dios Gazul,
> Lleve el diablo á Celindaja......
> Ha venido á su noticia
> Que hay cristianos en España?......
> Están Fátima y Jarifa
> Vendiendo higos y pasas,
> Y cuenta Lagarto Hernández
> Que danzan en el Alhambra!......
> Y al Cegrí, que con dos asnos
> De echar agua no se cansa,
> El otro disciplinante
> Píntale rompiendo lanzas!"   (No. 245)

In another ballad a different form of satire is employed.
Here it is the Moors themselves who resent the insults done
them by the Christian poets.   The angry Muza sallies
forth from the Tower of Comares with drawn sword, not
to kill the Abencerraje,

> "Mas por vengar el ultraje,
> Que le hacen los poetas
> En canciones y romances......
> 'Que me duelen ya los lomos
> De andar cargado de trajes,
> Que los poetas novicios
> Se desvelan en sacarme,
> Compuesto de más colores
> Que tapete de Levante......
> Pues me pintan, ya de verde,
> Ya de blanco, rojo y jalde'." (No. 253.)

Speaking of the poets' treatment of the Moors, another satirist exclaims:

> "Para qué los entapizan
> Y los cubren de gualdrapas
> De alamares, rapacejos,
> De listones, borlas, bandas?
> Déjenlos á los cuitados,
> Que se quejan que los cansan,
> Y que á caballo los suben
> Cargados de empresas varias."   (No. 256.)

Instead of such fanciful descriptions, says the satirist, it would be more proper to show them in their humble employments to which their masters had subjected them and of which this same ballad makes mention.

This was the literary triumph of the defeated and despised Moors. They had so invaded the romantic poetry of the sixteenth century that the very Christian poets themselves were compelled to cry "Enough!" A single ballad defends the presence of the Moors, and from it an interesting suggestion may be drawn:

> "No es bien que el Cid, ni Bernardo,
> Ni un Diego Ordóñez de Lara,
> Un valiente Arias Gonzalo,
> Un famoso Rodrigo Arias,
> Cuyas obras de ordinario
> Eran correr las campañas,
> Entren á danzar compuestos
> Entre el amor y las damas:
> A Muza le está bien esto,
> A Arbolán y Galiana,
> A los Cegríes y Aliatares,
> Que siempre de amor trataban."   (No. 246.)

This leads us to believe that when love and gallantry were in question the oriental color and Moorish setting were *de rigeur,* and meant no disrespect to the national heroes.   In fact, in the *romances moriscos* it is all tournaments and love-making; whereas in the ballads about the national heroes we are much more likely to find vigor and vitality. This handful of satiric ballads really brings us back to healthy reality after all the flights of romance, the theatrical pageantry of gaily decked Moors, of which we have been reading. The satire, with its return to the reality of the *Cid* and *Fernan Gonçalez,* dealt a death-blow to the Moors of romance. The next stage takes the Moors beyond the sphere of our study, quite out of anonymous literature. Once the trenchant pen of Cervantes had exposed the disgraceful spectacle of the subjects of a mighty Christian sovereign allowed to lie in the chains of the Berbery corsairs, we have to deal with personal authorship in a new sense. Cervantes was an agitator, and he wrote as an eye-witness of the atrocities committed and endured in Algiers. In his realistic *comedias* and *novelas* we may read of the burning shame which he felt for Christendom temporizing with the Infidels, and which led him to favor the cruel exile of the unhappy Moriscos by Philip the Third in 1610.

Such were the literary vicissitudes through which the Moors passed from the time of their first appearance in popular poetry until the political crusade of the seventeenth century drove their unhappy descendants from Spain. We cannot but feel that the Christian poets missed an opportunity. They have really told us little that is reliable about their Infidel neighbors. In all but the *romances moriscos* they are treated objectively, with but little attempt to penetrate the secrets of their strange civilization. When they tried to describe them subjectively, the poets totally missed the Moorish personality, and contented themselves with a conventional atmosphere of

Orientalismus which they threw about the Paynim chivalry.

Enough has been said to outline the treatment accorded to the Saracens at the hands of the mediaeval popular poets of southern Europe. Occasional descendants of the hordes that overran southern Europe penetrated into England, where the "unspeakable Turk" looks strange in a popular ballad or in an Elizabethan play. But after the period where we have dropped him, the Saracen passed from popular into historical literature. Travelers, novelists and dramatists continue to give us the corsairs and Turks of their own times. But the popular mediaeval legend of the Moors is at an end, and with it our subject.